CW00969746

THE
ENGLISH
COOKBOOK

by the same author

FEASTS
EXPORT – OR DIE?

CONTENTS

I

OLD & NEW

Food in England has changed significantly since Dorothy Hartley published her classic of that name in the early 1950s, but *English cooking* has not. Some helpful, some horrible, the changes have reflected growing interest in foreign cuisines, increasing availability of overseas produce, the spread of ethnic restaurants, and rampant development in all branches of the food industry. Except that the eggs come from batteries, however, and the bacon from Denmark, typical English dishes are more or less the same as they were at the beginning of the Industrial Revolution. And broadly this applies wherever British culinary tradition survives in the English-speaking world – Australia, New Zealand, the United States, Canada.

We miss a great deal through static loyalty to a stage-coach cuisine. French cooking has advanced creatively for 200 years, with each generation refining, re-assessing, refreshing the body gastronomic. At all levels it offers food for today, yet there has been no wholesale rejection of the past, just selective, questing evolution. The present book is an attempt to start such a process of renewal for English cooking and British culinary practice.

It is important that such renewal should take place. We owe much to Elizabeth David and her disciples, but we are not becoming French or Italian cooks; we are becoming Anglo-continental hybrids, with a touch of the orient. At best this sort of eclecticism creates imaginative new dishes and exciting adaptations, but all too easily it degenerates into just another manifestation of the depressing homogeneity which is making everywhere and

everything more and more the same. Good cooking is as susceptible to this process as junk food. So 'vivent les différences': may
multinational cookery and culinary jingoism flourish side by side.
Let's continue to have an ethnic cuisine of our own, but revitalise it
and stop relying on kitchen Esperanto.

What Is Wrong with Our Cooking?

We have a yeoman cuisine for a nation of car-drivers. The sturdy,
fattening fare which was ideal for our ploughing, fighting, hunt-
ing fathers has followed us to flats and semis. Fuel for physical
toil, inner warmth against falling snows and rising damp, our
famous dishes have been rendered anachronistic by labour-saving
machines, central heating and the slimmers' ethos. It is not that our
better effects have become mere archaisms; on the contrary, their
combinations of taste and texture are often inspired, but they are
overweighted by the past, encrusted by offices they no longer need
to perform. By reworking and renewing them, we can find more
apposite ways of enjoying our gastronomic heritage. What we
should develop now is a lighter, truer-tasting, more tempting
cookery based largely on familiar ingredients, and one which makes
better use of natural, national flavours as derived from farm and
garden, countryside and sea. Spoiling perfectly good food by under-
rating or overcooking it is, of course, another obsolete practice still
widespread in our kitchens.

In trying to evolve a new approach, I hope I have avoided change
for the sake of change, and preserved all that is best, most valid of
the yeoman tradition.

What Makes Cooking English?

It is easier to sense Englishness in cooking than to define exactly
what makes a dish English. Apart from grouse, hardly any of the
materials we use are exclusive to the British Isles, and relatively few
are even indigenous in the true sense of the word. Most of them, on
the other hand, do grow in and around Britain: apples, beef,
cabbage, Dover sole . . .

However, not everything which can be grown in a cold climate tastes English. For example, it is easier to cultivate coriander than parsley, but as leaf or seed, coriander tastes alien while good old umbelliferous parsley is as John Bullish as the gammon it so often accompanies. At the same time certain things which cannot be grown in the United Kingdom are inextricably linked with traditional English dishes – nutmeg with junket, cloves with apple sauce and bread sauce . . . English marmalade oranges come from Seville and owe little or nothing to English orangeries.

Thus the new English cookery will rely on traditional farm and garden produce, wild food from countryside and northern waters, and a select group of exotics which, over the years, have become as it were naturalised British. A number of other foods must therefore be resisted. Tastes and ingredients which are particularly associated with, say, French or Mediterranean, tropical or oriental cooking should almost all be banned – using Pernod or Calvados, for example, the marriage of tomatoes and basil, Indian and Indonesian spicing techniques (as opposed to 'Anglo-Indian' cookery). Also to be excluded are those immigrant species which have never acquired naturalised status, however popular they may be – avocado pears, aubergines, kiwi fruit, and so on. These call for a self-denying ordinance.

Guidelines

At the end of this book, there is a list of thoroughbred but northerly products and ingredients which continue to be the basic materials of English cooking. There is also a list of naturalised imports and a list of prohibited foods ('index ciborum prohibitorum') – foods which may be used for foreign and eclectic cooking but which remain un-English even if widely available in Britain today.

Guidelines rather than inflexible rules, these lists are inevitably subjective, but they have been very carefully considered. They have also been contested and refined by family, friends and fellow food reformers. As a result a list of 'borderlines' has also emerged – ingredients and products which cannot reasonably be banned from our cooking, but which should nevertheless be used with caution and perhaps reluctance. A typical example is garlic: new English cookery may employ garlic as a background ingredient but the final dish must never taste garlicky.

Certain ingredients and processes must also be indexed, or at least borderlined, because they are associated with heavy, over-rich, old-style cooking: flour-thickened sauces, for example, and fat-saturated pastry; suet may be used, symbolically and nostalgically, but in strictly limited quantities.

Finally there are numerous dishes, processes and materials which have their origins in continental Europe but which have now spread far and wide through Britain, the United States and wherever there is an interest in good cooking: soufflés and sorbets, sour cream and yogurt, pasta, pilaffs, mousselines. It would be cheating to claim that by making use of these one was renewing English cookery – one would merely be internationalising it. Accordingly most of these should be avoided.

In short, the new English cookery must be as unashamedly racist as, for instance, the genuine Tamil, Nepalese, Korean or Caribbean cuisines we can all now enjoy. Racial integration is a social imperative, but culinary apartheid enriches and intensifies the standard of life.

As to the lists themselves (pages 289–95), please look on them as general concepts rather than definitive rules. Having accepted the principle that restriction and limitation are implied by national – as opposed to multinational – cooking, please feel reasonably free to argue the toss about individual items, and to shift a few from one list to another if you wish.

Culinary Fats in New English Cookery

Animal fats have been used in Britain for centuries. Today they are somewhat under a cloud as suspected health hazards. Used prudently, however, beef dripping, pork lard, butter or bacon fat are often better than polyunsaturated vegetable oil, let alone soft margarine, for English-tasting food. Better but not essential.

The vegetable oil movement has gathered pace and many different varieties are now easily available. Some are more suitable than others for English cooking. As an all-purpose oil, sunflower seems about the best, and even if it is not always made from English-grown helianthus, still one can think cosily of those gentle, smiling giants nodding over their cottage gardens. At the time of writing, pure rape-seed oil – though it has come out very well in consumer tests – is not to be found in the average grocer's or supermarket as easily as our yellowing countryside would suggest. By all means try it when the opportunity arises. Like many of the oils, Flora-type margarine is ethnically neutral, and may, if preferred, be used instead of butter. A healthy compromise is to mix animal fat and vegetable oil approximately half and half: butter and oil for fish; dripping and oil for steak; lard and oil for pork chops. This raises the smoke point (which facilitates non-greasy frying) but preserves a characteristic 'meatiness'.

Though an ancient import, and God-given product, olive oil has never been used very much for cooking in England – only for mayonnaise, salads and suntans. With good olive oil the price it is, there is no reason to start now, and it would be un-English to do so. No such prohibition need apply to walnut or, especially, hazelnut oil now being sold in specialist shops. Both nuts grow here, but their oils do have most distinctive tastes, and they, too, are very expensive. Experiment with them by all means, though they are inessential.

Down with Frying?

'We never fry anything in my apartment – we only sauté,' said a San Franciscan in our kitchen.

'But is there any difference?'

'Sure is. Sautéing is much better for you, more delicate, more subtle – more French.'

No. Literally sauter means to jump, but in kitchen language it translates as to fry, and to use it – in English or American – instead of the word fry is mere euphemism. Frying is a dirty word in some quarters only because, badly done, it produces greasy, soggy, fat-saturated food. So do badly done sautés in France. If you use semi-rancid oil or tired, re-cycled fat, and cook at too low a temperature, the result will, of course, be greasy and unhealthy. If you use a little good, clean oil or fat (in some cases very, very little) and usually heat it to just below its smoke point, frying is a healthy as well as a quick and convenient method of cooking; closely akin to grilling. It is used all the time in modern French cooking.

Deep-frying is really a different process, but here too, the use of clean oil and high temperature produces crisp, dry, perfectly healthy food, which is only fattening if eaten constantly and in excessive quantity.

Cooking with Beer, Cider – and Wine

It's more English to cook with beer or cider than with wine; and if you must use wine, sherry, Madeira and port are more English than supermarket plonk. Pleasant and new, genuine English wine is too expensive to be used for everyday cooking. British sherry and British ruby wine can be used as substitutes for sherry and port; the best substitute for port, however, is a Spanish wine called

Tarragona – cheap but difficult to find. Montilla, also from Spain and relatively cheap, is another good sherry/Madeira substitute (dry, medium or sweet).

Unfortunately beer is a marginal and limited cooking medium. It does help certain things (including, oddly enough, batter), but is far too apt to donate an unwanted, hoppy taste. Bitter and light ale are particularly difficult to use effectively – difficult to lose. And if you have to hide one constituent in a sauce, do you need it at all? Sweetish brews like brown ale, mild and milk stout are the best. Michael Roberts devoted a whole book to beer cookery. It is full of enterprising ideas and ingenious ways round the problem, yet I have the unpatriotic suspicion that many of his dishes would be just as good without any beer at all. The best way of neutralising unwanted beery tastes is to co-opt plenty of vinegar, but that in itself is something of a giveaway. I have only used beer when I am convinced it is necessary to the final dish.

Cider, on the other hand, is a most versatile cooking medium, and is used throughout this book. It has the added advantage of being fairly cheap – and the nationally distributed brands all keep well once the bottle has been opened. Standard dry cider is adequate for most purposes; there is no need to use the wine-like luxury ciders. Sweet and medium sweet varieties are fine for puddings and syrups. Rough still cider is best of all.

Cooking with Shallots

Shallots (or 'eshallotts') have been used in English cooking since at least the seventeenth century, so we are justified in using them as well as the superficially more home-grown onion. As a general rule, they are better than onions for sauce-making, and for all the processes where you want an onion influence rather than an onion presence. Chopped fine, shallots melt into their surroundings as they cook, and more or less give up any separate identity. Onions are more resilient in texture and too sweet for some dishes; tenacious and assertive, they visibly retain their individual exist-ence, whether you want it or no. This means they have to be strained out of the sauce, or reluctantly tolerated. On the other hand they are significantly better than shallots for use as vegetables

9

in their own right – fried, roasted or boiled.

The difference between onions and shallots is not so great that in the recipes which follow one may not be substituted for the other in times of shortage. The ideal is to have plenty of each bulb always to hand, preferably in a dry out-house, though they also look convincing and businesslike hanging up in the kitchen.

Style and Character of the New Approach

The disciplines suggested for renewed English cooking lead to a cuisine of restricted range but very definite character as compared with the cosmopolitan approach – all-embracing in scope but increasingly blurred in definition. This renewed cooking has strong links with an insular past, particularly in its flavours, but is light and seductive. Though simple and traditional, the techniques employed incorporate modern ideas in order to bring out natural tastes and textures.

This cooking is less expensive than either Mrs Beeton's or the new international style. Dishes range in sophistication from straightforward family fare to relatively elaborate dinner-party food, though the division between the two is indistinct and perhaps unnecessary. As to simplicity, more than half the recipes take thirty minutes or less.

In its results this earthy, meaty cooking is certainly new; is it also nouvelle in the culinary sense?

Nouvelle Cuisine?

Yesterday's innovations become tomorrow's clichés. La nouvelle cuisine is already vieux chapeau according to some authorities; others claim that it never really existed or that, if it did, it wasn't all that new. My view is that it did and does exist as an important, innovative, albeit loosely defined, aspect of haute cuisine. It is also a reaction against the grosser forms – and customers – of haute cuisine.

While by no means rejecting cream, butter and eggs (except in its minceur manifestation), nouvelle cuisine is less rich, less ostentatious, less inclined to paint the lily. It respects natural tastes instead of clothing them in virtuoso but unnatural sauces. This is all to the good. The best nouveaux cuisiniers are superb, creative, reforming cooks – as well as brilliant businessmen. If the renewal of English cooking owes something to the lessons of Messieurs Troisgros, Guérard, Bocuse et al, so much the better.

Only the Best?

For commercial as well as gastronomic reasons, the nouveaux cuisiniers insist on using only the best of the best ingredients. In fact, they get up ridiculously early to make sure that they, and no one else, find the perfect foie gras, the ideal truffle, and crayfish from exactly the right chalk stream. This helps to justify their charges as well as to explain their success. Superb materials do tend to make fine meals.

Here, however, we are more concerned with the skills which can transform ordinary or indifferent ingredients into gastronomic magic. Accordingly most of the recipes in this book require nothing more than the standard of quality usually found in reputable shops and chain stores. At the same time they are wholly compatible with the real food movement which, from cottage industry to specialist shop, represents a welcome, if sometimes slightly dotty, backlash to standardisation and mass production.

11

Home Versus Restaurant Cooking

Because of the large choice they have to offer, multi-starred restaurants are in the fast-food business just as much as Colonel Sanders. Up-market fast food may require lengthy preparation and clever ways of decoration, but the final cooking time can only be a few minutes – roughly the time it takes for an expense account to start getting restless. Those few minutes often require complex and concentrated activity in the kitchen.

The same discipline does not apply when all meals are set meals with little or no choice, as in the home. Here, long slow cooking is perfectly possible, particularly when you know exactly how many people need to be fed and at what time. This does not mean that restaurant recipes and restaurant-style cooking are irrelevant to the home cook. So long as he or she feels able to put in a labour-intensive ten minutes at the stove just before serving dinner, any Roux brothers spectacular may be attempted. Ironically this means that such dishes are more practicable for everyday family life than for smart dinners or parties. The fast-food imperative also means using the most tender cuts of meat, which are the most expensive. You cannot cook skirt or brisket in ten minutes (or charge the earth for it).

These renewed English recipes have been devised for the home cook. Many, however, are perfectly suitable for restaurants and hotels.

Cosmetic Cookery

You can make a salmon look like Laura Ashley wallpaper, but it won't taste any better. You can make radishes look like roses, and 'turn' mushrooms to get a spiral effect; you can, but I can't and I won't. For 200 years the artificial decoration of food has been given more attention in some quarters than it deserves. The theory is correlation between eye and palate; make a cake look like the Taj Mahal and everyone will want to eat it. Surely this is pure piffle?

Cooking is an art in itself and does not need to copy other arts. The cook who tries to make his food as pretty as a picture is like a painter who embellishes his pictures with verse. Carême's dictum about confectionery being the highest form of architecture (probably just a joke) has a lot to answer for. When cooks assume the mantle of sculptors or architects they often reveal a pretentious vulgarity. The brothers Roux, for example, seem proud of the fact that they decorate rabbit dishes with little bunnies made of fried bread. Good tastes are easily clouded by bad taste. It must be admitted, however, that some of today's entrée designs have a Miro-esque quality which is not unpleasing – unless you happen to be very hungry.

Well-cooked food always looks good. It is perfectly in order to spend a minute or two titivating or decorating it further, but time-devouring pièces montées have nothing to do with good cooking or good eating. Their prime purpose is to make money or win prizes at competitions. But when the feast is finished and the oohs and ahs expire – no one has eaten the sculptor's handywork. (I was told in a very smart French kitchen that they often use the same radish-roses two or three times.) The dishes in this book are for eating, not for the colour photographer. They are also for the health-conscious as well as the food-lover.

Food and Health

'Alles ist Gift', as Paracelsus pointed out some 450 years ago. 'All substances are poisons; there is no such thing as a non-poison. It is the amount which distinguishes a poison from a remedy.' This applies to sugar and salt, polysaturated fats and roly-poly pudding. Cholesterol is vital to health, and the body will manufacture it out of turnips if starved of butter. It also kills. Fibre is good for you but too much will twist the lesser gut, and apples green are bad for you, though one a day . . .

As for the prevalence of heart disease and cancer, I blame doctors rather than diet. They have stopped us dying of almost everything else, but haven't been quite so clever with today's main killers – so they blame Mars bars and potato crisps.

Relatively low in fats, flour, sugar, salt; calling for fresh rather than processed ingredients, and no dubious additives, renewed English cooking is healthy but not faddily so. It does not claim to

13

obviate the need for balance and moderation which is implied in Paracelsus's caveat. Sensible balance in the menu is perhaps the wisest, healthiest and most enjoyable form of dieting.

Menu Composition

Menus of the affluent past seem designed more for the display of wealth and the dismay of kitchen staff than for eating. Queen Victoria used to offer thirty dishes regularly; the aristocracy took its cue from the royal household; the gentry copied the aristocracy; and the up-and-coming middle classes, according to their means, emulated the gentry – their guide and mentrix, Mrs Beeton, gives dinners for every month of the year of not less than twelve dishes.

The First World War brought 'a tendency towards simplicity in all the various meals of the day. Shortage of labour has had something to do with this and so also has later medical opinion as to the amount of food necessary to keep the body in health. A complete dinner consists of nine courses but it can be abridged without a great amount of loss. The hors d'œuvres, savoury, fish or soup can easily be dispensed with' (from *Good Cookery* by Mrs Francillon, first published in 1920). I particularly like that 'or', implying that you could safely cut down to a mere eight courses.

The other end of the social ladder, of course, was not quite so well fed, sometimes hardly fed at all. In between, the yeoman class and its counterpart in the towns dined on two or three courses as we do today.

We may dismiss those rich, immoderate menus to the dustbins of history, yet there is at least one aspect of them which deserves consideration. Each menu could embrace virtually the whole spectrum of eating possibilities – soup, fish, shellfish, poultry, eggs, meat, game, vegetables, offal, puddings, fruit, savoury, cheese. In practice it often lacked real contrast and repeated itself unimaginatively; but in theory it could offer the complete gastronomic experience. Surely a satisfying and challenging idea? Let's see how comprehensive a menu we can contrive today in, say, three courses, coming down from, say, seven elements: soup – fish – poultry – meat – game – pudding – savoury.

Soup and savoury are typically English ways of starting and finishing a serious meal, with savoury taking the place of (but frequently including) cheese. For different reasons, both are now under threat. The starters which are replacing soup can be regarded as promotion for the entrée or borrowings from the French; many people simply find them more interesting than soup. Savouries, needing last-minute preparation, tend to be too much trouble for today's pattern of entertainment. Seven courses are certainly too much trouble for the cook and too much food for the stomach. The next step reduces our menu to five courses: soup – fish – poultry or meat or game – pudding – savoury or cheese.

A more manageable meal, but still too much for most occasions and most appetites. It encompasses most of the main elements, but what if we reduce it to three courses: fish soup or fish starter – poultry or meat or game – pudding?

No cheese? Well, to my mind Cheddar and its English variants, meals in themselves, are redundant in this context – a ploughman's lunch at the end merely adds bulk to such a meal. There is a case for one of the English blues or for a piquant cheese savoury (which must be served hot; tepid cheese is horrid). Some people adore pudding, some adore cheese, so depending on circumstance, the final course may be: pudding or cheese (with fruit, nuts, celery, maybe) or savoury.

If you decide to solve this problem by having pudding and cheese (one of your guests is sure to love both), the English custom is to have the cheese last, but many people prefer it before the pudding unless they are being treated to port. It seems retrograde going back to cheese after a good pudding but climactic to go on to a really sapid savoury.

Dish Status

In revitalised English cookery, dishes do not have the fixed status that they had in the past. The same dish will serve as starter in one context and as main dish in another; perhaps as a savoury or side dish too. Most of the fish dishes in this book make excellent starters, as do some of the egg, salad and vegetable dishes. Savouries also make good starters, provided they are not too pungent; it's usually a mistake to begin with an assault on the palate. Equally many salads and starters, in adequate helpings, can provide the centrepiece of a meal. It is nowadays a commonplace that in restaurants the overtures are often more enticing than the principal works; experienced eaters-out sometimes confine themselves to the hors d'œuvres. However, a meat or game main dish still seems to me the central focus and most important element of English cooking.

Balancing Light and Heavy Dishes

Though English cooking should in future be considerably less solid than its ancestry, starchy or otherwise robust food ought by no means to be excluded. One aspect of the new approach is re-balance within a meal. A light starter or main dish may be followed by bread and butter pudding; a rich, substantial starter should be followed by a finely flavoured but slight main course. In short, it is not necessary that the main course itself be the most filling.

Cooking Techniques

It is assumed that would-be renewers of English cooking are familiar with the main cooking techniques: roasting and baking; boiling, poaching and steaming; grilling; frying; braising and stewing. The new approach calls for no unusual methods and no equipment more special than a liquidiser.

Most of the dishes and processes are simple but, please, they do require care, concentration and awareness. Here are recipes for cooks and culinary thoughts for food-lovers but not instructions for robots or programs for human computers. Reader, let us not assume a teacher–pupil relationship but a dialogue between equals. Within the context of any recipe, use your own judgement.

Kitchen Appliances

Modern, designed for today's living as these recipes are, their author is pathetically Luddite as regards gadgets. His liquidiser sounds like a jet engine running out of oil and his food processer never does what it's told; he's convinced that microwaves can damage your health and is sick and tired of having to unblock the waste guzzler. Sharp knives and a swivelly potato peeler are the aids most often used. Time may not be saved in food preparation, but at least it's not lost washing up horrid electrical gadgets.

Keeping Food Warm

Many dishes reach a stage when an important ingredient must be set aside and kept warm while another process, usually sauce-making, takes place. In some cases, the juices which seep out while the meat is keeping warm are valuable additions to the sauce. But keeping food warm is more easily said than done. The ideal is to have a spare oven warm enough for the purpose, though not so hot that cooking continues. But the only oven is being used for something else and is registering 300°C? No matter. Pre-heat a dish with lid so that it gets really hot right through; allow it to cool for a couple of minutes; then put in the meat (or whatever), and put the dish, covered, on to the warmest part of the stove which is just not hot enough to cook on. For the subsequent collection of meat juices, it is a slight help if the meat is raised on a grid.

Metrication and All That

We dither in metric/imperial limbo. Though emotionally drawn to our traditional weights and measures, I felt originally that renewal and modernisation of English ethnic cooking should be symbolised by acceptance of the new system. Accordingly I worked out all ingredients in grammes and centilitres, and intended merely to include a suitable conversion table in each chapter to act as an aide-mémoire. However, the publisher advises that both systems (one for older readers, one for younger?) should be included. We have put imperial first.

Inevitably the adoption of this double standard means compromise and occasional inconsistency. A convenient 'round' figure in one system converts to an inconvenient figure (even a vulgar fraction) in the other. But only in a very few recipes are quantities critical down to the last ½oz (14g). Readers may exercise their discretion.

Here is a useful tip for making conversions (and one which, so far as I know, has never appeared in print). However metric or unmetric you may be, the magic number 28 will lighten your darkness – because 28 grammes (actually 28·35) make one ounce, while 28 centilitres make half a pint. Therefore the following tables emerge by simple arithmetic:

28g	= 1oz		28cl	= ½ pint
56g	= 2oz		56cl	= 1 pint
224g	= 8oz		100cl	= 1·75 pints
448g	= 1lb		14cl	= ¼ pint
(1000g	= 2lb 3oz)		(2cl	= 1 tablespoon)

Most tables give the more accurate figures of 226g and 454g for 8oz and 1lb respectively, but the few grammes difference are of no account.

Quantities

Unless otherwise stated, recipes throughout this book are given in quantities which should be sufficient for four people with healthy appetites. Double the quantities for eight people; treble and divide by two for six.

Oven Temperatures

The theories and dishes of this British ethnic cookery have mostly been evolved and tested with the help of a loyal and ancient four-door Aga. The top right-hand oven was hot to very hot, the bottom right-hand oven was, well, medium; top left, lowish, and bottom left very low. What were their exact temperatures or their equivalents in electricity or gas regulo marks? I do have some vague idea, of course, but not an accurate one. And I'm afraid I don't much care either, since there was never very much I could do to adjust them up or down.

In practice, very few processes or recipes demand critically exact oven temperatures. Accordingly I have spared readers the 375°(F)/gas regulo 5/190°(C) formula, and resorted instead to 'hot oven', 'medium oven', 'low oven', and so on. Here, however, are some guidelines.

Low	100–150°C	200–300°F	gas mark ¼–2
Medium	150–200°C	300–400°F	gas mark 2–6
High	200–250°C	400–475°F	gas mark 6–9

Definitions and Terms

Culinary jargon has been kept to a minimum in these pages, but the following terms seem to have no English equivalent:

bain-marie – a basin or pan inside a larger basin or pan which is part-filled with water. The custard (or whatever) is put in the smaller pan and its cooking – in oven or on hob – is to some extent inhibited by the surrounding water.

chiffonade – individual leaves of spinach and other leaf vegetables are rolled into 'cigars' and then cut crossways or diagonally very finely indeed with a sharp knife. A form of shredding.

de-glaze – in new English cooking, this term means (1) the addition of vinegar or alcohol to pan juices after frying, grilling, or roasting, when the surplus fat has been poured off, or (2) the addition of vinegar or alcohol while frying or roasting continues. The first form of de-glazing is an important stage in sauce- and gravy-making; the second is used in making stock (before the introduction of water) and in certain forms of sauce-making to promote an emulsion between fats and other cooking juices.

julienne – root and other firm vegetables are cut into the thinnest of thin matchsticks – all the same length and width if possible.

2
BROTHS & CULLISES

The Importance of Broth

Good broth or stock is an essential part of new English cookery, a sort of gastronomic DNA. More than any other element it dictates the taste, texture and appearance of the dishes which follow. The principles of stock-making are not new, but they must be mastered and followed before traditional cooking can be reformed or revitalised.

Broth and stock are treated here as synonyms. Since stocks, in classic cookery, are meant to be clarified (and since 'stockpot', in England, implies a depressing perpetuation of leftovers), let us prefer the pleasanter word broth for the unclarified decoctions of renewed English cooking.

Contemporary writer-chefs have to some extent simplified the multi-stage rituals of stock-making in professional French kitchens, but they still demand the availability of four to eight different stocks (fonds or jus), each derived, in effect, from a full-blown soup or stew. It is impracticable for the domestic kitchen to follow such counsels of perfection. For the home cook, just one basic broth will suffice – household broth. By a simple process this can afterwards be elevated into a strong broth or cullis.

Compatibility of Broth Ingredients

House broth is made from bones and trimmings of meat, augmented by vegetables. Bones and meat may be cooked or uncooked; the vegetables should be raw.

Some ingredients go well together, some do not. The following are compatible: veal, beef, chicken, pork, duck, rabbit. They may be used singly or in combination. Ham and ham bones can be used too, but they do not make satisfactory broth by themselves – except as a form of brine for split peas or other dried pulses. Lamb and mutton should only be included when the stock is intended exclusively for lamb or mutton dishes. Lamb-flavoured broth can be fatal to sauces for beef or chicken, though beef or chicken broth can often enhance lamb dishes. Similarly strong game should only be included in broth intended for game dishes. The carcasses of under-hung pheasant and partridge are perfectly admissible.

Broth vegetables should include onions and carrots, plus (optionally) celery, leeks, turnips, tomatoes, garlic (not too much), herbs – but not potatoes, the cabbage family or Jerusalem artichokes.

Quantities, proportions and cooking times are not critical, since house broth is not meant to be consistent in taste, time after time. Use the suggestions below as a guide.

HOUSE BROTH

2¼lbs (1000g) veal or beef bones (sawn up) and meat trimmings
2 onions
2 large carrots
1 clove garlic
2 sticks celery
3½ tablespoons cider vinegar
3½pts (200cl) water
thyme or marjoram
bay leaf

Optional extras
1 chicken carcass
1 pig's trotter (split)
bacon rinds
ham scraps
leftovers from compatible meats

Cooking time: at least 3 hours

Put all the ingredients except vinegar, water and herbs into a very large pan or roasting tin and roast them in a hot oven for 20 minutes. When the bones are beginning to brown and sizzle, pour in the vinegar and let it all but evaporate. Then, transferring to a large saucepan if necessary, add the water and herbs and put the pan on the top of the stove. Bring the pan to a simmer with the lid on, removing the scum with a fine strainer as it rises to the surface. Skim regularly for the first 15 minutes; after that the broth can be

24

left to simmer away either on top of the stove or back in the oven, now medium to low. It must only just simmer and certainly not boil. Give it at least 3 hours, but up to 6 or 8, and keep the lid on until the last half hour or so.

Strain the broth into jugs or other vessels and allow it to cool. The fat is easy to remove when the stock is cold, and may be used as clarified dripping or put out for birds.

Broth will keep for up to a week in the refrigerator, much longer, of course, in a freezer. If it is to be kept several days before use, leave the fat in place so that it seals the broth from air.

Strength through Evaporation

As uncovered broth boils, its water content is gradually turned into steam. The remaining liquor, therefore, becomes less and less watery – that is, *stronger*. This process of reduction, the exact opposite of diluting a liquid by the addition of water, is the basis of syrupy, concentrated sauces. In new English cookery, reduction is not taken quite as far as for some French dishes, but it is an essential technique.

25

STRONG BROTH – OR 'CULLIS'

This may either be made as soon as the house broth has been strained off, or later, as and when needed. In its most basic form it is merely a continuation of the house-broth process but with the lid off, until the volume has been reduced by about two-thirds. It is improved if the starting broth is somewhat fortified, for instance with the following ingredients per 1¾pts (1 litre) of (preferably de-fatted) broth:

⅓pt (20cl) dry cider or 5 tablespoons sherry
5 tablespoons vinegar
2oz (56g) mushrooms
2 tomatoes
compatible meat, carcasses, giblets, as available

Cooking time: about 1 hour

Boil the ingredients for 45–60 minutes, so that they reduce to just under 1pt (56cl). If uncooked giblets or meat are introduced at this stage, the stock will require further skimming.

When sufficiently reduced, strain the strong broth into a jug and store in cool larder or refrigerator.

Further onions, carrots or other stock vegetables may also be included in this process.

It's sensible to make very large quantities of house broth from time to time, reduce most of it to strong broth, and freeze it against future use. Of course you can freeze it as house stock instead, if more convenient.

Cullis

The dictionary defines cullis as 'a strong broth made of meat, fowl, etc., boiled and strained'. Little used nowadays in English, the French form, coulis, is very much in vogue. Is there any chance of restoring the English word for culinary usage? Some may think this a lost cause or argue that 'strong broth', though less poetic, is more readily understood. Yes, but having a weakness for lost causes, I have allowed the word cullis to creep in, synonymously with strong broth or strong stock, in several of these recipes. Watch out for it.

Thickening Broths, Sauces and Gravies

A stock thickens as it reduces. Only if it is reduced considerably more than indicated above will it acquire the sticky, almost Bovril-like consistency – and intensity of taste – which classic haute cuisine sometimes demands. In English ethnic cooking, it is permissible slightly to anticipate that stage by using arrowroot. Neither flour nor cornflour should be used.

Arrowroot is an almost miraculous, under-used alternative to flour – the most digestible and least fattening of starches. One teaspoon will give a subtle, unctuous quality to half a pint or more of strong stock. The stock will not, of course, taste as strong as jus de viande, but it will feel like it in texture. We do not need it to taste as strong as a jus because we intend to use more of it in our sauces. Renewed English cookery provides delicious gravies rather than mini-sauces which barely lubricate.

Arrowroot, usually bought at chemists' rather than grocers', has no taste of its own, unlike cornflour.

Rules for Arrowroot

Mix 1 teaspoon of arrowroot and 1 tablespoon of cold water into a paste. Add half a cup of broth and stir the very thin paste which results into the rest of the (simmering) broth or cullis to be thickened. Alternatively dilute the thick paste with water.

One teaspoon of arrowroot will perceptibly thicken at least half a pint (28 cl) of house broth and up to twice as much cullis.

Arrowroot and water paste may also be added direct to sauces and gravies when extra body is required.

Removing Fat from Broth

The most thrifty way of removing unwanted fat is to cool the stock down to the point at which, having risen to the top, the fat solidifies. It can then be removed more or less in one piece with, say, a slice. When this is not practicable, the fat can be skimmed off with a spoon while the broth is still very hot, though not while it is simmering; a little of the stock will inevitably be wasted by this method.

An efficient but fiddly method is to employ a gros et maigre, the gravy boat with two spouts which enables one to pour broth from the bottom of the vessel and fat from the top. Finally kitchen paper can be passed across the surface to be de-fatted, but this always seems to take an awful lot of paper.

Stock Substitutes

In an imperfect world, most kitchens run out of broth from time to time. Stock cubes, tinned consommé (or other thin soup), and meat or yeast extract make passable instant stock. This can be fortified (and disguised) by a vegetable element such as tomato, onion or mushroom, perhaps in the form of a purée. Herbs and bay leaves can also be invoked.

The liquor produced in the boiling of vegetables is quite useful, particularly for making gravy to accompany a roast. And in this case, there is no need to exclude cabbage and cabbage family, providing they have not been overcooked.

However, it will make all the difference to your cooking if you do manage to have a jug of house or strong broth in the refrigerator most of the time, or keep a supply in the freezer.

The Recurring Problem of Fish Stock

In the serious professional kitchen, fish stocks are always available, but only in the most enthusiastic and fish-orientated of home kitchens is this the case. At home the preparation of fish stock is usually an ad hoc, last-minute chore – and a smelly one at that, unless you have a really good extractor system.

Fish stock is made by simmering head, skin, bones and trimmings of white fish with onion and bay leaf. Thyme or marjoram, peppercorns and cloves, wine or dry cider, and parsley stalks may also be added, as may the shells of, say, crabs or prawns. The concoction needs to be simmered for 20–30 minutes, and should be skimmed from time to time. And if you are sensitive to smells you will open the window and close the door before you start.

It is usually claimed that one should base a fish stock on the main ingredient of the dish about to be cooked, but this is not strictly necessary. In practice any unsmoked fish will do. Smoked fish may also be used circumspectly, but only when a distinct smoky flavour is thought an advantage to the sauce.

As to substitutes, both Knorr and Maggi are said to manufacture fish stock cubes, but they cannot be bought for love or money in the United Kingdom. Canned fish soups are mostly too creamy (or too distinctive in some other way) to be used in place of fish stock, though commercial soups can be used to improvise emergency sauces – for example, cream of lobster soup can be added to the cooking juices to provide 'lobster sauce' of a sort. Another substitute for genuine fish stock is house stock flavoured with anchovies or anchovy essence. Turtle soup is another short cut, but extravagant, and one which tells a tale . . .

In view of the difficulty, relatively few of the fish recipes in this book insist on fish stock.

Vegetable Broth

Useful broths can be made with plain vegetables, including vegetable peelings: onions, leeks, carrots, celery, turnips, parsnips, herbs, beetroot, tomatoes, peas and beans (and their pods), mushrooms. Various combinations of these may be used, but potatoes and most leaf vegetables should be avoided. Well-scrubbed potato *peel* makes a nutritional additive, however.

The cooking procedure is essentially the same as for house broth without the preliminary roasting. Simmer the vegetables – washed and roughly chopped but not peeled – in plenty of water for 45–60 minutes; then strain off the stock and discard the vegetables.

The longish time necessary to extract and commingle the vegetable tastes means that some of the nutritional values – vitamins for example – go up in steam. For many purposes quickly cooked vegetable purées are preferable to vegetable stock. In a sense, these are vegetarian equivalents of strong stock or cullis, but they are not produced by the reduction route.

29

Vegetable Cullis

The vegetables are either sweated in a little butter until they are just soft enough to blend into a purée, or they are simmered in a little salted water. In both cases they should be peeled (where applicable) and cut small or diced. As soon as they are soft to the fork, they should be blended in a liquidiser with some of their cooking liquor. In addition to salt and pepper, a touch of lemon juice helps most vegetable cullises.

There are several distinct applications for vegetable cullises. They can be used for thickening sauces or fortifying gravies, as vegetables in their own right, as stuffings or an element in stuffings, or as the basis for dips. Diluted with water or meat broth, they become simple soups.

Since these purées are so useful, it is a good idea to make them in bulk at times of seasonal glut or low prices. What is not needed for immediate consumption can be frozen in, say, ¼pt (14cl) containers. Cullises freeze better than unpuréed vegetables.

Which Vegetables?

Apart from cabbage, nearly all the usual cold-climate vegetables make good purées – by themselves or judiciously mixed. Mixtures of leaf, stalk, root and fungus provide a generalised taste suitable for gravies; but as vegetables or stuffings for vegetables, purées should be constituted so that one flavour predominates – tomato, spinach or leek, for example.

Dried pulses, of course, can be puréed into pease pudding or the equivalent. Heavier and thicker than purées made from fresh vegetables, they are a good base for winter soups but too hearty and assertive for typical vegetable cullis applications.

It is always best to use plump, young vegetables. As they grow old, most vegetables develop fibres, cores or hearts which resist being puréed. Some will ultimately submit to electric blending, but they all yield better results if the fibres are excluded from the end-product, as happens when a hair sieve or Mouli-légumes is used.

MIXED VEGETABLE PURÉE (or Cullis)

4 young parsnips (or turnips), peeled and diced
1 onion, peeled and finely chopped
4 large mushrooms with stalks, diced
spinach, a few leaves (or equivalent in watercress)
½oz (14g) butter
juice of ½ lemon
salt
pepper

Preparation and cooking time: about 40 minutes

Boil the root vegetables in salted water for 5 minutes. Drain, then sweat all the vegetables in butter in a pan with the lid on for 15–20 minutes, with the lemon juice, a little salt and plenty of pepper. Pour contents into liquidiser and blend to a purée.

The vegetables may be simmered in water instead of butter; if so, the purée should be further simmered with the lid off after the liquidising process, and so thickened.

TOMATO CULLIS

6 large tomatoes
1 shallot
oil for frying
3½ tablespoons cider vinegar
paprika
white pepper
thyme (or basil or marjoram)

Preparation time: 5 minutes; cooking time: 30 minutes

Peel the tomatoes. Cut them in quarters. Melt the shallot in oil for 4 minutes, then add cider vinegar and bubble it down to a gooey consistency. Add the tomatoes, pepper and herb. Cook, covered, over a low heat for 20 minutes. Blend in liquidiser. Thicken by further simmering if necessary, and season with salt to taste.

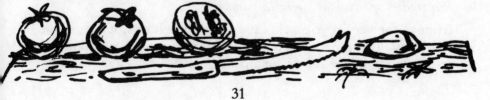

MUSHROOM PURÉE

1 lb (450 g) mushrooms, cleaned and chopped
1 sliver of garlic (say ¼ of an average clove)
1 oz (28 g) butter
salt and pepper
2 tablespoons lemon juice

Preparation time: 5 minutes; cooking time: 20 minutes

Melt mushrooms and garlic in butter for 5 minutes. Add remaining ingredients and cover saucepan. Simmer gently for 20 minutes. Pour contents of pan into liquidiser and blend.

If cultivated mushrooms are used, they will yield a light grey purée; field mushrooms, of course, give a much darker hue.

A dependable ingredient for many kinds of sauce and gravy, it is advisable to make mushroom purée in large quantities and freeze it in small containers or ice-cube trays (for future transference to plastic bags).

(Tomato cullis also should be made in bulk when tomatoes are cheap.)

WATERCRESS CULLIS

2 large bunches watercress, washed
¾ pt (42 cl) broth (page 24) or water
1 tablespoon double cream
1 teaspoon butter
1 teaspoon lemon juice

Preparation and cooking time: 15 minutes

Remove the very coarse stalks and the yellow leaves, if any, from watercress. Boil the cress in broth or water for 5 minutes. Drain but reserve some of the liquor for making purée.

Blend cress in liquidiser with a little of the liquor, or use a fine sieve, then return it to low heat in small saucepan. Add cream, butter and lemon juice. Stir well and raise to simmering point. Continue simmering and stirring if a thicker consistency is wanted.

SPINACH CULLIS

2 lbs (900 g) spinach
2 tablespoons double cream
½ oz (14 g) butter
salt
pepper
nutmeg

Preparation and cooking time: 15 minutes

Wash the spinach very carefully and cut out any coarse spines. Boil it for 2 minutes in a very large, uncovered pan of well-salted water – or cook it by one of the other methods discussed on pages 206–7.

When the spinach is cooked, turn off the heat and remove the vegetable from the water (as opposed to draining the water from the vegetable).

Purée the spinach in a blender with the warmed cream. Re-heat in saucepan with a little butter, a seasoning of pepper and (if liked) nutmeg.

Vegetables Which Make Good Cullises

artichokes (both kinds)
beetroot
broad beans
Brussels sprouts
carrots
cauliflower
celeriac
French beans
leeks
onions

parsnips
peas
spinach
split peas
turnips
watercress

celeriac and parsley
parsnip and watercress

33

Fruit Cullis

Many fruits also make excellent cullises – for use as ices, sauces or sauce constituents. The process is even simpler than for vegetable cullis, since in most cases the raw fruit merely has to be blended to a purée, and perhaps slightly sweetened. A touch of lemon juice sometimes helps to bring out the flavour of the fruit, and a shot of appropriate liqueur sometimes brings out the flavour of your guests.

Ideally fruit cullis should be strained through a fine sieve before use.

Among the best fruit for cullis-making are strawberries, raspberries, all the currants, gooseberries, blackberries, peaches and plums. Pears are good, too, but need to be cooked in sugar syrup before being liquidised. All these cullises freeze well – better than the un-puréed fruit in some cases.

3
STARTERS & SOUPS

examples of the genre. A mistake, I feel: the salmon, cod's roe, sprat, mackerel and so on are by no means the same in taste or texture, but they add little to each other when all on the same plate; on the contrary they are mutually negating, and tend to reduce each other to smoky-salt anonymity. However, they make excellent starters on their own, with lemon and some minimal garnish. The convention of serving horseradish with smoked trout, eel and mackerel is valid, and needs no updating.

Fish may be hot-smoked or cold-smoked. The former – trout, eel, mackerel and sprats – need no cooking; the principal cold-smoked fish are haddock, herring (kippers, bloaters) and salmon, of which all but salmon are usually cooked before being eaten. In fact, the cooking is not entirely necessary. Mackerel is the least attractive smoked fish in its hot-smoked (usually dyed) form – too oily and spongy, at least for me; but some fishmongers and smokehouses offer a single-smoked version. It is well worth seeking this out and serving it raw, even though you may be advised to cook it.

Tempting in their own right, most smoked fish also respond eagerly to titivation. A few recipes are given immediately below; the custard and syllabub techniques which follow are also applicable.

HADDOCK JULIENNE

8 oz (226 g) filleted smoked haddock
¼ pt (14 cl) lemon juice
2 or 3 young leeks
4 young carrots
3½ oz (100 g) green vegetables – baby French beans, cabbage, and so on

Preparation and marinating time: at least 2 hours

Using a very sharp knife, cut the haddock as you would smoked salmon but if anything slightly thicker. Put it with the lemon juice in a small bowl and leave it to marinate for at least 2 hours, preferably longer. Shred or julienne the vegetables so that they end up as matchsticks all of approximately the same length, and batch them by colour. Blanch each batch in boiling water for 1 minute, then drain it, refresh it in cold water and dry it. Still keep the colours separate.

To serve: drain the fish and pat it dry with kitchen paper. Arrange juliennes in red, white and green sections round each plate and surmount with the yellow haddock.

Only a small amount of sauce is required with this simple but characterful starter. Lost sauce (page 234) or cider vinegar sauce is particularly recommended. A vinaigrette made with 4 parts oil, 1 part lemon juice, 1 part mild mustard is also good, and may be heated up to blood temperature.

Cider Vinegar Sauce

Mix 1 tablespoon cider vinegar with 1 teaspoon of made English mustard. Stir in 3 tablespoons single cream. Heat to blood temperature and dribble 1 tablespoon of the sauce over each helping.

SMOKED SALMON DU BEDAT

Invented by my first employer – he used to eat it accompanied by heroic quantities of very pink gin – and genteelised or gentrified by myself into what wine merchant Simon Loftus calls 'one of the world's great sandwiches'.

hot toast
smoked salmon
mango chutney
hot, crisp, streaky bacon
cayenne pepper
butter

Preparation and cooking time: about 15 minutes

For each person, lightly butter 1 piece of toast, cover it (thickly) with smoked salmon, spread the salmon (thinly) with chutney, cover the chutney with bacon, sprinkle cayenne pepper on the bacon, and surmount with another piece of lightly buttered toast. Equally good as an open sandwich, in which case the single piece of toast should be medium-thick instead of medium-thin.

It isn't absolutely necessary to consume pink gin with this dish, but ardent spirits of some kind are perhaps better than wine or water.

39

TROUT AND BERRIES

Smoked trout is the poor relation of smoked salmon but the rich relative of smoked mackerel or sprats. It improves if jollied along by watercress purée, but is better still with a piquant gooseberry or blackberry sauce.

8 oz (226 g) gooseberries or blackberries (fresh or frozen)
¼ pt (14 cl) cider vinegar
1 shallot, finely chopped
1 tablespoon soft brown sugar (more if berries very sour)
¼ teaspoon cayenne pepper
1 dessertspoon mustard powder mixed with cider vinegar
1 teaspoon mustard seeds
1½ tablespoons oil for frying
4 smoked trout, skinned

Preparation and cooking time: about 30 minutes

Simmer fruit, vinegar, shallot, sugar and cayenne till fruit is cooked down to a jammy consistency, adding water if necessary. Stir in the made mustard. Fry the mustard seed in very hot oil. When the seed begins to pop, add the fruit, stir twice and remove from the heat.

The sauce should be spread over the upper side of each fish while it is still hot. Serve the trout with brown bread and branches of watercress. A crunch element like radish or raw young turnip is a pleasant addition.

A similar sauce can be made using blackberry or gooseberry jam but omitting the brown sugar and increasing the ration of vinegar and mustard.

COD'S ROE SCRAMBLE

Smoked cod's roe, creamed with butter, surrounded by lightly scrambled eggs, makes a beautiful starter in both senses. See page 138.

Fish Custards

Fish custards provide a luxurious starter at moderate cost. In general they can be regarded as self-help for the humbler fish rather

than platforms for marine aristocrats, not but what excellent versions can be made with salmon, sole and the major shellfish.

These custards can also be thought of as riceless kedgerees or potato-free fish pies. A brief digression on fish pie . . . When people say, as they often do, how much they adore fish pie, they are not talking about fish pie as normally understood. They are either being nostalgic about the golden, hungry days of childhood or, even more remote, yearning for the simple, gastronomic security of that ultimate table d'hôte, the womb. In short they idealise fish pie, forgetting the reality – bits of skin, tomato and off-white fish, needle-sharp bones and unyolked egg swimming around in béchamel substitute. ('Tone down or delete' is my pencilled comment on the first draft of that pearl-like insight. All right: good fish pies are possible, but for every one which I have eaten I've had ten horrors. Hot or cold, simple or complicated, fish custards are basically nicer than fish pie.)

The process involves poaching the fish in milk, thickening the milk with eggs (also, optionally, cream) and providing a suitable topping. Eggs are the key to thickening the milk, and at a pinch two eggs will set as much as one pint, although it is safer to use three eggs, and better still to use four. Two egg yolks have the same thickening power as one whole egg, and yolks only make for a richer custard. Once egg and milk have been conjoined, they must not be allowed to boil or the custard will be ruined. They can be cooked in a double saucepan, but a bain-marie in a medium-low oven needs less attention.

Fish custards may be made in pie dishes or (for quicker setting) individual ramekins. For a do-it-yourself bain-marie simply put dish or ramekins into a deepish baking tin and fill the tin with cold water, though not so high that there is any risk of water spilling into the milk mixture.

FINNAN CUSTARD

1 Finnan haddock
1 pt (56 cl) milk
3 or 4 eggs
5 tablespoons single cream (optional)
4 rashers streaky bacon or plain potato crisps

Preparation and cooking time: about 50 minutes

Pour cold milk over the haddock and bring it gradually up to simmering point. If it is allowed to boil over, everyone around will know what's cooking. About 6 minutes' simmering is enough, with the lid on. When the fish is cooked, remove it from the milk, allow it to cool a little, then bone and skin it carefully. Return bones and skin to the milk and simmer for a further 6 minutes, before straining off the milk.

Ideally the fish milk should be cooled to blood temperature. If time presses, however, it can be added pretty hot to the beaten eggs, providing the eggs are first well mixed with a coffee-cupful of warm milk or cream.

Having mixed eggs, milk and cream, put the flaked fish into a buttered pie dish or into ramekins and pour the custard mixture over it. Cover with greaseproof paper. Then place the whole in a larger vessel such as a roasting tin, and bake in a cool to moderate oven. After some 15 minutes, pour cold water into the outer vessel, to prevent overheating but allow quicker cooking. The custard should need a further 10 minutes (ramekins) to 15 minutes (pie dish).

Custards form their own (to me not unattractive) skin, but if you want a crunchy top, blanch streaky bacon in boiling water for 2 minutes, drain, then grill it till crisp and sprinkle it crushed on to the custard just before serving. Alternatively crush plain potato crisps and bake or grill them before scattering on top of the custard. If serving the custard cold, decorate it with little strips of smoked salmon, unpeeled shrimps, or watercress.

Eat with silver teaspons.

Custard Variations and Additions

Custards can be made with most fish and can embrace various extra flavourings provided these do not upset the chemistry of the dish. Unsmoked white fish such as cod makes a good custard, but requires chopped parsley aplenty (or dill or chervil). The addition of a few peeled shrimps is an attractive and economic frill which provides an additional texture. More expensive fish such as scallops are also welcome. Putting a pinch of saffron into the milk improves colour and compounds flavour. Anchovy essence gives valued zip to bland fish. Well-seasoned custards composed of mussels and whiting or cockles and crab are very acceptable, especially eaten cold, and not expensive. The cockles and mussels should only be cooked just long enough to open the shells.

Herring, mackerel and the oily fish do not seem suited to the custard treatment.

Vegetables may be added – raw, cultivated mushrooms, for example, or blanched asparagus tips, though you may consider using asparagus in this way is ostentatious.

Custards are excellent cold. They make a charming summer lunch, with salad, as well as a good first course for dinner. It should be borne in mind that cold dishes usually need more seasoning than their hot counterparts.

CURRIED FISH CUSTARD

While hot curries are unacceptable at the beginning of a meal, a mild, creamy curry flavour will harm no one's palate and will intrigue most people.

2 onions, fairly small
butter for frying
oil from an anchovy tin, for frying
2 teaspoons commercial curry powder (e.g. Vencat) or curry paste
lemon juice
5 tablespoons cream
1 lb (450 g) white fish (filleted for preference)*
1 pt (56 cl) milk
3 or 4 eggs
1 teaspoon mustard seed

Preparation and cooking time: about 45 minutes

Fry the chopped onion in a little butter and oil for 5 minutes, not too fiercely. Add the curry powder and continue cooking slowly for 10 minutes (5 for curry paste), stirring so that the powder absorbs most of the fat. De-glaze with a little lemon juice, then work cream into the resulting paste.

Meanwhile cook the fish in milk, as in the Finnan custard recipe (see page 42). When the fish is cooked (about 6 minutes), stir the fishy milk into the curry-cream mixture (or vice versa). Flake the fish and put a portion into each ramekin (or the whole lot into a pie dish).

Beat the eggs and amalgamate with the milk/cream/curry mixture. Pour this over the fish, cover with greaseproof paper, and bake in lowish oven in a bain-marie for 25 minutes, filling the roasting pan with cold water after 10–15 minutes.

Before serving, fry mustard seed in a little smoking hot oil for 1 minute. Have a lid standing by and as soon as seed starts popping smack on the lid but turn off the heat. Sprinkle burnt mustard seed but not the oil over the custard(s).

---

* If unfilleted fish is used for this recipe, allow at least 1 lb 2 oz (500 g) and discard skin and bones after simmering the fish in milk.

Savoury Syllabubs

Whipped cream flavoured with lemon and alcohol but not sweetened makes a heavenly vehicle for fish which is firm of texture or positive in taste, such as monkfish or salmon. Savoury syllabubs improve with keeping and should be made some hours before they are needed, being kept cool but only refrigerated in hot or thundery weather. The cream can be fortified by mustard, horseradish, herbs, anchovy, and decorated with pickles, chutney or slivers of smoked salmon.

Syllabubs are not recommended for soft white fish such as cod or plaice, but they work well with smoked fish and most shellfish. Since no cooking is involved, they are particularly suitable for bivalves like mussels, which are susceptible to overcooking.

PRAWN SYLLABUB

8 oz (226 g) prawns, cooked and shelled
juice of 1 lemon
tabasco or cayenne pepper
1 teaspoon mustard powder
scant ½ pt (25 cl) double cream
salt
paprika
garden cress or mustard and cress

Marinating time: 1 hour (optional); preparation time: about 25 minutes

Fresh, large prawns are best but frozen ones are also fine for this dish, all except the very small ones from south-east Asia (which are only suitable for spicy oriental food). If time permits marinate the prawns in some of the lemon juice and a couple of shakes of tabasco (or a pinch of cayenne) for 1–2 hours before use.

Mix the mustard powder with lemon juice to a thinnish paste. After 20 minutes, dilute it further with lemon juice so that it is about as runny as single cream.

Whip the double cream until it is stiff. Stir in the mustard and season lightly with salt and paprika. Add the prawns and most of the cress or mustard and cress. Distribute syllabub into individual glasses and leave in a cool place. Before serving strew each glass with more cress. Serve with thinly sliced brown bread and butter.

COCKLES AND MUSSELS AND CRESS

24 mussels
32 cockles (or small clams)
¾pt (42cl) house broth (page 24, chicken if possible)
2 large bunches watercress
a few young spinach leaves
1 large lemon

Preparation and cooking time: about 25 minutes (longer if using fresh, unwashed bivalves)

Of course it is best to collect your cockles and mussels alive alive oh from some unspoilt rocky shore, but if for any reason this is impracticable, and if your fishmonger has no bivalves in the shell, frozen ones will do very well. The timings given below are for frozen shellfish, in fact. Fresh ones must be cleaned and cooked till they open. Their juices must subsequently be allowed to rest, so that the sand settles on the bottom. Most of the juices can then be poured off and used for the watercress cullis. However, if you use the frozen variety, you will need some chicken stock instead of the cooking liquor.

Poach the cockles and mussels in chicken stock for 1 minute then plunge them into cold water. Keep the stock.

Remove coarse stalks from the watercress and discoloured leaves. Chop the rest roughly and blanch with the spinach leaves in boiling stock for 5 minutes. Drain the cress. Continue boiling the stock and reduce by half.

Blend the cress to a purée, using some of the stock as a lubricant and a little lemon juice. If the resulting purée is too watery – this will depend on your machine, ours seems to require an awful lot of liquid in order to blend efficiently – reduce it by simmering.

This dish may be served cold, but is better hot or warm. The purée can happily take a little cream or butter (introduced over a low heat). Re-heat the cockles and mussels in a little butter too, and even flare them with Irish whiskey (or Scotch if Molly Malone isn't watching). Spoon purée round the perimeter of each plate in a thick band and put the bivalves in the island in the middle.

JOBISKA

Edward Lear's Pobble was consoled for his loss of toes by Aunt
Jobiska's eggs and buttercups fried with fish. But what sort of fish?
Living so near the Bristol Channel, it might have been elvers, but
scallops would make a runcible alternative, as would crayfish,
prawns, the white meat of crab, lobster, sole, or members of the
shark family.

4 tablespoons rice (brown if liked)
8 or more scallops depending on size
6 rashers lean bacon
6 eggs
butter for cooking
salt and pepper
Angostura bitters

Cooking time: about 25 minutes

Boil the rice for about 10 minutes in plenty of salted water, draining
it as soon as it is edible. (Brown rice takes twice as long as ordinary
rice but should not be overcooked.)

Poach the scallops for 3 minutes. If using frozen 'queen' scallops,
leave them whole (about 6 per person); if using large fresh ones, cut
them into 'toes' about ⅓ in (1 cm) thick.

Cut rind-free bacon into small pieces, and beat up the eggs as for
scrambling. Using a large, deep pan fry the bacon in plenty of
butter, adding the scallops after 3–4 minutes, then the eggs and the
rice. Stir continually to scramble the eggs over a low heat. Season
with pepper, Angostura bitters and a little salt. As soon as the egg is
beginning creamily to set, remove pan from the heat, stir in a little
melted butter – and serve on hot plates.

Fish Cocktails

Corrupted by ketchup, polluted by proxies, sullied by salad cream,
the prawn cocktail has long since become a symbol of Philistine
affluence at table (though this does less than justice to the Philis-
tines, by the way, who were a gastronomically cultured minority
and were responsible for introducing both vine and olive to

Palestine; they have been reviled down the centuries because of partisan historians such as Jeremiah and Ezekiel). Yet a good prawn or shellfish cocktail makes an ideal start to a wide variety of meals – the cliché, as so often, is based on genuine insight. Syllabubs are one way out of the dilemma. Using an unwhipped cream-and-hardboiled-egg-yolk sauce is another.

PRAWN COCKTAIL RENEWED

½pt (28 cl) lost sauce (page 234)
1 tablespoon chives
7 oz (200g/¾ pt) prawns (shelled)
1 teaspoon cayenne pepper
lemon juice
4 large unshelled prawns
small cucumber

Preparation time: about 20 minutes; refrigeration and marinating time: at least 1 hour

Prepare lost sauce, add chopped chives, and refrigerate for at least 1 hour. Toss the prawns in cayenne and lemon juice.

To serve: mix prawns and sauce. Spoon mixture into individual glasses. Decorate with a single unpeeled prawn and serve with fingers of unpeeled cucumber.

This cocktail is equally good with fresh shrimps, pink or brown. They should be de-headed and tailed but need not be shelled. Lost sauce is excellent with most shellfish but should not be used with the brown meat of crab as it forms too rich a mixture.

Potted Fish

After grievous commercialisation into paste, true potted fish was almost forgotten, except that potted shrimps put up a valiant fight for survival. Several years ago, Elizabeth David set about restoring the practice of potting, and I shall not trespass long on her territory. However, her characteristic monograph on the subject is now unobtainable, and since potted fish makes a beguiling, very English starter, I shall attempt to summarise the rules.

Lightly cooked and seasoned (often with mace), the fish is

blended with butter, and chilled in a pot or pots, preferably of white china. Unless the potted fish is to be eaten almost at once, it should be sealed with a thickish layer of clarified butter. Like this it will keep for several weeks unrefrigerated. Before being blended with butter, the fish should be as dry as possible and it should be packed into its pots tightly so that all air is excluded.

Good subjects for potting include salmon, lobster, smoked haddock, kippers, shrimps and small prawns, smoked trout and freshwater fish such as char. Toast and lemon are the accompaniments.

POTTED TROUT

A good treatment for farmed trout.

2 trout
1 tablespoon cider vinegar
butter
mace
horseradish (grated)
pepper

Cooking and preparation time: about 25 minutes

Put the cleaned fish into cold water with the cider vinegar. Bring to a very gentle boil and simmer for 4 minutes. Remove the fish from the water and when they are cool, skin, bone and weigh them. Break up the flesh and mix it with rather less than its own weight in soft or just melted butter. Season with mace, horseradish and pepper but not assertively so. Potted food should be understated. Blend butter and fish either with a fork or in a mixer or a mortar; then pot it in – pots. Seal with clarified butter if it is to be eaten more than 2 days hence.

Please do not use commercial horseradish relish for this dish.

Shrimps

Note the second s, indicating little pink or brown crustaceans taken by the million from places like Morecambe Bay and the Wash, rather than the many varieties of prawn which are collectively identified as shrimp (no second s) in the American-speaking world.

Fresh shrimps – brown are meant to be best but I'm not sure I would know the difference blindfold – are cheap, delicious and fun. They are easy to serve – just put them in bowls and let everyone deal with their own. Do not dream of peeling them.

The best way to eat shrimps, of course, is to hold head and tail between finger and thumb, and bite the bit in the middle. So long as the shrimps are fresh, the shells are not only edible, but the source of appetising crunch. What is vital is that they are bought from a conscientious fishmonger the day they are served. True they will keep overnight, but the next day the shells will be scaly and tough; the only thing then is to peel them resignedly and put them in a sauce or curry.

As nibbles with drinks or as simple starters, shrimps are quite happy by themselves, with bread and butter, and salt seasoned by red and black pepper. For more ebullient beginnings, they can be accompanied by their seaside classmates, whelks, winkles and other cheerful little gastropods.

SEASHORE D'ŒUVRES

3 eggs
4 tablespoons turnip purée
1 tablespoon tomato cullis (page 31)
1 tablespoon lemon juice
1 tablespoon orange juice
parsley
1½ tablespoons dry sherry
1 shallot peeled and chopped small
Worcestershire sauce

a selection of cooked lesser shellfish, viz.

whelks	cockles
winkles	shrimps
mussels	clams

carrots and watercress to garnish

Preparation time: about 25 minutes

Hardboil 2 eggs. Mash their yolks with the third, raw yolk. Blend egg mixture with tomato and turnip purées. Add lemon and orange juice, chopped parsley, sherry, shallot and a dash of Worcestershire sauce. Season to taste and use as a zestful bed for the shellfish.

50

Remove whelks from their shells and cut off the little, hard, round coverpieces. Cut each whelk in half. Leave winkles in shells and provide pins for their extraction. Cockles and mussels should also be shelled, or served on the half shell.

A garnish of raw young carrots and watercress is suitable for this do-it-yourself hors d'œuvres. Try out different vegetable purées, according to season.

COCKLE WARMERS

4 large onions
4 rashers back bacon
oil
36–40 cockles (frozen will do)
1 egg
pepper
2 rashers streaky bacon
house stock (page 24)
whisky (optional)

Preparation and cooking time: about 1¼ hours

Bake the onions for about ¾ of an hour in a hot oven. When they are cool enough, remove the outer skins, take off the top as if they were eggs, but using a very sharp knife, and scoop out most of the insides of the onions, leaving at least 2 thicknesses as 'shell' for subsequent stuffing.

Blanch the back bacon in boiling water for 1 minute. Dry it on kitchen paper, then fry it in a little oil – 1 minute on each side. Finally dice the bacon, removing rind, and add it to the onion pulp. Also add the cockles, the egg and pepper. Stir and mash the mixture; then stuff it into the onion shells. Cover each onion with half a rasher of streaky bacon, having dribbled a teaspoon of whisky into it beforehand, if you feel so disposed. Bake for 15 minutes in a medium oven, with a little house stock in the bottom of the pan.

Notes: if using fresh cockles in the shell, only cook them long enough (in water or steam) to open the shells.

Mussels may be used instead of cockles.

Potatoes may be used instead of onions and will make a more substantial dish, but will need longer initial cooking (1¼ hours) and some chopped chives or lightly fried onion in the stuffing.

51

Pickled Salmon

While smoked salmon remains the most widely popular British ethnic luxury, travellers to Scandinavia often decide they like pickled salmon even better. Pickled salmon, in fact, has an Anglo-Saxon pedigree going back to the Middle Ages, but the form seems to have died out in the last century, when the laws of supply and demand began to promote salmon from poor man's protein to up-market show piece.

A basic Swedish version is given below, followed by an Anglicised variation. Both make wonderful starters or, with plenty of plain boiled potatoes, simple but expensive main courses. Both methods can be applied to large trout.

PICKLED SALMON (Swedish Method)

2lb 3oz (1kg) salmon or a whole sea-trout
½oz (14g) white peppercorns
3oz (84g) salt
1½oz (42g) white sugar
large bunch fresh dill
2 tablespoons English mustard
3 tablespoons white sugar
4 tablespoons vinegar or lemon juice
½pt (28cl) olive oil or olive and sunflower oil mixed

Preparation time: 30 minutes; pickling time: at least 24 hours

Cut the salmon laterally and extract all bones, to make 2 fillets.

Grind the peppercorns in a mortar; add the salt, sugar and dill, including the dill stalks (the pickle mixture).

Cut a large piece of kitchen foil and sprinkle one-quarter of the pickle mixture on to it; place a piece of fish, skin down, on the pickle mixture. Rub about half the pickle mixture on to the cut sides of both salmon fillets and place the second one, skin side up, on top of the first. The remaining pickle mixture goes on the skin side of the upper fillet and the foil is wrapped round so that it encloses the salmon tightly.

Weight down the fish between 2 plates or boards and leave it for 24–48 hours in a cold place. Before serving, throw away the salty liquor and wash the fish carefully, rubbing off adhering bits of pepper. Carve it in rather thick slices. Serve with a mustard, sugar and dill-flavoured vinaigrette and hot boiled potatoes.

After they have carved the fish down to the skin, Swedes sometimes cut the skin into little strips and fry them till crisp.

PICKLED SALMON (English)

1¼lb (600g) or more middle-cut salmon or a sea-trout
2oz (56g) salt
1oz (28g) caster sugar
½oz (14g) mustard powder
1 tablespoon mustard seed
1 teaspoon cayenne pepper
1 teaspoon white peppercorns
4 bay leaves

Preparation time: 30 minutes; pickling time: at least 24 hours

Cut the fish horizontally and remove all bones, leaving yourself with 2 thick fillets each with skin on one side.

In a mortar or mixing basin grind together the salt, sugar, mustard powder, mustard seed, cayenne, white pepper and bay leaves (the pickle mixture).

Cut a piece of kitchen foil large enough easily to enwrap the two pieces of fish. Spoon one-quarter of the pickle mixture on to the foil and put half of the fish, skin downwards, on to it. Put half the pickle mixture on to the cut side of the first piece of fish and place the second piece of fish, skin upwards, on to the mixture. Pull the foil up around the fish so that only the skin of the upper half (of the sandwich) is visible, and over this pour the remaining quarter of pickle. Fold the foil, parcel-like, so that fish and pickle are completely enclosed. Place parcel in a shallow dish; put another dish atop the parcel and weight it down very firmly. Store in a cool larder for 24–48 hours, turning the fish over once or twice.

Before serving, wash the fish free of adhering salt and spices, using quite a lot of cold, running water. Then pat it dry with a towel or kitchen paper.

Carve the pickled salmon diagonally downwards to the skin in slices about ⅛in (½cm) thick (that is, appreciably thicker than one usually cuts smoked salmon).

Serve with a mustardy, lemony vinaigrette and a new potato or two.

53

Salmagundy

Apparently my wife and I were by no means the first to revive salmagundy when, back in the mid-1970s and with a friend's unstinted if disputatious assistance, we made in a mere five hours enough of this medieval hors d'œuvres to sustain some four score of Aldeburgh Festival supporters through an evening of Mozart and Hummel. At the time I was convinced that no one had attempted the feat since the Wars of the Roses, but since then I have come across several adaptations of salmagundy by contemporary cookery writers.

In essence the dish is a combination of fish, eggs, chicken, citrus, pickle and greenery. It should contain nothing which derives from the New World, nor any non-indigenous foods which were not tolerably familiar before 1800 (at the latest). Salmagundy seems to have gone out just as the Industrial Revolution was coming in. The simple version given below will take considerably less than five hours to assemble and works equally well as a sumptuous first course or out-of-doors main course instead of salade niçoise yet again.

ESSSENTIAL SALMAGUNDY

cooked chicken
pickled herring
hardboiled eggs
apple
lemon
leaves of spinach, lettuce, nasturtium as available
pickled onion and/or walnut
cucumber
oil, vinegar and mustard for dressing

Preparation time: about 1 hour

The idea is to form a mound by layering the different ingredients, with a leafy element at top and bottom. Starting from the bottom, a good sequence of layers would be: lettuce; herring; chopped egg white; slices of pickled onion or walnut; spinach leaves; egg yolk; chicken; lettuce; cucumber; lemon and apple; lettuce.

Depending on how much you are making, repeat the layers as necessary. Before putting final layer of greenery in place, dribble a mustardy vinaigrette generously into the mound. Decorate the green top layer with nasturtiums or other edible flowers.

Further ingredients which may, with advantage, be used are anchovies, tongue, ham, pork, veal, raisins, radish or turnip.

CRAB CRUMBLE

2 cloves garlic (squeezed through garlic press)
1 heaped teaspoon cayenne pepper
4 teaspoons Urchfont-type mustard
2 teaspoons anchovy essence
3 tablespoons lemon juice
3 tablespoons sherry

2 large cooked crabs (or 3 or 4 smaller ones)
6 tablespoons soft breadcrumbs
4 tablespoons chopped parsley
spinach or sorrel, a few leaves
mustard powder
2oz (56g) refrigerated butter cut in small cubes

Preparation time: about 1 hour; cooking time: 20 minutes

Mix the first group of ingredients together in a pudding bowl. Remove all the meat from crabs and mix it very thoroughly with the condiments in pudding bowl. Add 4 tablespoons of bread-crumbs, 4 tablespoons of chopped parsley and the sorrel or spinach leaves cut into a chiffonade (see page 20). Leave the mixture to breathe and blend for at least 30 minutes.

To serve: either put the crab mixture back into crabshells, or into scallop shells, or into a pie dish. In each case scatter the surface with a mixture of the remaining breadcrumbs and mustard powder and dot it with the cubes of butter. Warm through in a medium oven but finish under the grill, watching carefully or the crumbs will burn the moment you turn your back.

Note: use plenty of parsley and other greenery. Crab dishes easily get too dense.

If this is being used as more than a starter, for example as one of 2 or 3 main offerings at a lunch or buffet, the cayenne/mustard content can be increased to something like 'devil' proportions.

STUFFED BIVALVES

The best stuffing for molluscs remains the garlic-butter-parsley mixture associated with snails. It is sensationally good with mussels and clams – but undeniably French. Here are a few non-garlicky stuffings which also make bivalves into delicious hot starters.

4 rashers streaky bacon, crisply grilled
6 tablespoons spinach cullis (page 33)
2 spring onions, chopped
black pepper
2 tablespoons breadcrumbs

Crumble the bacon and mix it with spinach purée. Season the mixture with spring onions and pepper, then spoon a little into each opened bivalve. Sprinkle lightly with breadcrumbs. Grill.

2) Use the above mixture, but substitute tomato cullis for spinach.

3) Use a vegetable purée flavoured with mild curry paste.

4) Mix together chopped parsley, chopped chives, butter, cream cheese and a pinch of cayenne pepper.

These are all suitable for mussels, cockles and clams – which should be opened in a saucepan with a very small amount of boiling water, but cooked only long enough to part the shells; or for Portuguese oysters or scallops. Open them raw with an oyster knife.

FISH FARCE

6 sardines
1 oz (28 g) ground hazelnuts
1 shallot, very finely chopped
parsley, chopped
pepper
anchovy essence
1 large, firm lettuce
4 fillets plaice
scant ½ pt (25 cl) chicken cullis or fish stock (pages 26, 28)

optional
1 tablespoon cider vinegar or lemon juice
1 oz (28 g) butter
2 tablespoons single cream

Preparation and cooking time: 30 minutes

Make a farce (stuffing) by mashing together the sardines, hazelnuts, shallot, parsley, pepper and a shake of anchovy essence.

Select 4 lettuce leaves and blanch them for a few seconds in boiling water. Plunge them into cold water, then dry them on kitchen paper.

Put 1 fillet of plaice on to each lettuce leaf and spread it with farce. Roll leaves and fish into little Swiss rolls, secure them with cocktail sticks or cotton thread, and pack them into a small ovenproof dish. Moisten them with a little fish stock or chicken cullis. Cover with greaseproof paper and bake in a medium oven for 15 minutes.

A sauce is not essential, but the juices may be reduced by brisk boiling with a tablespoon of cider vinegar or lemon juice and then thickened with the butter and lastly the cream.

SARDINE CAKES

Sardines on toast, sardine sandwiches and straight sardines are the usual ways of serving these wonderful, tinned fish. Sardine cakes are delicious, and so is sardine and potato salad (virtually a cold version of sardine cakes).

4 large potatoes
milk
2 spring onions
parsley
6 tinned sardines
salt and pepper
flour
oil for frying

Preparation and cooking time: 30 minutes

Peel and boil the potatoes. Mash them with a very little milk but add no butter.

Chop the spring onions and the parsley very finely. Break up the sardines. Mash potatoes, sardines, parsley and onion together, and season with salt and pepper. Divide the mixture into 4, and form thin fish-cake shapes. Dust these with flour and fry in very hot oil till brown and crisp on both sides.

Serve with a zest or gusto selected from pages 237–44.

SARDINE AND POTATO SALAD

Make a potato salad (page 222), but pour oil from the sardine tin on to the potatoes while they are still hot. Include 2–3 spring onions in the salad and parsley or dill plus hardboiled eggs, if the occasion is suitable. The sardines may be added whole but are more convenient cut in halves or thirds.

Don't underrate potatoes as a first course. This is the right sort of dish to start with if you are planning a light main dish.

The best tinned sardines come from France and these are still packed in olive oil. Iberian and North African sardines are cheaper but well worth eating, as long as they are not packed in tomato sauce.

LYNN TOMATOES

A natural dish for early autumn or late summer when tomatoes and shrimps are both plentiful.

8–10 tomatoes, depending on size
5 tablespoons dry cider
½ clove garlic, chopped
salt
pepper
paprika
3½oz (100g) streaky bacon
bay leaf
1 dessertspoon mustard powder
½pt (28cl) single cream
7oz (200g/¾pt) peeled shrimps
1½ tablespoons Rose's lime juice
20 unpeeled shrimps
parsley, chopped

Preparation and cooking time: about 45 minutes

Cut the tomatoes in half horizontally and scoop out the pips and some of the flesh, being careful not to damage the remaining shells. Unless the tomatoes are very small (hardly worth stuffing) or very large, allow 3 half tomatoes per portion. The remaining tomatoes should be chopped coarsely and put in a saucepan with the tomato scoopings, the dry cider, garlic, salt, pepper and paprika – and simmered for 30 minutes.

Meanwhile de-rind the bacon and cut it into very small pieces. Fry it gently without extra fat but with a little crumpled-up bay leaf. Make mustard-cream by mixing mustard powder with cream and diluting to a very thin paste with more cream (using 5 tablespoonsful to a dessertspoonful of mustard).

Strain the tomato mixture on to the bacon by rubbing it through a fine sieve; add the peeled shrimps; add the mustard cream and the lime juice; cook very gently for 5 minutes, stirring.

Take pan off heat. Retrieve the shrimps and bacon pieces with a perforated spoon (tilt the pan so that sauce runs to bottom) and stuff them into the tomato shells.

To serve, bake the stuffed tomato shells for 5 minutes in a hot oven, pour the reheated sauce over them, and decorate with the unpeeled shrimps and parsley.

Note: if you precook the tomato shells, they may split and disintegrate when you stuff and recook them.

WATERCRESS TERRINE

watercress cullis (page 32) made from 2 bunches of cress
2½ tablespoons single cream
2 eggs
1 tablespoon cream cheese (optional)

Preparation and cooking time: 25 minutes; cooling time: 1 hour

Mix all the ingredients well and put the mixture into 4 buttered ramekins. Bake these in a bain-marie in a medium oven for just under 20 minutes, covered with greaseproof paper.

Leave them to cool, then turn them out on individual plates. These are lovely on their own but are very compatible with home-made tomato cullis or ketchup.

Note: virtually all vegetable cullises can be turned into little terrines by the addition of egg.

TOMATO CAVALIERS

Tomatoes and bacon have an affinity which need not be confined to breakfast.

8 rashers streaky bacon
1 scant oz (25 g) butter
2 shallots
2 very large tomatoes
7 oz (200 g) cooking tomatoes, any size
thyme
salt
pepper
cayenne pepper
1 teaspoon sugar
1 scant tablespoon cider vinegar

Preparation and cooking time: 1 hour

Grill, fry or bake the bacon till it is crisp but not burnt. Keep to one side. Transfer any bacon fat produced by this process to a saucepan and add the butter. Melt the chopped shallots in the saucepan.

Blanch the large tomatoes in boiling water for a minute, then peel them. Cut them in half laterally. Scoop out pips and pulp but leave shells as for stuffing. Add the pulp to the shallots in the saucepan together with the cooking tomatoes, roughly chopped, the thyme, salt, pepper, cayenne, sugar and vinegar. Simmer gently for at least half an hour with the lid off, stirring occasionally. The sauce should be highly seasoned, sharp and thyme-scented. When it is cooked and slightly reduced strain and rub it through a fine sieve, so that there are no pips or skin in the final dish. Reduce the sauce further till there is little more than a good tablespoonful per person.

Carefully bisect each bacon rasher and arrange 4 halves vertically in each of the large tomatoes. Put sauce in the middle and sprinkle with fresh thyme. 5 minutes before serving, re-heat the tomatoes in a hot oven.

Note: you may certainly use fresh basil instead of thyme, though it is not strictly an English herb, alas.

STREAKY CABBAGE

6–8 rashers streaky bacon
oil
10 large, crisp cabbage leaves, or the equivalent in smaller ones
1 teaspoon mustard seed
3 tablespoons cider vinegar
dash Worcestershire sauce

Preparation and cooking time: 20 minutes

Quarter and de-rind the bacon rashers. Blanch them for 1 minute in boiling water. Take them out of the water, pat dry on kitchen paper, and roast or fry in a little oil using, if possible, a thick-bottomed iron casserole or the equivalent. Let them sizzle to a nice brown but not carbonise.

Meanwhile separate the cabbage leaves, remove thick, coarse stalk, and cut them in halves or quarters according to their size. Blanch them for 3 minutes in boiling water (the same as was used for blanching the bacon). Then drain them and plunge them into very cold water. Take them out of the cold water, pat them dry, and note the brilliance of their colour.

Remove the crisp bacon from casserole. Sprinkle mustard seed into the hot remaining oil and fat. As soon as the seed begins to pop, add the cabbage. Stir encouragingly and reduce the heat enough to prevent any burning. After 2 minutes add the vinegar and Worcestershire sauce. Let it bubble for a minute then reduce the heat again and cook for about 5 minutes before adding the bacon, and cooking for a further 3–4 minutes.

A sophisticated dinner-party starter using very prosaic materials.

A SUMMER'S TAIL

1 oxtail, cut by the butcher
2 large onions
5 tablespoons cider vinegar
3½pts (200cl) house broth (page 24)
4 carrots
bay leaf
thyme
1 teaspoon black peppercorns
chopped parsley
chopped chives
pickled walnuts
pepper
salt
wineglass port (optional)

Initial cooking time: 3 hours; cooking and preparation time: minimum 12 hours

Roast the oxtail in a large casserole in a hot oven. After 10 minutes add the onions, quartered but unpeeled. After another 10 minutes add the cider vinegar. When the vinegar has bubbled down to a syrup, add the stock, already hot but not boiling. Also add carrots, bay leaf, thyme and peppercorns. Reduce heat of oven; cover the pan, and cook for about 2 hours. Skim the stew 2 or 3 times at the beginning of the process. When the meat is ready to fall off the bone, remove all the pieces of oxtail but allow the stew to cook on and reduce for a further 30 minutes. Then take the pan out of the oven (of course the dish may be cooked on top of the stove), strain into a jug, and leave it to get cold. In short forget about it for several hours or overnight.

Remove all fat from cooking liquor; it should come away in 2 or 3 thick pieces. Has the broth underneath formed a firm or a runny jelly? If the latter, it needs further reduction by brisk boiling.

Remove every particle of fat from the pieces of tail. Take all the meat off the bone and shred it with the fingers. Mix it in a bowl with chopped parsley, chives and a few little pieces of pickled walnut. Then put the mixture into a mould. Do not pack it in terribly tightly.

Taste the liquor in which the oxtail cooked, adding pepper and salt to make it fairly pungent. A glass of port wine would almost certainly help it. If you put in port let it cook for a few minutes. Pour the liquor, hot but not boiling, into the mould. Allow about 2 hours for the brawn to cool and set. Then turn it out on to a plate.

Better than pig's head brawn, this dish must be thought about and begun well in advance as it is a lengthy process, albeit an easy one.

BLACK AND WHITE

1 onion, peeled and chopped
butter and/or bacon fat for frying
1 oz (28 g) jumbo oatmeal
1 oz (28 g) breadcrumbs
1 black pudding
1 white pudding (or 2 large pork sausages)
8 rashers streaky bacon

Cooking time: 15–20 minutes

A substantial starter which can equally well serve as a main – or only – course.

Fry the onion golden brown in quite a lot of fat (this isn't a particularly healthy dish). Add the oatmeal and crumbs and cook for at least 7 minutes to make a form of what they call skirlie north of the Border.

Cut the puddings in rings not more than ¾ in (2 cm) thick. Grill them and the bacon on both sides.

To serve: put skirlie on to a plate or platter. Arrange slices of pudding in alternate colours round the perimeter and bacon in the middle.

Though by no means essential, the following sauce makes a spectacular addendum.

2 tablespoons whisky
4 tablespoons meat cullis (page 26)
1 oz (28 g) butter
¼ pt (14 cl) mustard–cream (page 232)

Add whisky to stock in saucepan and boil till they have reduced to less than 2 tablespoonsful. Stir in the butter, then the mustard cream.

Outside Scotland, black puddings are more easy to find than white (or 'mealy') puddings, but the latter are worth seeking out.

Soup

As a soup-hating child, I pondered apprehensively the fate of Augustus, the chubby lad in *Struwwelpeter* who faded away because, like me, he would not eat the horrid stuff. Permitted alternative forms of nourishment, in the end I grew up to be a good, big boy, despite the dire warnings. I even came round to soup, realising that the moral of Augustus remained valid even if his fate was, in practice, eluctable. Soup is nourishing and nurturing.

If eating has two purposes, one to sustain life and health, the other to afford pleasure, then soup tends to fulfil the first office more than the second. Above subsistence level, of course, most dishes contain both functional and diversionary elements; soup can be fun. On the whole, however, it has a serious job and belongs to functional meals rather than jollies. For example, on normal working days at home we very often have soup and cheese for lunch. At dinner, soups have to be rather special to earn their keep.

Turtle Soup

Turtle is the best English soup, so here goes: 'Procure a fine, lively, fat turtle, weighing about 120 lbs – this weight being considered the best as the fat is not liable to be impregnated with that disagreeable strong savour objected to in fish of larger size; on the other hand turtle of very small size seldom possess sufficient fat or substance to make them worth dressing. When time permits, kill the turtle overnight . . .'

No, no. Forget Francatelli.* Turtles are a delightful – endangered – species. It is possible that one day turtle-farming in the tropics may be established as morally acceptable and ecologically sound. Until then, let's leave real turtle soup to John Lusty and the Lord Mayor of London (and perhaps boycott both).

Even in Victorian times this great soup posed logistical problems for all but the grandest kitchens. Mock turtle, in which the

---

* One of Queen Victoria's chefs, author of *The Modern Cook* (1846) and other works.

gelatinous meat from calves' heads, cunningly fortified with anchovy, took the place of the reptile, was devised as a substitute. Lewis Carroll immortalised the mock turtle, but the soup called for skilled cranial surgery as well as bursting larders and scullions aplenty, and has understandably been abandoned by modern cooks.

A mock mock-turtle soup follows – suitable for today, quite simple and very good.

MOCK MOCK-TURTLE SOUP

2 medium onions, chopped small
1 oz (28 g) beef dripping
1 lb (450 g) lean stewing beef, cubed
4 oz (110 g) ham, diced
¼ pt (14 cl) Madeira or cream sherry
¼ pt (14 cl) water
3½ pts (200 cl) house broth (page 24)
2 carrots
small packet dried fungi
parsley
marjoram
tin anchovies
1 lemon

Preparation and cooking time: 2½ hours

If you haven't enough broth, augment it by adding a can of consommé.

Soften the onion in beef dripping in a large saucepan; add beef and ham and fry until browned 'all over' (as recipes usually say; in practice this is impossible unless you deep fry). Add the sherry together with the same quantity of water and boil fast until the liquid is reduced to a glaze. Then add the broth (or broth and consommé), carrots and fungi. Bring to the boil, skim, then simmer for 2 hours with lid on. A medium oven, as for casseroles, is suitable for this operation; the length of cooking is not critical but must be long enough for the meat to relinquish all its goodness. Remove lid for last 30 minutes.

Strain the liquor through the finest sieve available or through muslin.

Remove tough stalks from the herbs; chop 4 anchovy fillets, and using half a cup of the liquor make a herb purée in the blender. Add the juice of a lemon to the purée, then amalgamate purée and liquor. Re-heat, taste for seasoning, and add a further glass of sherry or Madeira before serving.

Optional but impressive: mash 4 hardboiled egg yolks with 1 raw yolk and most of the oil from the anchovy tin. Roll this into little balls and drop the balls – mock turtle eggs – into the soup 3 minutes before serving.

The marine flavour of the soup is unobtrusive. To make it more overt, increase the anchovy content by adding 1–2 fillets or some anchovy essence.

Cullis Broths

The kitchen which is well supplied with good broth and vegetable cullises can produce beautiful soup on demand. Diluted with broth, any vegetable purée becomes a fresh-tasting, sensible soup in seconds. Family soup. The addition of cream or the incorporation, without boiling, of eggs bestows a touch of class without social pretension – guest soup! For soup-making, the importance of having a selection of home-puréed, home-frozen cullises can hardly be overstressed.

Cullis broths may be fortified or varied in many ways apart from the cream and egg options. Herbs, finely chopped chicken or ham, most leftover vegetables, finely chopped (julienned) fresh vegetables, fresh fungi, sherry, grated cheese and curry flavours can all be introduced. Such soups can be anything from heartily thick to delicately thin depending on the needs of the moment.

VEGETABLE SOUP

6 tablespoons mixed vegetable purée (page 31)
1½pts (84cl) house broth (page 24)
3 tablespoons single cream
chopped chives
2 tablespoons sherry

Heat broth and purée to simmering point. Stir well. Add cream, fresh herbs and/or sherry if required.

LIGHTLY CURRIED SOUP

The new-wave French cooks discovered curry powder and were naïvely excited by it. Under the influence of Indian friends, I more or less gave up using the stuff years ago – on the grounds that it was Anglicised and un-Indian. That in itself validates the discreet use of curry powder in new *English* cooking; as does nostalgia for the British Raj.

The simplest cullis-broth can be enhanced by mild currification. Since it needs less cooking, I tend to use curry paste rather than curry powder for soups. If using powder, remember it must be fried (preferably with onion) for at least 8 minutes before the broth is added.

1 onion
2 tablespoons butter or oil
2 teaspoons mild curry paste
1 pt (56 cl) vegetable cullis (page 31)
1 pt (56 cl) house broth (page 24)
¼ pt (14 cl) single cream
juice of 1 lemon
salt and black pepper

Cooking time: 15 minutes

Fry the onion for about 7 minutes in butter or oil before adding the curry paste. Stir paste and onions together, then add vegetable cullis and heat it through. Add the broth and simmer for 5 minutes. Enrich with cream, sharpen with lemon, and season with salt and black pepper, as necessary.

Almost any vegetable purée may be used. The degree of curry spicing may be increased, but these soups should not be chilli hot.

SPROUT SOUP

1 medium onion, chopped
½oz (14g) butter or bacon fat
2oz (56g) ham or lean bacon, diced
8oz (226g) Brussels sprouts
5 tablespoons dry cider
1¾pts (100cl) house broth (page 24)

Cooking time: 15–20 minutes

Fry the onion in butter or bacon fat until golden, then add the ham.
Cook but do not brown it, stirring carefully.

Remove outer and discoloured leaves from the sprouts. Shred the
sprouts very finely, removing thick pieces of stalk. Add the sprouts
to onion and ham and stir-fry for 1 minute. Add the cider and let it
bubble down to almost nothing. Add the broth. Bring it up to the
boil and the soup is ready.

BEETROOT SOUP

2 medium-large beetroots, peeled, uncooked, cubed
1 turnip, peeled and cubed
1 clove garlic
1 onion, peeled and chopped
1¾pts (100cl) house broth (page 24)
scant ½pt (25cl) double cream (whipped)
1 lemon
1½oz (40g) grated horseradish
1 orange (not too sweet)
salt and pepper
4 cardamom pods

Preparation time: 10 minutes; cooking time: 30 minutes

Simmer the vegetables in broth until they are soft enough to blend.
Purée them in blender, using some of the broth.

Make horseradish sauce using whipped cream, juice of half a
lemon and the freshly grated horseradish.

Return beet and turnip purée to the broth in the pan and re-heat
with juice of 1 orange and half a lemon. Season with salt, pepper
and crushed cardamom.

Serve the soup in bowls with a good dollop of horseradish cream in the centre.

Note: admittedly cardamom is not one of the more usual Anglicised spices, but it has a special affinity with beetroot. It has been imported from the east for centuries and plays an important part in the cuisine of Scandinavia and Germany. It's extremely good with beetroot salads.

MULLIGATAWNY

A favourite English soup throughout the nineteenth century, but now tandoorised into oblivion, mulligatawny was an elaborate, usually thick, soup served with a separate dish of boiled rice. Some recipes call for 3–4 hours' cooking. Here is a 20-minute version.

2 onions, chopped
1 clove garlic
2–3 tablespoons oil
curry paste (or powder)
1 tablespoon syrup from jar of mango chutney
2 lemons
2pts (112cl) chicken stock
2 tablespoons boiled rice
2oz (56g) cooked, shredded chicken
single cream (optional)

Cooking time: 20 minutes

Fry the onion and garlic in oil until golden. Add a good dessert-spoonful of curry paste and cook with the onions 1–2 minutes. Add the chutney syrup and the juice of 2 lemons. Bubble the mixture for 1–2 minutes and amalgamate thoroughly. Add the chicken stock and simmer for 10 minutes. After 5 minutes, add the boiled rice. Before serving throw in the chicken – and some cream if you like.

SCOTCH BROTH

1 lb 2 oz (500 g) stewing lamb or mutton (e.g. neck)
3 pts (170 cl) house broth (page 24)
4 oz (112 g) pearl barley
scant ½ pt (25 cl) brown ale
2 large onions, not peeled
4 large carrots, whole
1 turnip, not peeled, halved
1 head celery
8 small carrots, julienned
1 leek, julienned
1 handful finely shredded cabbage
3 tablespoons green ginger wine
chopped parsley

Preparation and cooking time: 1¾ hours

Put the meat, stock, barley, beer, onions, carrots, turnip and celery into a pan, bring to simmering point, and cook gently (uncovered) for 1½–2 hours, skimming as necessary. When thoroughly cooked, remove the vegetables and meat, leaving the barley in the broth. Skim off any fat. Dice about 4 tablespoonsful of lean meat and return it to the pan together with the julienned vegetables and the cabbage. Boil briskly for 5 minutes. Before serving add the green ginger wine and some parsley.

This procedure can be adopted for beef, rabbit or pigeon, but if using game, include also an element of ham or bacon.

SOUP D'ÉTAT

A richly satisfying combination of oxtail and game which, in one version, makes a luxurious starter, and in another a hearty main course. Start preparing the dish the day before it is going to be eaten.

1 oxtail, cut up by the butcher
2 hind legs of hare
1 pigeon
2 onions, peeled
3 carrots, peeled
1 turnip, peeled

70

½ beetroot, peeled
1 leek, trimmed
2 sticks celery, trimmed
scant tablespoon peppercorns
scant tablespoon juniper berries
bay leaf
6 oz (168 g) prunes
pot of Indian tea
1 tablespoon black treacle
5 tablespoons whisky
3½ tablespoons Rose's lime juice
chopped fresh herbs
bunch raw carrots

Preparation and cooking time: 24 hours

In a large pan suitable for oven and hotplate, start roasting the oxtail in a hot oven. When the fat begins to run, add hare, pigeon and onions. They should brown but not burn. After about 20 minutes transfer to hotplate or ring, add carrot, turnip, beetroot, leek, celery, and cover with plenty of cold water. Bring up to simmering point and skim carefully and regularly for 15 minutes. When the broth is bubbling clear, add the peppercorns, juniper berries and a bay leaf. Put on the lid and transfer to medium oven. Some 2 hours later, add the prunes, having soaked them in Indian tea the while. Now leave the lid off and continue cooking for an hour. If, at the 3-hour stage, the meat comes easily away from the bones, remove oxtail, hare and pigeon, and strain off the broth, reserving the vegetables. If the meat needs further cooking (some oxtails take 4 hours or more), delay this process as long as necessary.

Soup d'état as starter: next day (or several hours later) remove the solidified fat from the cold broth. Re-heat 2 pints and boil rapidly to reduce by one-third, adding the treacle, whisky and lime juice. Taste for seasoning. Just before serving, add chopped fresh herbs.

As main course: remove all fat from broth. Whizz retained vegetables to a purée. De-fat, bone and chop up the oxtail meat, the hare and the pigeon meat. Wash and dice a bunch of raw carrots (young if possible). Put all these ingredients into saucepan, add treacle, whisky and lime juice as above, and simmer till carrots are just cooked.

Proportions given will feed at least 6 people.

CHICKEN TEA

Without knowing it, Baron Justus von Liebig, the great nineteenth-century chemist, was an innovatory cook. It happened like this. My great-grandfather and his sister, Emma, were staying with Liebig, their father's friend, at his Munich house in 1852. Emma unfortunately caught typhoid fever and for weeks lay at death's door, attended by one Dr Pfeufer. As the end approached, Pfeufer said to Liebig, 'I have no hope of saving the young girl's life. The crisis is past, but she is so weak she cannot digest any food. The only chance of recovery is to find a food which the patient can assimilate. Medicine can do nothing – perhaps science can.'

Liebig, who naturally felt responsible for his English friend's daughter, thought he might be able to prepare a sort of chicken tea which would assist digestion, so he made a special 'extract of meat, without coagulating the albumen', using chicken, cold water and muriatic acid. The patient, given a teaspoonful every half hour, was able to assimilate it, since 'by a chemical process the food was (already) digested', and gradually got better. Indeed Emma Muspratt made such a complete recovery that she was subsequently complimented by ex-King Ludwig of Bavaria on her close resemblance to his former dear friend, Lola Montez, while the commercial process which saved her was adapted and commercialised in Britain as Liebig's Extract of Meat, and that's how Oxo was born.*

So reach for your muriatic acid . . . or try the following recipe, which, though free of HCl, commemorates an oft-repeated family story.

2 pts (112 cl) house broth (page 24)
10 tablespoons hock
2 medium carrots, julienned
2 oz (56 g) breast of chicken, cooked and julienned
1 lemon, the rind julienned
China tea (made, not too strong)

Cooking time: 10 minutes

Use a very chickeny broth, free of all fat. In a saucepan reduce the hock to half its original volume, then add the broth and bring to the

* From E.K. Muspratt, *My Life and Work* (Bodley Head, 1900).

boil along with the carrot, chicken and lemon. After 2 minutes, remove pan from the heat and add a good cup of china tea (no milk). Serve in teacups with saucers and wedges of lemon.

Fish Soups

For a soup-conscious island surrounded by fish, Britain has produced surprisingly few fish soups. It is quite easy to adapt bouilla-baisse and its Mediterranean siblings to northern fish, and so produce pungent, cross-Channel cousins, but by no stretch can such soups be called English. No English dish ever tastes of garlic, for example, and our use of tomatoes is restrained. Similarly fish bisques and veloutés can be adumbrated in northern climes but, quintessentially French, they cannot be part of English ethnic cookery.

The fish soups suggested below are suitable as starters to quite elaborate meals as well as soups for everyday eating.

FISHMONGER SOUP

1 lb 6 oz (620 g) white fish (cleaned, on the bone, with heads if possible)
5 oz (140 g/½ pt) shrimps
4 tablespoons chopped parsley
⅓ pt (20 cl) dry cider
1 lemon
small clove garlic
1 onion, coarsely chopped
1 leek
2 carrots
2 sticks celery
1 large potato, peeled and diced
3 anchovy fillets

Preparation and cooking time: 40 minutes

Reserve about one-quarter of the fish (including shrimps). Remove its skin and bones; cut it into small chunks. Peel the shrimps. Reserve parsley, cider and lemon.

Cover the remaining ingredients with cold water and bring to the boil. Skim as necessary. Simmer about 20 minutes. Then put everything, skin, bones, heads and all, through a Mouli or blender. Return to saucepan and simmer for another 5 minutes, before pressing the broth through a fine sieve.

Return the strained broth to pan. Add dry cider, lemon juice and the reserved chunks of fish. Poach for about 5 minutes then add peeled shrimps and parsley. Serve as soon as you like.

So long as it is in good condition, cheap fish is suitable for this soup and different species may be combined promiscuously. Reserve the best and firmest for poaching as chunks.

Variations and Additions

Add a dessertspoon of powdered turmeric at the beginning. This gives a golden colour and a mild, but not curry-flavoured, spiciness. A few wisps of saffron may also be considered.

Add mussels or clams, lightly cooked, at the final stage, with their cooking juices.

Use fennel or dill instead of (or as well as) parsley.

MACKEREL SOUP

1 large (or 2 small) fresh mackerel
½ smoked mackerel (cold-smoked or uncooked if possible)
1¾ pts (100 cl) milk
2 spring onions or shallots
2 teaspoons coarsely ground white pepper
½ oz (14 g) butter
1 tablespoon oatmeal
bay leaf
½ pt (28 cl) single cream
chopped parsley or chives
freshly grated horseradish

Preparation time: 35 minutes; cooking time: 25 minutes

Clean and split the fresh mackerel. Cover it and the smoked mackerel with ¾ pt (42 cl) milk in a saucepan. Leave for 30 minutes then slowly heat up to simmering point. Hold the simmer for 2 minutes, then remove fish and throw away the milk (or give it to the cat). This process removes most of the oiliness from mackerel. Cut the fresh mackerel into large pieces.

Fry the onions and pepper in a large saucepan in butter. When the onion is soft (don't let it go brown) throw in a scant tablespoon of oatmeal – just enough to take up the butter. Gradually add fresh milk, stirring to prevent the formation of lumps; somewhat over 1 pint in all. Add the fresh mackerel and bay leaf. Simmer gently for 10 minutes with lid on. Remove the pieces of fish and take pan off heat. Discard skin and bone from fish. Blend fish and entire contents of pan to a thin purée in blender or suitable appliance. Return to heat and add the cream.

Meanwhile grill the smoked mackerel until it is nice and brown. Throw away the skin. Cut the fish into small diagonal croûtons and divide these between the soup bowls. Pour the soup over the smoked mackerel and top with chopped parsley or chives. Serve grated horseradish separately.

75

CRAB SOUP

2 cooked crabs
2 medium potatoes
⅓ pt (20 cl) dry cider
½ tablespoon cider vinegar
milk
black pepper
cayenne pepper
anchovy essence
¼ pt (14 cl) single cream
lemon
toasted croûtons

Preparation time: 30 minutes; cooking time: 15–20 minutes

Extract all the crab meat and separate white from brown. Meat from the fat part of the claws should be kept as intact as possible, so that you have 8 largish pieces. Clean outer shell and claws. Break up and pound the crab remains and boil them for 12 minutes in 1 pt (56 cl) water, dry cider and cider vinegar. Include potatoes, peeled and diced. When potatoes are soft, strain broth from shell; remove potatoes.

Blend the cooked potato with enough warm milk to make a purée. Add brown crab meat and blend again briefly. Combine blended ingredients with the crab-shell broth, add all the white meat except that from the fat part of the claws. Season with black pepper, cayenne and anchovy essence. Heat through, add cream, simmer for about 1 minute.

Serve in bowls with 2 pieces of claw meat per person, plus wedges of lemon and a few toasted croûtons.

If you are lucky enough to have crabs with red coral (females in summer), pound the coral to a paste with butter, parsley and chives. Divide the result into 4 and put 1 portion into each bowl.

CULLEN SKINK

This is not a new recipe but a rationalised version of perhaps the best indigenous fish soup. It ought to be better known. Like many good soups it hails from Scotland – Cullen is a village on the Moray Firth, skink means broth.

2 medium potatoes
1 large onion
1 smoked haddock (on the bone)
1¼ pts (70 cl) milk
¼ pt (14 cl) single cream
chopped parsley
½ oz (14 g) butter
1 or 4 eggs (optional)

Cooking time: 30 minutes

Peel and quarter the potatoes and onion. Place them with the fish in a saucepan and cover with 1 pt (56 cl) milk and ½ pt (28 cl) water. Bring up to simmering point and cook for about 12 minutes before removing the fish. Leave potato and onion to carry on cooking for another 5 minutes. Carefully remove bones and skin from fish. When cooked, remove potato and onion from broth but return fish bones and skin to it. Let these cook 5 minutes or a little longer, then strain the broth, discarding skin and bones.

Blend potato, onion and some of the broth to a purée. Return this to saucepan with the remainder of the fresh milk, half the cream and the fish broth. Also add the flaked fish and half the parsley. Heat to near boiling point. So long as you do not boil the soup, a beaten egg may be included at this stage to finish the soup luxuriously. Just before serving, stir in the butter.

Incorporate the rest of the cream and the rest of the parsley as a garnish in soup bowls when serving.

These quantities give 4 hearty helpings but will easily be enough for 6 if the soup is to be followed by a substantial main course.

Without either cream or eggs, an austere version of this soup is still very good indeed. Extra potato can be employed to make it more filling. Cullen skink can also be made with Arbroath smokies.

A lightly poached egg in each plate, makes this soup a meal in itself.

SHRIMP SOUP

10 oz (280 g/1 pt) shrimps
2 pts (112 cl) milk
1 tablespoon tomato cullis (page 31) or concentrate
1 anchovy fillet
tabasco
paprika
4 rashers streaky bacon

Cooking time: 15–20 minutes

Cover the shrimps in milk (but keep back a few). Bring them to the boil. Transfer them heads, shell and all, to a blender or food processor, with some of the milk, the tomato and the anchovy – and whizz to a purée. This will have to be done in 2 or 3 batches. Return the mixture to saucepan, add the rest of the milk, sharpen with tabasco and paprika, and simmer for 5 minutes. Strain through a fine sieve.

Peel the shrimps kept back and remove heads and tails. (Use the biggest for this.) Sprinkle them with paprika and heat through in a dry (fatless) frying pan over a brisk heat. At the same time grill the streaky bacon crisp.

Strain the soup. Pour it into bowls and top with shrimps and crumpled bacon. If you have some home-made tomato cullis, stir a teaspoonful into each bowl before adding shrimps and bacon.

FISH MULLIGATAWNY

1 onion, chopped
1 tablespoon oil
1 tablespoon turmeric
1–2 teaspoons curry paste, or to taste
1 teaspoon black peppercorns, crushed
1 lb (450 g) white fish, boned and skinned
juice of 1 lemon
1 tablespoon Rose's lime juice
1¾ pts (100 cl) fish stock (from bones and skin, see page 28) or water
anchovy essence
¼ pt (14 cl) single cream
3–4 tablespoons plain boiled rice

Cooking time: 25 minutes

Using a saucepan or deep-sided frying pan rather than an ordinary frying pan, fry the onion in oil for about 7 minutes but not so that it browns. Add turmeric, curry paste and peppercorns. Cook on for a further 5 minutes, then add the fish, cut into small chunks. Stir so that the fish gets impregnated with the spices. After 2–3 minutes add lemon and lime juice to de-glaze the remaining oil, and when the juices have bubbled down a little add the fish stock or water. Simmer for 7–8 minutes, until the fish is cooked, but not falling apart. Add a dash or two of anchovy essence. Before serving add the cream and simmer for 30 seconds, then the boiled rice.

Junket as Cold Soup

Unsweetened junket makes a refreshing and delicious cold soup – every bit as good as (and a jolly sight more English than) Crosse & Blackwell's (dependable) consommé or mock gazpacho made with Libby's tomato juice. The junket needs to be slightly salt, slightly lemony and may well include a hint of dry sherry. Cold junkets are improved by cream – half milk, half single cream is a good ratio, but the proportions are by no means critical and milk only is very acceptable. Nutmeg is optional. Sometimes a bay leaf should be allowed to pass through the milk while it is being warmed, but not to linger beyond the moment rennet is added.

Junket is a good vehicle for fresh herbs, nasturtium leaves, spring onions, edible flowers, radishes and most of the vegetables which can be enjoyed raw.

BASIC PROCEDURE

To one pint of milk or milk-and-cream add the juice of a small lemon, and, if liked, a small glass of sherry. Season lightly with salt and white pepper. Bring the milk up to blood temperature on stove then remove from heat and add a teaspoon of rennet (unflavoured). It should then be poured into soup bowls or custard glasses in which you have already put a scattering of herbs, flowers or chopped raw vegetables. Junket sets quite quickly and does not need refrigeration.

CUCUMBER JUNKET

1 cucumber
salt
chives
mint
1 tablespoon brandy
1 lemon
tabasco
¾ pt (42 cl) milk plus ¼ pt (14 cl) single cream, or 1 pt (56 cl) milk
1 teaspoon rennet (or a little more)

Preparation time: 35 minutes; cooking and cooling time: at least 45 minutes

Wash but don't peel the cucumber. Cut it into long chips and salt these generously to extract water. After 30 minutes drain, dry and dice them. Chop the chives and mint. Put a tablespoon of cucumber and a scattering of herbs in each soup bowl.

Add brandy, salt, lemon juice and tabasco to milk (and cream). Raise this to blood temperature (98°F), add rennet and remove from heat. Pour milk mixture into bowls and leave to set. Before serving, scatter herbs on surface of junket, also a nasturtium flower if available.

4
FISH & SHELLFISH

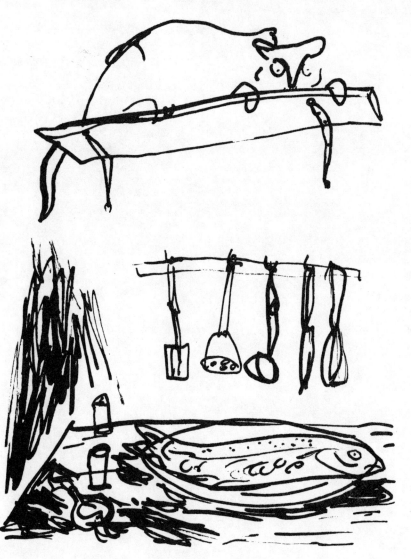

The Need for Change

The static, reactionary side of British cooking is particularly marked in its treatment of fish. Nowhere is the need for reform more urgent. For most of history fish has been abundant and cheap – oysters and salmon were poor man's fare in Dickens's day – yet hardly any great national dishes have emerged in recent centuries, apart from fish and chips (born 1870, still going wrong). If certain improvements have taken place since the Second World War, they can mostly be traced (via Elizabeth David) to French or Italian influences, or to the colonisation of these islands by oriental cooks. Of indigenous evolution there has been none; and resuscitation of ancient recipes from provincial archives has for the most part served only to explain the desuetude of the dish concerned. Culinary archaeology is not the answer: we must think for ourselves.

Today, of course, overpopulation on land is leading to under-population at sea. Scallops have joined oysters in the luxury class; the pilchard's progress has led to its destruction; herring and even cod are fast on the tails of sole, salmon and turbot. At the same time, interest in fish has never been greater. Cause and effect? Or well-deserved irony? If only we could exercise contemporary enthusiasm on yesterday's fishmongers' slabs – and at yesterday's prices.

Fish farming offers some hope. Farmed rainbow trout may never compare in natural taste with freshly hooked 'brownies', but they maintain supplies and inhibit price rises to some extent. Compensatory cooking, for example by using the new recipe inspired by Izaak Walton's original (page 100), can do much to remedy inherent deficiencies. Half of Norway's salmon is fjord-farmed already, and farming techniques are being developed for many other species, including sea-trout, lobsters and crayfish. It is surely more realistic to expand this industry than to hope that Russia, Denmark and Japan will restrict their factory ships.

New English fish cookery seeks to improve our ways without merely copying others, to evolve interesting new dishes from familiar – often humble – local produce, and to show how our fish cooking can be reformed deliciously, while remaining straight-forward and, in essence, traditional.

A Key Formula

The new fish cookery in France is largely based on one simple formula. Restaurant chefs add their individual gloss to it, earning laurels according to the success and originality of the variations they conceive, but the syntax of the dish is always the same. In a recent book,* the Dorchester's presiding genius gives 20 variations on the theme (in a fish section containing 26 recipes in all). The author is Swiss not French, but the formula he exploits belongs to no particular nation. It can equally well produce magnificent dishes with an Anglo-Saxon or northern flavour. The thing is – it works, it's quick, and the result is always appreciated. Here it is.

For convenience and speed (especially in restaurants), the fish is filleted and usually skinned. The fillets are cooked for the minimum time, typically in a mixture of fish stock and white wine, though not very much of either, and with a little finely chopped shallot. When just done, they are removed and kept warm while the cooking juices are reduced over brisk heat. After this first reduc-tion, cream is added; then there is a second reduction. The sauce is then finished with cold butter.

Variations are achieved principally by introducing extra ingre-dients and flavours during one or more of the last three stages – vermouth, brandy, herbs, fungi, shellfish, citrus. Particular favourites among these aids in the new French school are Noilly Prat, truffles, crayfish and basil. The beurre blanc method, in which butter rather than cream is added to the reduced (acidulated) cooking liquor, is a minor variant – and some chefs include cream in their beurres blancs.

The interested cook will see at once possibilities and limitations in this formula. It can be adapted to accommodate ingredients which happen to be in the larder, in season, or in somebody's

* Anton Mosimann, *Cuisine à la carte* (Macmillan, 1983).

particular esteem. However, a family likeness pervades all its manifestations.

In expensive restaurants the formula is normally applied to expensive fish and very expensive trimmings, but it works equally well with lesser breeds. Arguably, indeed, the humbler the fish, the more it responds to this kind of treatment. Under the title Three-Star Fish, which follows, there is a basic English version of the formula, and some pointers to possible variations. Mastering this easy routine is the surest way to a reputation for sophisticated originality in the fish department.

On or Off the Bone?

As remarked in Chapter 1, innovative restaurant chefs are leaders of the fast-food industry. Their customers are prepared to pay handsomely but not to wait long before starting to eat. Accordingly, first courses must be more or less instant, and even main courses must be quickly finished, though both may include preparatory processes which are time-consuming.

This is the discipline which leads to the filleting of sole and other noble fish – fillets being quicker to cook, easier to handle, more convenient for portion control, and (in some cases) more accessible to elegant decoration. Gastronomic considerations alone would normally suggest cooking the fish whole, since removal of skin and bone also detracts from the taste. In its purest form, serious fish cookery returns the lost taste by using skin, bones and head to make stock, and using the stock either as a cooking medium or as an element in the final sauce, or both.

The cutting and cooking of suitable fish into steaks is dictated by similar considerations. Salmon and tunny fish, for example, are easier to deal with as steaks than as fillets, and can be cooked in the time it takes to sip a glass of sherry.

In the home kitchen, filleting is perfectly valid but is only essential with fish which are too large to be cooked whole. Gastronomic and aesthetic calculations both lead to cooking on the bone if possible. Nor are whole fish necessarily less convenient than fillets in the domestic, as opposed to the restaurant, context. They hold their shape and texture better than fillets, and the fact that they take longer to cook is often an advantage at a dinner or lunch party. Moreover, whole fish look more characterful than disembodied slabs of fillet. One of the reasons some chefs indulge in elaborate garnishings which have little connection with cooking is their need to disguise the anaemic appearance of a pale fillet covered by creamy sauce. (They also do it because they are good at it, and because they can thereby charge more for the finished product.)

Choosing Fish

The best thing is to catch it yourself, or to be there waiting on the quay when fishing boats land; then you can be sure it's fresh.

Assuming you have to resort to a fishmonger, the rule is to look each fish in the eye. If perfectly fresh, it will stare back through a convex retina; if old or stale, its eye will be concave; flat eyes indicate that the fish is past peak freshness but still worth eating.

One reason unscrupulous shopkeepers fillet so much of their fish is to prevent customers from seeing those tell-tale concavities. Plenty of whole, unbeheaded fish are a sign of the scrupulous supplier.

Another sign of the caring fishmonger: nearly all fish should be gutted before you arrive. In general, fish should be cleaned as soon as they have been killed. Guts taint the flesh. Trout left ungutted, for example, become virtually unsaleable within five hours. Herring are a partial exception to this rule, and salmon should only be gutted if caught at sea rather than in the river.

Frozen fish – difficult to avoid these days – usually come into the intermediate (flat-eyed) category in relation to freshness. Happily most fish freeze fairly well. Once frozen, they will never be as good as *fresh* fresh fish but should be better than elderly unfrozen fish.

The fresher the better does not apply to skate, the one fish which is unattractively tough unless 'hung' for two or three days.

The Interchangeability of Fish Recipes

A sauce or technique which complements (and compliments) one type of fish can often be applied to several others. Trout and sole, for example, are as different as two fish can be, yet they respond equally well to the classic meunière treatment.

This is ideologically unsatisfactory. The romantic ideal is for each recipe to be a unique marriage of ingredients and methods, the alteration of which, in the smallest particular, will change and probably ruin everything. Very few recipes are as perfect as that, however, and certainly not mine. In chemistry, water is always H_2O and common salt sodium chloride, but in the kitchen there are no such certainties. Ah, you may say, that is because cookery is an art not a science . . .

Yes indeed, and how gratifying to make virtue out of deficiency, to turn confession into claim. Thank you, and please feel free to make as many intelligent swaps and adaptations of these recipes as you like.

A parallel form of interchangeability is that while all the dishes in this chapter can be used as the principal course of a meal, many of them are equally appropriate, in smaller helpings, as first courses.

THREE-STAR FISH

The quintessence of new fish cooking for domestic kitchens, this recipe can be adapted to soft fish like cod, firm fish like sole, oily fish like mackerel, to salmon and trout and to all kinds of freshwater fish. The individual character bestowable in the final stages should be dictated by the nature of the fish being featured, but in practice often depends on what is to hand or on whim. It is helpful but not essential to start by making some fish stock (page 28).

2 shallots
½oz (14g) butter
4 cod steaks, or 4 pieces (each 4½oz/150g off bone, 7oz/200g on bone) of some other fish, e.g. monkfish
5 tablespoons fish stock (or water)
5 tablespoons dry cider
¼pt (14cl) double cream
seasoning
squeeze of lemon
1oz (28g) butter

Preparation and cooking time: about 20 minutes

Chop the shallots very finely and melt them for 2 minutes in a little butter – use a baking dish or frying pan for this. Add the fish, whole or filleted, the fish stock, and the dry cider – 2½ tablespoonsful of liquid per person. The fish may be cooked under or over heat, or in a medium-hot oven. In domestic kitchens, wrapping in buttered foil with the shallots and cooking liquid and using the oven is often best. Fillets need less cooking time than whole fish; neither need very much, unless they are dense-fleshed, like tunny: say 5 minutes for fillets of plaice, 10–12 minutes for fillets of sole or turbot; 8–20 minutes for whole fish depending on size.

As soon as the fish is cooked, transfer it to warm individual plates or a serving dish, cover and keep it hottish (but not so hot that it dries out or goes on cooking). Transfer the remaining juices to a convenient vessel for sauce-making.

Bring the juices to the boil and reduce for 1–2 minutes. Remove from heat, add cream, return pan to stove and reduce again. Taste – and season with salt, pepper and lemon juice as necessary. Finally finish and emulsify with cold butter in 2 or 3 pieces, stirring and shaking constantly over brisk but not too fierce heat, so that a custardy consistency is attained. This will provide a neutral but elegant sauce which goes well with all but the richest fish. Some ways in which it can be sharpened, heightened and accentuated are indicated below. Many others will occur to the inventive cook.

THREE-STAR VARIATIONS

Shrimps
A handful of peeled shrimps or small north Atlantic prawns is added to the sauce while the butter and cream are emulsifying.

Lesser Shellfish
Lightly cooked cockles, clams, mussels and/or winkles can be added instead of shrimps as above. In this case introduce a generous glass of their cooking liquor (strained free of sand) at the first reduction stage, and continue the reduction by an extra 2–3 minutes.

The Great Shellfish
In times of glut, the lily may be painted by introducing lobster, scallops, oysters, etc., to the sauce. Likewise . . .

Crayfish
These decorative little freshwater crustaceans are an obsession with top French chefs. Their lobster-like texture (the fishes' not the chefs') gives tactile distinction without having much effect on the taste. But they *look* jolly expensive. Difficult to find unless you have your own stream.

Parsley
Plenty of chopped parsley stirred into the sauce at the last moment is a cheap but most attractive titivation.

Watercress
The chopped leaves and tender parts of stalk can be used in the same way as parsley, but a watercress purée is better. Introduce it after the cream and stir in carefully.

89

Other Herbs

Fennel, basil, chives and dill all go well with several kinds of fish.

Fungi

White button mushrooms are very much at home in three-star sauces, as are chanterelles and ceps. Field mushrooms are too powerful in taste and colour.

Mustard or Horseradish

Both lose pungency when exposed to heat, so introduce them at the end of the saucification process, having already mixed them with a little cream as a vehicle. One or other but not both is almost essential to rich, oily fish.

Smoked Fish

Slivers of kipper, bloater, buckling or Arbroath smokie will impress and tantalise visitors from continental Europe. Smoked eel and smoked mackerel may also be used.

Whisky

This is a further indulgence for the smoked-fish option. Add Scotch while the cream is reducing and before introducing the smoked fish.

SEASIDE SOLE

On both sides of the Channel, minor shellfish are associated with seaside holidays, whether they are retrieved from the rocks at low tide or purchased from stalls, but in France a good many find their way to serious kitchens and become the 'normande' or 'dieppoise' part of marine masterpieces, whereas in England they are vandalised with vinegar. Here is a way of marrying the aquatic chorus line into the aristocracy.*

* Or into the middle classes – use lemon soles, dabs, plaice and so on instead of Dover soles, and cook for only 10–12 minutes.

4 Dover soles
2 shallots
5 tablespoons dry cider
2oz (56g) minor shellfish such as mussels, cockles, winkles, whelks or
  shrimps
lemon juice
¼pt (14cl) cream
1oz (28g) butter
Angostura bitters

Cooking time: 20–5 minutes

Bake the soles with a little chopped shallot in a baking dish, moistened by the dry cider, for about 15 minutes in a medium oven, covered with buttered paper.

Wash the shellfish (if uncooked) as carefully as possible and cook them, all except the shrimps, with a little water and lemon. When the bivalves open, remove all the fish with a perforated spoon; only a few minutes' cooking is required. In the unlikely event of your shrimps being bought uncooked, cook them too, in the same water as the other fish; about 3 minutes. When they are cool enough, remove cockles, mussels and whelks from their shells, and rinse in cold water. Peel most of the shrimps, but leave a few unpeeled for decoration. Leave winkles in shell. Keep the cooking liquor but pour it off so that sand and sediment are left at bottom of saucepan.

When the soles are cooked, add the liquor from their baking dish to the shellfish liquor and boil hard to reduce by half. Add cream to the liquor and let it simmer, stirring the while with a wooden spoon. Add a knob of butter, still stirring, then the shellfish, then a dash or two of Angostura bitters. Having kept the soles warm, serve them on individual plates, with the sauce, decorated by unpeeled shrimps.

SHARK IN BAY

No need to be wary of shark in the kitchen: monkfish, porbeagle, tope and dogfish are firm of texture and fine of flavour. Poor man's Dublin Bay prawn. And don't underestimate bay leaves. The bay tree thrives strangely in a cold climate and offers a spice-like, almost tropical indigeneity, yet generations of northern cooks have relegated its leaves to ritual half-life in the *bouquet garni*. It deserves better treatment; bay is one of the great flavourings.

2 shallots
6–8 bay leaves, preferably fresh
1 tablespoon butter and oil, mixed
salt and pepper
1½lbs (700g) tope or monkfish, cut into rounds at least 1in (2½cm) thick
2 tablespoons gin
2½ tablespoons Rose's lime juice
¼pt (14cl) double cream

Preparation and cooking time: 15–20 minutes

Chop the shallots very finely and cut the bay leaves into tiny pieces (if dry, crunch them up).

Fry them gently in a mixture of oil and butter, seasoning well with salt and pepper. After about 7 minutes, increase the heat and add the fish. Fry it for 3 minutes on each side. Then flare the pan with 2 tablespoonsful of warm gin – for some reason gin seems to burn much longer than other spirits – and when the flames die down, add 2½ tablespoonsful lime juice.

This recipe can be used for most firm-fleshed fish. It is the basis for bay leaf sauce (page 227) for use with grilled, baked or poached fish.

Fish and Chips

Fish and chips may now be available on the Costa Brava and most of the other places which have been rendered as unforeign as possible by the international tourist industry, but people who still seek out 'the abroad', the genuine article, tend to feel the need for a good fish and chip shop as soon as they return home. Dating from

about 1870, fish and chips is one of the few great British gastronomic institutions which are comparatively new. Often, however,
the chips are soggy, the batter is heavy and the fish, within its
contorted casing, disappointingly diminutive or doubtfully fresh.
I have even heard people claim that they like their chips soggy.

BEER BATTER

1 oz (28 g) plain flour
5 tablespoons beer or water
salt

Preparation time: 25 minutes

The purpose of batter in fish and chips is to preserve the taste, juices
and texture of the species being fried. If it also provides a pleasant
texture of its own and a taste which enhances the fish, all to the
good. A very light, crisp texture which holds these properties for as
long as possible is the goal; thick, flabby batter has no place in
improved English cookery.

After experimenting with a dozen different batter formulations, I
think I have found one which meets all requirements. It involves
neither eggs nor milk, let alone yeast, butter or bicarbonate of soda.
Just seasoned flour – and beer.

A tablespoonful of plain flour mixed with 3–4 tablespoonsful of
bitter or light ale will make just enough batter for 4 people. The
initial mixing must discourage the formation of lumps, but once
a smooth paste is formed, the rest of the beer can be poured in
rapidly and the mixture may be whisked. It is just right when it falls
from uplifted whisk in a thin but cohesive stream. Leave it for 20
minutes before frying begins.

Beer batter is characterful, fries golden-brown and crisp, retains
its texture in oven or newspaper. Its taste may be sharpened by
anchovy essence, lemon juice or tabasco, and the flour should be
well salted before use.

The same process works nearly as well with water in place of
beer. When fried, water batter is paler in colour and marginally less
meaty but just as light and crisp in texture. Above all remember –
no eggs, or the fish will be coated in flour-thickened omelette; no
milk, or the batter will be leathern.

93

Which Came First?

The idea which follows may seem a more or less blatant borrowing from ethnic Italian or ethnic Japanese cooking. I deny this. Until given irrefutable proof to the contrary, I shall always maintain that both fritto misto mare and tempura are, in turn, blatant and unacknowledged borrowings, nay hi-jacks, from the fish-and-chips partnership which originated in or around Wapping a hundred years ago. That they are both improvements on the original, is gratefully acknowledged, however.

SMALL FRY

Beer batter will enhance fish fried whole or in one-person helpings. In new English cooking, however, the ideal is to offer several different fish, including at least one of the lesser shellfish, fried in much smaller portions, together with a vegetable or two. Serve with a special zest or gusto (pages 237–44) instead of vinegar.

Of course, for simple, family meals one species of fish remains in order, but more than one adds interest without necessarily increasing the cost. Fish to be considered include cod, coley, conger, dogfish ('rock salmon'), fresh haddock, hake, plaice, skate, sprats and whiting. Among the cheaper shellfish, cockles, clams and mussels can all be used – shelled, of course, but as little pre-cooked as possible. Prawns are good, too, but shrimps and whitebait* are too fiddly for batter.

1½lbs (700g) frying fish, mixed if possible
10oz (300g) vegetables for frying
batter (see beer batter, page 93)
1½pts (84cl) oil for frying

This is one of the dishes where it is best to use filleted fish, though little numbers such as smelts and sprats can be fried whole, with or without their heads, and it is impossible to fillet skate. The fish should be cut into pieces which, when fried, will make one, two or three mouthfuls. After being dipped into batter, they should be

* If particularly liked, however, a few whitebait may also be included. They should be tossed in seasoned flour and deep fried (but not battered).

94

deep-fried for 2–3 minutes, lifted out of the oil, drained on to absorbent paper (or shaken free of oil in a metal strainer), and fried again for a further 2–3 minutes. For the first frying, only 2–3 pieces should be cooked at the same time – more will weld themselves to each other. Depending on the size of the pan, at least twice as many pieces may be fried simultaneously second time round, as they are no longer mutually adhesive.

Vegetables should be treated in a similar way – cut into slivers or bite-sizes, dipped into batter, and twice fried. Most should be blanched first in boiling water for a minute but can otherwise be almost raw. Good vegetables to use include broccoli, carrots, celery, spring onions, leeks, cauliflower and turnip.

Small Fry de Luxe
Luxury fish are also very good cooked as above – for birthdays and special occasions. They come into the reprehensible category of simple but expensive food. Fish to consider include fillets of sole, halibut, brill or turbot; trout, monkfish, scallops, large prawns and, again, mussels. I have also found that smoked eel is an excellent recruit to small fry de luxe.

Chips
Not strictly necessary with small fry, but popular with non-slimmers, especially the under-25 age group. I enjoy a good chip myself but am fairly poor at – and bored by – cooking them; so I had better not advise on the subject. Nasty chips are already ubiquitous.

ENGLISH FRIES

These combine some of the crispness of French fries with the taste, texture and nutritional value of true potato. They are easy to prepare and should be eaten as an interesting vegetable rather than mountainous filler-upper.

Medium-sized potatoes, scrubbed but not peeled, should be halved, halved and halved again (into eighths), so that each portion has one uncut facet with peel intact. They should then be boiled for 5–6 minutes, drained, dried and deep-fried twice, as for chips.

Deep-frying Vessels

The traditional deep-frying pan with basket cooks fish and chips satisfactorily of course, but calls for a lot of oil and takes a long time to heat up. Using it often seems a bit of a performance.

The trendy wok is a good alternative. It takes less oil and heats up very quickly. I prefer it. Two cupsful of oil in the bottom of a wok will be enough for cooking fish, but you will need more if you have been talked into making lots of chips or English fries.

Baked Fish

An underrated way of cooking fish, baking encourages invention and easily yields enhancing sauces. The following procedure, closely related to the three-star formula, can be applied to most fresh- and salt-water species, whole or divided, on the bone or filleted.

The best opening gambit is to sprinkle fragments of vegetable, typically shallot or carrot, and strands of herb on to lightly buttered aluminium foil, and to place the fish, cleaned and, if appropriate, scaled, on top. A little dry cider is added next and a seasoning of salt and pepper. Finally the foil is closed – hermetic sealing is unnecessary but one wants to preserve most of the cooking vapours.

The dish is baked in a moderate oven for 10–25 minutes, depending on size. It wants neither to be rushed nor to be overcooked. Large beasts take longer than small, soft-fleshed fish cook faster than firm-fleshed.

As soon as the fish is cooked, remove it to a warm plate and use the juices in the foil as the basis of a quick sauce, probably transferring them to a saucepan. The juices, which may need a little brisk reduction and a jolt of lemon or vinegar, can essentially be saucified either by a vegetable cullis or by cream and/or butter. Additional ingredients such as herbs, fungi, shellfish, smoked fish, anchovy, bacon, citrus fruit, spices, savoury butters, give the sauce individual character and the process almost infinite variability. Vegetable purées which are particularly suitable as saucifiers for baked fish include mushroom, celeriac and parsley, watercress and, of course, tomato. The vegetable-purée sauce option will be preferred by slimmers and cholesterophobes to the cream/butter option.

Baking in Salt

This is an excellent way to cook whole, firm-fleshed, élitist fish such as sea-bass or chick turbot; but the process does not produce liquor on which to base a sauce. One answer is a hot vegetable cullis, loosened by fish stock, sharpened by lemon, and perhaps pricked by anchovy. The white butter procedure (page 226) is also a great standby, on its own or as a vehicle for herbs, small shellfish or smoky flavours.

Put a thick layer of rock salt in the bottom of a baking dish. Place the fish on the salt and cover it with another very thick layer of salt. Bake in a hot oven for about 20 minutes. The salt will solidify.

The whole thing should be transferred to a serving platter for taking to table. Removing the salt taxes the ingenuity and provides a mildly tantalising challenge before you start eating.

Instead of unadulterated salt, a mixture two-thirds salt/one-third plain flour is sometimes used.

Boiled or Poached Fish

The hot-blooded mugging of perfectly innocent fish by water boiling with venom typifies the contempt for food and indifference to suffering which is English cooking at its worst. The very thought of boiled cod or whiting sends shudders down the spine . . . and yet, the gentle poaching of fish is a pure, tender, healthy process which can preserve and enhance natural flavours.

To poach effectively you either need enough simmering hot liquid for it to maintain, or very quickly regain, its temperature when the (cold) fish is introduced, or you can start cooking the fish in considerably less cold water and bring it to a sub-simmer gradually. The second method is simpler but the first is perhaps marginally better at safeguarding the full virtue of the fish. Either way the fish need surprisingly little cooking – 3–4 minutes for a trout, 8–10 for a codling or fresh haddock.

On no account should the cooking water be thrown away. In the past few minutes it has become stock and it has stolen taste from the fish. Keep the fish itself hot and retrieve the stolen taste by boiling away most of the unwanted water. Then use the concentrated fish stock to make a sauce – with cream or cullis as discussed under baked fish on page 96 and on page 226.

In new English cooking it is by no means necessary to poach in plain water. A mixture of water and dry cider, with a tablespoon of cider vinegar, not only gives something to the fish but also gives you a much more interesting basis for the eventual sauce. Similarly bay leaves, herbs and some member of the onion tribe can all improve the end-product. It is also possible to poach in beer – see Walton trout, page 100.

THE PIECE OF COD WHICH PASSETH ALL UNDERSTANDING

My father used to make this joke whenever we had cod, as did his father before him; I make it, too, and I dare say my sons will follow suit in due course, though they tend to sigh and groan whenever they hear it now.

½lb (226g) Jerusalem artichokes
1 whole codling (or large piece of cod on the bone, at least 1¾lbs (800g)
1 small clove garlic
2 shallots
2 sticks celery
1pt (56cl) milk
salt and pepper
saffron
¼pt (14cl) single cream
2 egg yolks
butter

Preparation and cooking time: 35–40 minutes

Scrub the artichokes and cut them in half. Boil for 5 minutes, then plunge them in cold water. This makes them a little easier to peel. Peel and cut into pieces the size of large broad beans.

Put the fish in a baking dish on top of the cut-up garlic, shallots and celery. Add the milk, slightly salted, and half of the artichoke 'beans'; bake in a medium oven for up to 20 minutes, basting occasionally. It is important not to overcook cod, and if you are adapting this dish to cod steaks, barely 15 minutes will be sufficient.

Transfer the cooked fish and keep it warm in a serving dish. Liquidise the artichokes and other vegetables along with about a cupful of the cooking milk. Re-heat the resulting purée in a saucepan with a good pinch of saffron, half a cup of cream, and a little more of the cooking milk. To finish the sauce, whisk 2 egg yolks with the remaining cream and stir them into the purée. Now that eggs are present, the sauce must not be allowed to boil. Keep just below simmering point, and stir until it thickens to a custard.

Meanwhile the remaining artichoke beans should be lightly salted and peppered and fried in butter. They are used as a garnish.

Pour the sauce round (but perhaps not over) the fish in its platter and put the artichokes around the perimeter and along the back of the cod (if whole).

SHRIMPLIFIED TURBOT

5 oz (140 g/½ pt) shrimps
lemon juice
4 oz (112 g) white button mushrooms, chopped small
4 oz (112 g) carrots, julienned
4 oz (112 g) leek, julienned
1 oz (28 g) butter
1 chick turbot 3½–5 lbs/1·6–2·25 kg) on the bone
¼ pt (14 cl) dry cider
salt and cayenne pepper

Preparation and cooking time: 25–30 minutes

Peel the shrimps. Use heads, tails and shells to make a quick fish stock, just covering them with water and boiling for 10–15 minutes, with a squeeze of lemon juice.

Sweat most of the mushroom, carrot and leek juliennes in butter for 5 minutes. Add enough shrimp stock to simmer efficiently, and cook till the vegetables are soft enough for liquidising.

Meanwhile, bake the turbot wrapped in well-buttered foil, with the remaining carrot, mushroom and leek, moistened with the cider. Allow some 20 minutes in a medium-hot oven.

Blend vegetables and cooking liquor to a purée and return it to saucepan. When the turbot is cooked, transfer it to a hot dish. Add the cooking juices from the foil to the purée and simmer for 2 minutes. Taste for seasoning – use cayenne rather than black pepper. Add the shrimps and a small knob of butter, shaking the pan. As soon as the butter has dissolved and the shrimps are hot, pour the sauce round the turbot, and serve.

WALTON TROUT

Doubt has been cast, by Henry Williamson, on just how reliable a fly-fisherman the compleat angler really was, but his way of cooking trout is the basis of a new dish which stands up to critical attention and works wonders with farmed or frozen specimens.

1 pt (56 cl) mild or brown ale
5 tablespoons vinegar
good sprig of rosemary
1 teaspoon salt
4 trout
½ oz (14 g) soft brown sugar
1 saltspoon mace or nutmeg
1 teaspoon arrowroot
3½ oz (100 g) butter
1 oz (28 g) grated horseradish, or more

Cooking time: 15 minutes

Put beer, vinegar, rosemary and salt into saucepan and raise to simmering point. Simmer for 3–4 minutes before inserting the fish, ideally in a basket, and cooking them very gently for 4 minutes. Then remove pan from the heat and leave the fish in the liquor another 2 minutes.

Remove the fish and keep them hot. Add sugar and nutmeg or mace to the beer, re-heat, and reduce by at least one-third by rapid boiling. Add the arrowroot dissolved in a little water. After reduction and still over a high heat add the butter in 3 or 4 refrigerated knobs one by one, stirring to produce a well-emulsified sauce.

Pour the sauce over the fish and sprinkle very generously with grated horseradish.

ALBERT HERRING

Food and drink play an important part in Britten's opera: Mrs Herring is the village greengrocer; Albert is first seen bearing a load of turnips; the butcher's boy pinches fruit for the baker's daughter; and the hero's liberating downfall is brought about by lemonade

100

laced with rum. These elements provide a dish worthy of all that is best in herring.

6 oz (168 g) peeled turnip
6 oz (168 g) peeled apple
4 herrings
cooking oil or butter
salt and pepper
1 oz (28 g) butter
2½ tablespoons rum
2 lemons
⅓ pt (20 cl) fish stock (page 28) or broth flavoured with anchovy
1 teaspoon arrowroot
½ orange
1 tablespoon very runny made English mustard
1 peach (optional)

Preparation and cooking time: 25 minutes

Cut the turnips into wedge-shaped eighths and boil them for about 5 minutes. They should be young turnips if possible; if mature, throw away the boiling water and re-boil in fresh, salted water for a further 3 minutes. Cut the apple into similar eighths and keep it on one side in cold, acidulated water.

Brush the whole herrings (cleaned, de-scaled) with cooking oil or melted butter and sprinkle with salt and pepper. Grill them to an enticing brown – about 3 minutes on each side under a hot grill. When they are cooked, remove them to an oval fish platter, arranging them diagonally, head to tail. Keep warm.

For the sauce, add butter, salt and pepper to the juices left in grilling pan, and when the butter has melted transfer all to a frying pan or smallish saucepan. Fry the turnip and apple segments 2 minutes on each side, flare with warm rum, then arrange the segments around the fish. Add juice of 1 lemon to pan and bubble fast for 1 minute before adding fish stock and arrowroot dissolved in a little water. Boil rapidly to reduce by about one-third, adding the juice of half an orange. Finally remove the sauce from heat and stir in the rather mild, runny mustard. Pour sauce over fish.

Romantics may surmount each herring with a sliver of peach, explaining to their guests that Sid and Nancy go off to eat peaches between kisses in Act II. Cynics may prefer the astringency of lemon wedges.

101

MACKEREL AU MAQUEREAU

2 shallots
4 fresh mackerel, gutted, heads removed
salt
¼pt (14cl) dry cider
¼ smoked mackerel (about 3oz/84g), all bones removed
2 lemons
¼pt (14cl) double cream
2 tablespoons grated horseradish

Cooking time: 20 minutes

Chop the shallots finely and bake them in a moderate oven for 3–4 minutes in a buttered roasting pan.

Split the fresh mackerel and flatten them so that they look like headless kippers. Put them in the roasting pan with the shallots, sprinkle with salt, add the cider, and cover with foil. Bake for 12–15 minutes.

Remove the fish when cooked (leaving the shallot and juices); keep fish warm. Finish the sauce on top of the stove by adding the smoked mackerel, finely shredded, and cooking it for 1 minute, the juice of 2 lemons and cooking (fast) for another minute, and the cream – allow 2 minutes' bubbling.

Finally remove pan from heat and stir in horseradish. To serve, dribble sauce down the centre of each split mackerel.

It adds to the pleasure (but also the labour) of this dish if the mackerel are removed from the oven after only 8 minutes, that is before they are fully cooked, painted with melted butter, sprinkled with red pepper, and finished – flesh side up, of course, under a fierce grill.

BLACKEREL

4 mackerel
⅓pt (20 cl) pickled walnut vinegar
4 spring onions (or 2 shallots)
1 onion
oil and butter for frying
½oz (14 g) soft brown sugar
¼pt (14 cl) Guinness
1 tablespoon black treacle
Worcestershire sauce
1 teaspoon arrowroot or 1 oz (28 g) butter
cayenne pepper
powdered ginger
2–3 pickled walnuts
8–12 sprigs parsley

Preparation and marinating time: 65 minutes; cooking time: 25 minutes

Clean and split the mackerel. Marinate them for at least 1 hour in vinegar from a jar of pickled walnuts, with chopped spring onions.

For the sauce: fry the onion (chopped small) in a mixture of oil and butter until it is brown rather than golden, then caramelise it with brown sugar, lowering the heat. Add half the marinade from the mackerel and bubble it fast to de-glaze; then add the rest of the marinade, the Guinness, the treacle, the Worcestershire sauce (2 or 3 jerks) and simmer it for 10–15 minutes. The sauce may be thickened either with butter, just before the end, or with arrowroot dissolved in water.

Having dried the mackerel on kitchen paper, dust them with cayenne and powdered ginger. While the sauce is simmering, grill them, flesh side up for 10–15 minutes. They should be rather well done and slightly blackened.

Serve fish and sauce separately, garnishing the fish with morsels of pickled walnut and whole sprigs of parsley.

GRILLED HERRINGS WITH
SCOTCH GUSTO

4 herrings
4 teaspoons made English mustard
1½ lemons
1 scant teaspoon black peppercorns, crushed
oil from 1½ tins of anchovies
3½ tablespoons whisky
2 pairs soft herring roes
4 anchovy fillets
1 shallot
1 tablespoon chopped parsley
2 egg yolks

Preparation time: 15 minutes; cooking time: 8 minutes

Clean and decapitate the herrings.

Mix mustard, juice of half a lemon, black pepper, anchovy oil (half tin), and whisky and put a quarter of the mixture to one side for brushing on the fish. Use the remaining three-quarters to make Scotch gusto with the herring roes and other ingredients as described on page 240.

Brush the herrings on both sides with the mixture and grill them briskly till they are nice and brown. Serve with the gusto.

Salmon and Sea-Trout

Greatest fish of northern waters – some would say of all waters – salmon have survived generations of criminal assault in British kitchens. They have been overcooked, over-cucumbered, over-praised, overfished and overpriced, yet they remain the pride of hosts and the great expectation of guests. (On balance I prefer the sea-trout.)

When cooking a salmon it is important to prevent it drying out and solidifying; in saucing and garnishing it, the prime objective should be to complement its rich density. The practice of serving mayonnaise with cold salmon and hollandaise with hot may be justifiable, even advisable, with dry, improperly cooked fish, but verges on the gross with salmon which is moist and succulent. More appropriate sauces are suggested on pages 235–6.

Smoked and pickled salmon are every bit as good as fresh at its best and in practice less likely to disappoint. Commercial smokers usually know their business and have fumigated salmon into the most popular of all luxury fish. Compared with oysters, lobsters and caviar it is not all that expensive, but if anything I would rather have pickled salmon, perhaps because outside Scandinavia, it is still little known. A Swedish recipe and an Anglican alternative are given on pages 52–3.

TO COOK A WHOLE SALMON OR SEA-TROUT FOR EATING COLD

The fish should be gutted, scaled, washed, then put into a fish kettle and covered with cold water. Salt, pepper, bay leaf and onion may be added, though that is becoming a culinary ritual. The water must be brought to the boil and left to boil gently for just 3 minutes. Then the fish kettle is removed from the stove altogether and the fish left to cool in the cooking water. The process takes ages, but however large the salmon, however small the sea-trout, the fish will be perfectly cooked by the time it and the water are cold right through.

If the salmon is too big or the kettle too small, the fish may be cut into suitable lengths, but in that case it should be wrapped tightly in lightly oiled foil.

A WHOLE SALMON TO BE EATEN HOT

Foil is advisable whether or not fish fits kettle, and should be buttered as well as seasoned. This time the water is brought to boiling point before the well-wrapped fish is put into it. Simmering should be timed to some 5 minutes per lb (450 g) for salmon and sea-trout of 5 lbs or less, but 3–4 minutes per lb for larger fish. Maximum cooking time no matter how large the salmon is 50 minutes.

Alternatively, foil-wrapped fish may be baked in a medium oven for 1 hour or 12 minutes per pound, whichever is longer. Clearly if the fish is cut into lengths, it is the weight of each piece, rather than the total weight which dictates cooking time. (Timing advice based on Jane Grigson's *Fish Cookery*.)

105

SALMON STEAKS

These, too, should be wrapped in foil and baked for about 20 minutes in a medium oven. They may be assisted by herbs, shallot, melted butter, lemon or sherry, and salt and pepper, before being wrapped.

SALMON SYMPOSIUM

Just as the raw material itself can leap up waterfalls, this relatively complex dish shows the gastronomic heights to which salmon can ascend. It is well worth the trouble and expense, but may suggest that salmon and mayonnaise is actually rather a misalliance.

8 salmon steaks not more than 1 inch (2½cm) thick
4 good slices of smoked salmon
1 cucumber, peeled and grated
1 leek, julienned
2 carrots, julienned
1oz (28g) butter, melted
1 lemon
2 large and 12 small slices of pickled salmon (or extra smoked salmon)
1 shallot
5 tablespoons whisky
¼pt (14cl) double cream
½oz (14g) butter (unmelted)
boiled new potatoes
parsley or dill

Preparation time: 20–5 minutes; cooking time: 20 minutes

Allow 2 thin salmon steaks or escalopes per person. Form each pair, lightly seasoned, into a sandwich with smoked salmon in the middle. A large piece of buttered foil is required for each sandwich.

Spread a quarter of the grated cucumber in the centre of each piece of foil. Place the sandwiches on top of the cucumber, and strew leek and carrot on top of the sandwiches. Draw the foil up round the fish and just before enclosing it completely, spoon one-quarter of the melted butter and one-quarter of the lemon's juice on to each sandwich. Then fold each parcel tightly so that nothing can escape; place them all in a suitable dish, and bake in a medium oven for 20 minutes.

Meanwhile dice the large pieces of pickled salmon and chop the shallot finely. Pack them both into a large wine glass and pour in the whisky. Leave this cocktail to commune for 20 minutes.

When the salmon sandwiches are cooked, remove them to warm plates with their vegetable toppings but without any cucumber. Empty all the juices and cucumber pulp from foils into the baking dish, boil it for 1–2 minutes then strain it through a fine sieve into a saucepan, squeezing the pulp with a wooden spoon. Add the pickled salmon and whisky. Simmer for 5 minutes, then add the cream. Simmer for 3 minutes, then add the butter (that is, finishing the sauce in the basic way described on page 226).

To serve: pour a little of the sauce round or over each sandwich. Put boiled potatoes round the sandwiches and intersperse these with the smaller slices of pickled salmon. Sprinkle with parsley or fresh dill. Any other vegetables would be de trop.

COALITION OF SALMON

14 oz (400 g) cooked salmon
4 oz (112 g) smoked salmon
4 oz (112 g) pickled salmon
salmon roe or red lumpfish roe
parsley, dill, or other green herb
4 baby leeks
4 baby turnips
12 bright red radishes
other raw or very lightly cooked vegetables, as available, including asparagus

Preparation time: 1 hour 10 minutes (sauce), 20 minutes (fish and vegetables)

Simpler than salmon symposium, this also shows off the versatility of a too often stereotyped fish. It is eaten cold, and is more a test of design ability than culinary skill. Smoked, pickled and freshly poached salmon must be disposed decoratively on the plate, accompanied by salad material so that the whole forms an attractive palette of reds and greens.

The best sauce to use is this version of lost sauce (see also page 234): mix 2 hardboiled egg yolks with 1 raw yolk and some salmon roe or red lumpfish roe. Add cream gradually, as you would add oil for a mayonnaise but not quite so cautiously, and spike the resulting sauce with salt, pepper, lemon juice and made English mustard. Refrigerate it for at least 1 hour before consumption.

107

SOLE SCORZONERA

Some people assume Scorzonera to be an Adriatic seaport, others that it's a form of acne; they may be right, but it is also a vegetable very like salsify but with a nasty black-brown skin.

4 Dover soles, on the bone
1 lb (450 g) scorzonera or salsify
⅓ pt (20 cl) dry cider
2 oz (56 g) butter
salt and pepper
2½ tablespoons gin
1 lemon

Preparation and cooking time: 20–5 minutes

Bake the soles in the oven, lightly buttered, with a little cider, and covered by foil. They will take about 15 minutes. Remove foil for last 5 minutes and baste with butter.

The scorzonera should be washed, then boiled for 12 minutes, and plunged into cold water. It should then be skinned (scorzonera is easier to peel than salsify) and cut into roundels about ¾ inch (2 cm) thick.

Fry the scorzonera roundels in well-seasoned butter, and when they are nice and golden, flare them with the gin. As the flames die down, add the lemon juice, the rest of the cider and the juices in the baking pan.

Put the soles on a large plate, surround them with the scorzonera croûtons and pour a little of the scant but delicious sauce over each fish.

SECRET SOLE

This is another salsify/scorzonera recipe, but few people will guess the mystery ingredient. According to books, by the way, salsify is nicknamed 'vegetable oyster'; no one actually calls it that.

1 lb 5 oz (600 g) salsify or scorzonera
¼ pt (14 cl) cream
¼ pt (14 cl) fish stock (page 28)
salt and pepper
saffron
Rose's lime juice
4 Dover soles
2 oz (56 g) butter

Preparation and cooking time: 20 minutes

Wash, boil and peel the salsify as in the recipe above. Chop it small, then liquidise it in blender with cream and fish stock. Return it to the pan with salt, pepper and a good pinch of saffron. Add an overflowing teaspoon of Rose's lime juice and simmer the purée so that it thickens a little and takes on colour from the saffron.

Meanwhile grill the soles, having first brushed them with melted butter. After they are cooked, remove them to a warm platter. Add more butter to the juices in the grilling pan and a scant teaspoon of Rose's lime juice. Heat this over a high flame so that the butter almost burns. Dribble butter and lime juice on each fish and surround them by the scorzonera purée.

109

REFORM BRILL

1 lb 5 oz (600 g) fillet of brill (1¾ lbs/800 g on bone)
butter for cooking and sauce-making
salt and pepper
1½ oz (40 g) white breadcrumbs
4 tablespoons chopped parsley
3 rashers lean bacon, finely diced
1 shallot
5 tablespoons cooking port
1 bloater (or kipper)
3 or 4 gherkins, chopped small
2 tablespoons cider vinegar
⅓ pt (20 cl) fish stock (page 28)

Preparation and cooking time: 25 minutes

Brill can be almost as enormous as turbot or halibut, so they are usually sold and cooked as fillets or steaks.

Brush the (skinned) surface of the fish with melted butter, season with salt and pepper, and sprinkle with a mixture of breadcrumbs, parsley and bacon. Firm this coating into the fish.

Bake the brill in a buttered, shallot-strewn dish, moistened with 2½ tablespoons of port, for 12–15 minutes in a medium-hot oven. (Use a Pyrex-type dish which fits the fish comfortably rather than a roasting pan.)

Blanch the bloater in boiling water for 1 minute. It can then be skinned and filleted quite easily. Cut the flesh into small, flaky pieces. If kipper is used, blanch it in boiling water twice before filleting and cutting up the flesh.

When the brill is cooked, remove from oven and keep it warm in a serving dish. Add 2 oz (56 g) butter to the fish-cooking juices in baking dish and transfer them to a saucepan. Add the flaked bloater and cook in the buttery juices for 2 minutes. Then add a generous milling of black pepper and the rest of the port. When the wine has bubbled for a minute, add the gherkin and the cider vinegar. Bubble for a further minute, then add the fish stock. Simmer this for 3 minutes before adding 2 or 3 walnuts of cold butter. Pour the resulting sauce over the fish.

Can be adapted to halibut, turbot, Dover sole.

Shellfish

While the formidable Mme Prunier described thirty French ways of serving oysters and forty-eight different lobster dishes, in English cooking we take our shellfish raw or boiled and seldom assist it with any but the simplest of dressings – lemon juice, melted butter, oil and vinegar, mayonnaise. Both positions are extreme: the French imputing too much versatility to shellfish; the English too little. New English cookery notes that bivalves can be improved by being stuffed, that crustaceans and scallops respond merrily to whisky or gin, but it tacitly acknowledges the limitations imposed by shell and texture.

HOT BUTTERED LOBSTER

2 good lobsters (cooked)
4 tinned anchovies
½ clove garlic
5 oz (140 g) butter
¼ teaspoon nutmeg or mace
cayenne pepper
1 lemon
2½ tablespoons whisky or gin
2 oz (56 g) soft white breadcrumbs
parsley

Preparation time: 15 minutes; cooking time: 15–20 minutes

This is a renewal of one of the relatively few hot lobster dishes found in old English cookery books, in this case Mrs Glasse.*

Extract all the meat from the lobsters, retaining the 4 half shells.

Chop the anchovies and garlic very finely. Fry them in a little of the butter – quite gently for about 3 minutes. Then add the rest of the butter, the nutmeg or mace and a strong seasoning of cayenne. Add the lobster meat and heat it through. Squeeze the lemon and add the juice to lobster. Heat the whisky or gin and pour it flaming into the lobster mixture, shaking the pan. When the flames cease, start adding breadcrumbs with a tablespoon. Add just enough to absorb most of the butter; add chopped parsley.

Transfer the buttered lobster to the (heated) lobster shells. Sprinkle the tops with cayenne, parsley and breadcrumbs (in that order), and finish under the grill.

HOT BUTTERED CRAB

The same form of buttering up is deserved by crab, but it is best to omit all or most of the brown meat, unless you want a very rich dish indeed. Use the brown meat for crab butter with, say, baked fish. (Mix the brown meat with an equal quantity of softened butter. Season with lemon juice and cayenne.) Allow one decent-sized crab per person.

All the firm-fleshed fish are excellent prepared in this way –

* Hannah Glasse, *The Art of Cookery Made Plain and Easy; A New Edition* (Miller, Law & Cater, London; Wilson & Spence, York, 1789).

halibut, brill, turbot, monkfish, etc. The dish is always rich and needs to be extravagantly seasoned with anchovy and pepper. Plain boiled potatoes are the only accompaniment it needs, or possibly boiled rice.

GINNY PRAWNS

Simple and sinful, this forms a main course with large, king or giant prawns, an excellent starter with smaller specimens.

shallots (small one per person)
½oz (14g) butter per person
cayenne pepper
prawns (a generous helping for each person)
1 tablespoon gin per person
2 tablespoons cream per person
lemon juice

Preparation and cooking time: 15 minutes

Gently fry the chopped shallot in butter, with a shot of cayenne. Add the peeled and cooked prawns. Toss them in the butter and when there is no doubt that they are hot right through, flare them with warmed gin. When the flames die, add the cream, and, stirring the while, cook it quite fast for upwards of 2 minutes. Before serving, sharpen with lemon juice.

Most other shellfish are excellent if finished with gin and cream, however they have been cooked initially.

When served as a main course, ginny prawns can be accompanied by boiled and thinly sliced Jerusalem artichokes.

113

STEWED MUSSELS

With acknowledgments to umpteen variations on moules mari-
nières.

4½ lbs (2 kg) mussels, in their shells
1 onion
½ pt (30 cl) dry cider
large bunch of parsley
bunch of watercress
gin
¼ pt (14 cl) single cream
1 oz (28 g) butter

⅓ pt (20 cl) leek cullis
black pepper
2 egg yolks

Preparation time: 30 minutes; cooking time: 25 minutes

Clean and de-beard the mussels.

Put chopped onion and cider into a very large saucepan and
simmer them for at least 5 minutes, covered. Add the mussels, in
batches if need be, and raise heat to maximum. Remove mussels as
soon as they open and discard the upper shells, leaving as much of
the mussel liquor in the pan as possible. It's useful to have asbestos
hands at this stage.

When all the mussels are ready, strain off the cooking liquid,
leaving any sand in the bottom of the pan. Put the mussels in a large
bowl and keep them hot without letting them go on cooking.

Use the strained cooking liquor to make a sauce with:

1) chopped parsley, chopped watercress, a nip of gin and cream.
Add all these to the liquor and boil for 2 minutes; stir in a knob of
butter, and pour the sauce over the mussels. Or

2) add the cooking liquor to a good leek cullis; simmer them
together with a good teaspoon of ground black pepper. Then
remove from the heat and stir in 2 egg yolks. Pour over the
mussels.

For other shellfish recipes, see pages 45–8, 50–1 and 55–6.

5
POULTRY & EGGS

Earthy, traditional wisdom: roasting chickens are usually young cocks six to twelve weeks old, but young hens are better eating; older hens can also be roasted (when sent to market for not laying properly); if they go off the lay or become broody, hens can still be roasted, but are better pot-roasted or casseroled; last season's cocks, and hens which have had more than one laying season, are for boiling . . .

Distilled from Dorothy Hartley's *Food in England* (1953), these natural ground rules were formulated when the broiler chicken was still a scowl in the heart of some agro-chemist. Since then fowl-raising has become foul industry. Once a luxury, chicken today is plentiful, cheap, convenient, seasonless – and, according to some, totally without taste. There are gastronomic as well as ethical reasons for boycotting the mass-produced bird, so they claim.

The Other Side of the Question

Those who keep their own farmyard hens in the approved, natural way, often think longingly of the oven-ready, supermarket bird – white and tender, however clumsily it may be cooked. Lacking in flavour? Maybe, but lacking also the plastic skin, rubber breasts and purple drumsticks of free-range liberty. Left to their own devices, chickens are muscle-bound athletes in youth, leathery malcontents in maturity. If only one could grow eggs from seed.

As a farmer's husband, I know the pros and cons. For many years, my ecological, economical wife kept our household on a siege footing as far as chicken was concerned, with glut succeeding famine on the egg front. The principal question was how to reconcile the pleasures of gastronomy with the rigours of self-sufficiency. Conversion of most OAPs (old-age poultry) into stock was the best solution, but when thrift called the tune, it was long, slow simmering, followed by stock reduction and use of the resulting cullis to make a sauce.

We no longer keep chickens, thank goodness.

117

Meanwhile most reputable dealers sell real roasting birds at reasonable prices. These must always be preferred to mass-produced broilers.

CHICKEN LOAF

1 chicken
½pt (28 cl) lost sauce (page 234)
1 cucumber
1 lettuce (or some young spinach leaves)
bunch of radishes
4 pickled walnuts
1 white tin loaf
7oz (200g) cooked ham
fresh herbs (tarragon if possible)
butter
salt and pepper

Preparation and cooking time: 2 hours

Roast, pot-roast or poach the chicken, according to its age.

Prepare the lost sauce with cream, eggs and lemon juice. Put it to set in the refrigerator.

Quarter and salt the cucumber and set it to drain.

When the chicken is cooked, leave it to get cool. Wash and dry the cucumber; cut it into slices. Wash and dry the lettuce; shred it. Slice the radishes and the pickled walnuts. Cut top off loaf and scoop the bread out so that you are left with an oblong receptacle.

When it is cool, carve the chicken into small, thin slices, removing the skin. Slice the ham very thinly. Chop fresh herbs.

Butter the base and walls of the loaf on the inside. Fill it with alternate layers of chicken, sauce, ham, salad materials, more sauce, and so on, dotting the contents with particles of black walnut and sprinkling with herbs. Season generously with pepper, circumspectly with salt. When the loaf is full, put the top on as a lid and tie it down with string. Brush the outside walls with melted butter (or butter and oil); put it on a rack and bake it in a very hot oven for 3–4 minutes – to crispen the crust without cooking the contents. Serve cold, cut in slices, preferably out of doors in the sunshine.

Apart from chicken and ham, the ingredients of this dish are by no means critical. A wide variety of salad materials can be used. Tongue is an excellent addition. Hardboiled eggs? It can also be made with cold, lean veal instead of chicken, or, of course, cold pheasant.

ROAST COCK-A-LEEKIE

8 leeks
butter
1¾ pts (100 cl) chicken stock, giblets and extra chicken carcass
4 prunes
1 roasting chicken
oil
salt and pepper
sugar

Preparation time: 10 minutes; cooking time: 1 hour

Discard the inedible parts of the leeks and cut the white parts whole from the 4 best specimens. Chop all the rest small, green included, wash very carefully, and drain. Put the chopped leek to sweat in a covered saucepan for about 30 minutes with a knob of butter and a slight moistening of stock or water.

Prepare a chicken cullis (page 24) ideally by adding giblets and a chicken carcass to 1¾ pts (100 cl) of existing stock (reserving a coffee-cupful of stock for later), and boiling it down to ½ pt (30 cl). During this process, cook the prunes and the reserved lengths of leek in the cullis for 5 minutes.

Roast the chicken, basting with a mixture of butter and oil, in a hot oven for 45 minutes or until cooked. Sprinkle the outside skin with salt and pepper before the roasting and at least once as it cooks. Time this process so that the chicken has a few minutes to rest before it is eaten.

Glaze the blanched leeks and prunes in a small, shallow pan with a knob of butter, the reserved stock, salt and a sprinkling of sugar. Cover with greaseproof paper and put the pan on a lowish heat for about 15 minutes. Turn the leeks once or twice and remove paper towards the end to allow most of the moisture to evaporate.

Liquidise the green leeks which have been sweating. If possible rub them through a sieve to remove fibres. Re-heat in saucepan; add the strained chicken cullis to make sauce. It is in order to finish the sauce with cream, but it is very good without cream.

Instead of being glazed, the blanched prunes and leeks may be roasted with the chicken for 10–15 minutes.

119

ROAST COCK-A-LEEKIE SUPRÊME

8 prunes
2 tablespoons Drambuie or whisky
¼pt (14cl) Indian tea
1 roasting chicken
½oz (14g) soft brown sugar
4 leeks chopped small, washed
½pt (28cl) dry cider
2½pts (150cl) house stock (page 24) or water
parsley, bay leaf and thyme
4 leeks trimmed (white parts only), whole
butter
coffee cup chicken stock
salt and sugar
1 large, peeled potato
¼pt (14cl) single cream
½oz (14g) butter

Preparation and cooking time: 3½–4 hours

Luxurious to eat and simple to cook, you must start to prepare this dish about 4 hours before it is served.

Macerate prunes in Drambuie diluted by tea – just enough to cover the fruit.

Roast the chicken for 30 minutes in a hot oven. Let it cool until handleable then cut breasts, legs and thighs from bird. Chop remainder of chicken into about 6 pieces and continue roasting, along with the liver and giblets. After 10 minutes sprinkle with brown sugar. After another 10 minutes add chopped leeks and stir. After another 10 minutes add the cider. When the cider has more or less evaporated, transfer everything to a large saucepan, adding the house stock or water, and herbs. (Swill out the roasting pan with a little water to make sure you transfer everything to the pan.) Simmer with the lid on for an hour, at least, and boil with the lid off for a further 40 minutes, reducing the volume to a scant pt (50cl). Strain the reduced stock into a bowl. As it cools, remove fat with spoon or absorbent kitchen paper.

Blanch and glaze the trimmed leeks as in the previous recipe.

Cut the potato into small cubes and cook these with the prunes in the reduced chicken stock. After 10 minutes, remove prunes. Liquidise the cooked potato with a little of the stock and return to pan. Add cream and simmer; add whisky–tea mixture and boil off the alcohol; finish sauce with butter.

Reheat the chicken breast, legs and thighs, having cut breasts into 2 portions and having bisected the leg/thigh joints. Ideally the chicken should be brushed with melted butter and grilled for 2 minutes skin side down, 3 minutes skin side up – but the re-heating may be done in oven or on hob. Each person has a portion of breast and either a drumstick or thigh.

ABREAST OF THE THYME

2 large or 4 small chicken breasts
salt and pepper
thyme (1 teaspoon dried or 3 sprigs fresh)
butter
1 large pink gin (at least 2 tablespoons)
scant ½pt (25cl) house broth (page 24, chicken if possible)
¼pt (14cl) double cream

Cooking time: 20 minutes

The chicken breasts may be taken from a whole bird or birds, or be bought as breasts (for speed and convenience). Beat them flat into escalopes with a rolling pin. Season them with salt, pepper and some thyme. Fry them gently in butter (or butter and oil mixed), 4–5 minutes on each side according to size. Remove them to a warm serving dish.

De-glaze the frying pan with the pink gin. Then add the chicken stock and the rest of the thyme. Boil down to about one-quarter of its previous volume before adding the cream. Bring cream to boil, then finish the sauce with a knob of butter and a further shake from the Angostura bottle.

121

CHICKEN WITH THYME AND LEMON SAUCE

1 roasting chicken
1½ lemons
butter and oil for roasting
house broth
shallot
thyme
4 tablespoons sherry
1 egg yolk

Cooking time 60–70 minutes

Rub the chicken with the half lemon; then cut the half into 2 quarters. Put 1 quarter inside the chicken together with a piece of butter. Roast the chicken, basting with a mixture of melted butter and oil and the juice from remaining quarter of lemon.

While bird is roasting, boil its liver and giblets in house broth (page 24) with a shallot and plenty of thyme. Skim as necessary.

Pare the whole lemon. Cut the pith-free rind into tiny slivers. Blanch them in boiling water and set aside. Squeeze all juice from pared lemon.

When the chicken is done, put it on a serving plate and de-glaze the roasting pan with lemon juice and sherry. Strain the reduced chicken giblet stock into the pan and continue reducing, with an extra pinch of thyme.

Put egg yolk into top half of a double saucepan. Add a tablespoon of warm water acidulated with lemon juice; stir with wooden spoon. Remove chicken and thyme stock from heat. Cool it by pouring it back and forth between 2 saucepans, then gradually add it to the egg yolk. After putting hot water in the bottom of the double pan, put the egg mixture on top, add the lemon slivers, and cook over a very low heat, stirring until the sauce thickens slightly. Don't boil it or let it simmer!

DREADNOUGHT CHICKEN

When the system breaks down and you suddenly have to prepare a reasonably special meal from the shelves of your nearest super-market, fear not nor despair. Take the plunge and buy the dreaded broiler. Also:

1 loaf factory bread
1 packet Cheddar cheese
1 packet bacon
2 lemons
1 small carton of UHT cream

You will also need mustard powder, an egg, soft brown sugar and a tot of whisky or rum, but let's hope the system hasn't broken down so badly that you need to buy these too.

Preparation and cooking time: 1 hour

Make a stuffing composed of 4 parts breadcrumbs, 2 parts grated cheese, 1 part chopped bacon. Bind it with an egg; season with pepper and mustard powder. Put it in the chicken and roast in a hot oven for 50 minutes, having rubbed the bird with salt.

While the chicken is cooking make if possible both a lemon gusto (page 239) and a mustard-cream (page 232). The former provides an astringent contrast to the rich stuffing; the latter complements and blends with it. (If you only have time to make one, go for the gusto.)

Served with boiled or roast potatoes and a salad, this is a meal you may supply with equanimity to the hungry, the greedy and the fastidious.

Herbs and an onion element may very happily be included in the stuffing.

COQ AU CIDRE

young roasting chicken cut in 4 pieces
4oz (112g) bacon, cubed
8–12 small onions or shallots, peeled
1½ tablespoons gin
1 tablespoon cider vinegar
1pt (56cl) dry cider
white pepper
3½oz (100g) white mushrooms
bacon fat, butter or lard for frying

Cooking time: 1 hour

Fry the bacon gently (in a braising pan which goes into the oven) and when its fat begins to run add the chicken pieces. Fry them on both sides, adding the peeled little onions. Pour in the warm gin and set it alight. When the flame dies down, add a tablespoonful of cider vinegar. Arrange each piece of chicken so that it is skin side up. When the vinegar has gone, add cider to come roughly two-thirds up each piece of chicken. Season with milled white pepper. Bring to a simmer. Cover the pan and transfer to medium oven for about 45 minutes.

Halve or quarter the mushrooms and melt them in butter or bacon fat (only a little) till they just begin to cook. When the chicken has been cooking for half an hour, add the mushrooms, remove the lid, and raise the oven temperature to hot.

COQ AU CIDRE (older birds)

1 boiling fowl
2 medium onions, peeled and quartered
2 large carrots, scraped
1 stick celery
2oz (56g) bacon
thyme or marjoram
1¾pts (100cl) dry cider
1lb (450g) mushrooms

Preparation and cooking time: 2½ hours

Put bird in close-fitting casserole with its giblets. Pack in onions, carrots, celery, bacon (or salt pork), thyme or marjoram. Pour in dry cider. Assuming this does not quite submerge the bird, top up with water or broth. Simmer, skimming as necessary, till the chicken is cooked – about 1½ hours maybe.

While the bird is cooking, prepare a mushroom purée (page 32) but keep a few good mushrooms aside.

Remove the cooked bird and let the remaining juices settle in casserole. Spoon off any fat which rises to the top. (It doesn't matter if you lose some of the stock underneath.) Then return casserole to a high flame and reduce with lid off till you only have about ¾ pt (40 cl). Strain this on to the mushroom purée in a second pan. Add the mushrooms kept aside, quartered, and simmer for 2 minutes.

Divide the chicken into large pieces, discarding the breast bone and skin. Put them in an ovenproof serving dish. Pour the mushroom and cider sauce over them and heat through in oven till everyone is ready for supper.

BARNYARD BOLLITO

old hen(s)
selection of onions, carrots, celery, mushrooms, garlic
piece of ham or bacon
⅓ pt (20 cl) double cream
2 eggs
2 cloves
1 small onion
white pepper
large bunch parsley, finely chopped

Cooking time: 2–4 hours

In a large pan cover the bird or birds with water, add the vegetables, then the ham or bacon (in one piece) and cook slowly for 1½–3 hours according to the obduracy of the chicken. Skim the surface as necessary. Keep a lid on for at least the first hour.

When at last the chicken meat is ready to come away from the bone without resistance, help it to do so. Return carcass, bones and skin to the pan and boil rapidly without lid, to reduce the broth to a cullis.

Meanwhile assess the chicken meat. The white meat should be attractively edible in its own right; some of the dark may be very sinewy and should be returned to the boiling saucepan. The better dark meat may be left as it is or be minced. Dice the bacon or ham.

125

Cut the white meat up as for a fricassee. Put chicken and ham into an ovenproof dish and cover until use.

When the boiling stock is very well reduced, say to a scant pint, strain it into a jug. Let it cool long enough for the fat to be removed. Use the chicken cullis with cream and eggs, cloves, onion and pepper to make a no-bread sauce (page 231). This takes about 20 minutes and gives you plenty of time to re-heat the chicken in a low oven. When the sauce is ready, add parsley and pour it over the chicken.

POACHED TURKEY

Not for Christmas dinner perhaps, but poached turkey, hot or cold, makes a lovely summery meal whatever the weather outside.

1 small turkey, fresh rather than frozen, with giblets
chicken stock or water
2 large onions
4 large carrots
2 sticks celery
thyme or marjoram
salt
fresh seasonal vegetables such as peas, French beans, cauliflower, broccoli
   (enough for four helpings)
arrowroot (optional)
1 lemon

Preparation and cooking time: 2 hours

Cover turkey (including giblets) with water or stock. Add onions, carrots, celery, herbs and some salt. Bring to near boiling point and simmer gently for about 1½ hours, skimming with care.

When the bird is cooked, strain three-quarters of the broth into another saucepan. Cover turkey and set it to one side; discard carrots, onions, celery and giblets which are now in the strainer; bring new pan to a fierce boil. Throw the seasonal vegetables into the boiling broth and cook them for 7–10 minutes. Remove vegetables to a warm, buttered serving dish. Continue boiling the broth for at least 5, preferably 10–15, minutes, thickening it, if desired, with arrowroot. Taste the broth for seasoning and before serving it with the turkey and vegetables, add the juice of one small lemon.

Alternative sauces for poached turkey include no-bread sauce (page 231), green summer sauce (page 236), and mustard-cream (page 232). Sauce methods 2 and 5 (page 226) also apply, while the Troisgros frères of Roanne suggest truffles with walnut vinaigrette (and they should know).

Duckling and Duck

Along with muscular chickens, we also used to rear Muscovy ducks. Drier and less fatty than the Aylesbury clan, they were marvellously meaty birds – a well-grown drake would feed six people or more. Muscovies are cultivated for the table in France but not elsewhere (unless there are untrumpeted duck farms on the Île de Moscou). Supermarket ducks look plump but only feed two or three, at most four people. Their meat is rich and tender, however, and the skin can be made appetizingly crisp.

If you can allow half a duck to each person, the 'suprême' procedure is well worth following, since it yields much better sauces than more thrifty conventional methods (see duck and green peas below).

Unless they are Muscovies, ducks and duckling need no extra fat when they are roasted. Instead they should be placed on a rack or grid above the roasting pan. Potatoes, turnips or onions can be cooked underneath the bird.

Wild duck (teal, widgeon and mallard) are almost fatless and best cooked by the game suprême method (page 184) or roasted well larded with fat bacon.

ROAST DUCK WITH SAGE AND ONION SAUCE

1 oven-ready duck
salt and pepper
1 shallot
1 carrot
cider
4 sage leaves
2 large onions, skinned and halved
1 tablespoon vinegar

Cooking time: 60–70 minutes

Roast the duck in a hot oven on a grid above the roasting pan. After 15 minutes pierce the skin in several places to assist the flow of fat into the pan beneath. At the same time, sprinkle the skin with salt and pepper.

Put giblets, liver, shallot and carrot to make duck broth. Boil in water, broth, or a mixture of water and cider for 30 minutes, skimming the surface as necessary. Put a sage leaf with this broth.

Peel and slice the large onions. Blanch them in boiling water for 2 minutes; drain thoroughly and put onions in roasting pan (under the duck) with 3 sage leaves embedded in them. Reduce oven temperature to medium. Over the next 30–40 minutes, keep an eye on the onions – they should mush down and take on colour but not burn. If necessary moisten with water or cider.

When the duck is cooked, allow it to rest on a hot plate in a warm place. Make sauce by adding a tablespoon of vinegar to the onions, now over a high flame. Then add the strained duck broth. Remove the sage leaves.

DUCK AND GREEN PEAS

1 duck
2 tablespoons cider vinegar
¼ pt (14 cl) dry cider
9 oz (250 g) shelled peas plus their pods
8 spring onions, trimmed
1½ tablespoons British medium sherry
¼ pt (14 cl) double cream

Preparation and cooking time: 1½ hours

Roast the duck for 30 minutes in a hot oven. Remove and rest it for 10 minutes. Carve off breast and legs. Hack up remainder of bird and roast for a further 10 minutes. Pour off and reserve excess fat. De-glaze pan with cider vinegar then transfer to saucepan. Pour cider into roasting dish and stir with wooden spoon to retrieve all duck essences. Add to saucepan and barely cover the remainder of the duck with water. Add the peapods and a little more water if necessary. Boil fast for 30 minutes with lid off, reducing it to about ½ pt (30 cl) of duck cullis.

Simmer shelled peas and spring onions very gently in duck fat for 10 minutes. Add sherry and turn up the heat. When the duck cullis is ready, strain it into the peas. Finish the peas with cream.

Meanwhile grill or fry the duck legs for 3 minutes on each side, having lightly brushed them with duck fat. Cook the breasts for 1½ minutes on each side, similarly; then carve each into 3 or 4 fillets.

Each person receives a leg and 3 or 4 fillets of breast – so the whole bird feeds only 2 people (but those 2 have a very nice time).

BRAMBLED DUCK

¼pt (14cl) cider
¼pt (14cl) cider vinegar
4oz (112g) blackberries
1oz (28g) caster sugar
1 duck, with liver and giblets
3 large tomatoes, halved
1 onion, halved
1 apple, quartered
3 shallots, chopped

Preparation and cooking time: 1½ hours

Heat the cider and vinegar to boiling point then pour them over the blackberries. Stir in the sugar. Allow the berries to cool for an hour, then strain off the liquor, reserving it and the berries.

While berries are cooling, roast the bird in a very hot oven for 30 minutes. Remove and rest it for 10 minutes. Carve off breast and legs. Divide legs at joint with poultry scissors. Reserve the fat which has run from the duck.

Meanwhile start a duck broth with liver and giblets and 1pt (56cl) water, removing scum as broth comes to the boil. After carving duck, add carcass and wings, broken up, to the broth. Also add the tomatoes, onion and apple. Boil fast for a further 30 minutes to obtain a good concentrated stock.

Fry the shallots in a little duck fat over medium heat for 7 minutes, in a saucepan. De-glaze with 3 tablespoons of the black-berry vinegar and bubble this down to a syrup before adding remainder of vinegar. Boil rapidly till there are only 2 tablespoons of liquid remaining. Strain in the duck and tomato broth, which by now should be almost a cullis. Simmer the resulting sauce, taste for seasoning and thicken with arrowroot if need be.

Meanwhile grill or fry the duck breast and legs as in the

preceding recipe. Finally add the blackberries to the sauce, and carve the breast into fillets.

LAME DUCK

When a duck has gone to pieces, that is when it's jointed, it can be helped by beer, treacle and prunes . . .

2 tablespoons black treacle
2 tablespoons cider vinegar
⅓ pt (20 cl) sweet stout
8 prunes
12 coarsely crushed peppercorns
1 onion
1 apple
4 or more joints of duck
giblets, neck and wings (or 1 extra joint) for broth
butter
salt and pepper
1 oz (28 g) blackcurrants (or blackberries)

Preparation and marinating time: at least 12 hours; cooking time: 45 minutes

Dissolve treacle in vinegar over medium heat; add stout, prunes, pepper, sliced onion, chopped apple. Heat the brew to less than simmering point but more than blood temperature, stirring and mixing well. Pour it over the pieces of duck and let them marinate in it for 12–24 hours.

Prepare duck broth from giblets, neck and wings. Use quite a lot of water for this but reduce it to about ½ pt (30 cl). If you have bought duck ready-jointed, make sure you ask for the giblets, or buy an extra joint for stock.

Remove duck from marinade, also the onion slices, and dry on kitchen paper. Deep fry the duck joints for 90 seconds each. Drain on kitchen paper.

Melt the slices of onion in a little butter in a braising pan or dish. Put the duck on top of the onions. Add duck stock so that it comes two-thirds up the duck. Make sure the duck is skin side up. Season with salt and pepper, and cook uncovered in a medium to hot oven for 20 minutes. Then add the prunes. Cook for a further 20 minutes with lid off. Just before serving, scatter in a few blackcurrants or blackberries.

STRETCHED DUCK

1 duck
3 large onions
sage or thyme
house stock or water
3½oz (100g) bacon
7oz (200g) pot barley
3½oz (100g) green split peas
salt and pepper

Cooking and preparation time: at least 3 hours

Roast the duck for 40 minutes on rack above roasting pan. At the same time, start making duck broth with liver, giblets, 1 onion, sage and house stock or water. Slice 2 onions and cook them under the duck rack for the last 20 minutes of roasting. Cook bacon similarly, in large thick slices, for the last 10 minutes of roasting.

After letting it rest for 10 minutes, carve the duck. Cut the duck skin into small pieces and continue roasting these, well salted, till they are all crisp. Remove as much meat as possible, then hack up the carcass and bones. Add these to the duck broth and continue simmering for at least 30 minutes.

When duck broth is good and rich, strain it into a large saucepan in which you have already put the barley and split peas. Top up with water if necessary. Season with salt and pepper. Barley and peas will need at least 1½ hours cooking. Add the par-cooked onions and bacon. After 90 minutes' simmering, taste the barley and peas. They may need a little more time. Shortly before serving, stir in the carved duck and crisp duck skin. Pour off excess liquor (if any) from the barley. Add fat and juices from roasting pan. Taste for seasoning.

A good-humoured, filling and economical dish, this will feed at least 6. By increasing the amount of barley and split peas, a duck can be stretched further, to 8 or maybe 10 people.

A similar effect can be obtained with pork instead of duck, or with goose. The dish is a distant cousin of the cassoulet, and can take sausages, herbs, garlic, and so on.

132

Eggs and Bacon

A potent combination, eggs and bacon can be cooked appallingly and yet remain palatable. The method indicated below makes a very presentable lunch or family dish, and could also be used as a dinner starter – for example when fish forms the main course.

Eggs and bacon can be so good, it's a pity not to take a little trouble over them sometimes.

EGGS AND BACON AND EGGS

4 rashers streaky bacon
4 rashers back bacon
8 eggs
salt and black pepper
butter
2 slices white bread

Cooking time: 10 minutes

Grill, fry or roast the bacon so that streaky becomes crisp but back is moist and supple.

Scramble half the eggs seasoned with a little salt and plenty of black pepper, using plenty of butter. The best scrambled eggs are made by steady stirring over very low heat, and can take up to half an hour. One seldom has the patience for this. The other 4 eggs should (in order of preference) be baked in individual buttered cocottes, poached or fried. The bread should be cut into triangles and fried, if possible in clarified butter.

Arrange the components on individual plates with the whole egg centred, the rashers on either side, east and west, a mound of scrambled egg to the north, and the fried bread south – or some other symmetry.

Various additions and variations are eminently possible: chives can be added to the scrambling eggs; mustard seed can be fried and scattered over both eggs; slivers of smoked salmon will convince guests they are eating a starter of rank and polish; a chiffonade of sorrel may be stirred into the scrambled egg just before serving; with a spinach purée this goes a long way to becoming a serious main course.

A SAUSAGE, EGG AND BACON VARIATION

8 chipolatas
8 rashers bacon
bacon fat (if possible)
4 slices white bread
butter or clarified butter
2oz (56g) cooked ham
8 eggs
pepper
chives (optional)
cream (optional)
vinegar
Worcestershire sauce
English mustard

Cooking time: 15–20 minutes

Fry the sausages and bacon in bacon fat if available.

Fry triangles of crustless white bread in butter or clarified butter. Keep them warm with the bacon and sausages.

Chop cooked ham very finely. Add it to eggs and beat them prior to scrambling. Add pepper. Scramble the eggs slowly and add, optionally, a few chopped chives, a little cream.

Make a mini sauce by de-glazing the sausage and bacon pan with vinegar and a drop of Worcestershire sauce. Then reduce the heat and finish sauce by adding butter and – off the heat – made English mustard.

As a change you could put chopped anchovy into the scrambled egg, or fresh green peas, or baby broad beans.

Trickle the sauce over the sausages and bacon.

A green purée of watercress, sorrel or spinach goes very well with this. Or the purée could be a combination of all three leaves. Drink cider.

SASSENACH EGGS

Scotch eggs, like station sandwiches, stare balefully at potential customers, defying consumption by any but the hunger-crazed. Yet eggs encased in sausage or forcemeat can be delicious enough to tempt us all.

4 coddled eggs
3oz (84g) lean ham or bacon
2oz (56g) fat ham
2oz (56g) soft wholemeal breadcrumbs
4 tablespoons parsley
flour seasoned with pepper
deep fat or oil for frying

Preparation and cooking time: 20 minutes

Boil the eggs for 5 minutes. Plunge into cold water. When cold, crack the shells very carefully and remove. The whites should be set but the yolks inside still fairly runny. Do not use very fresh eggs for this because the shells are difficult to remove.

Mince the ham or bacon and fat ham but keep them separate. Mix lean ham, crumbs and chopped parsley in bowl; then start adding the minced fat, using only enough to bind the mixture. Season it with pepper. Mould one-quarter of the mixture round each coddled egg. Dust with seasoned flour. Deep-fry until crisp and golden.

Can, of course, be eaten cold, but they are better eaten hot with tomato and thyme gusto (page 238) or tomato zest (page 244).

DEVILLED EGGS

6 eggs
devil butter (page 176)
4 teaspoons dry breadcrumbs
devil pepper (page 176)
mustard and cress, or parsley or watercress

Preparation and cooking time: 15 minutes

Hardboil the eggs. Cool them in cold water, then shell them. Cut them in half and remove the yolks.

Pound the yolks with the devil butter – which should be soft – and the breadcrumbs. Refill the whites with this mixture, piling them convexly. Sprinkle the eggs with devil pepper.

Serve 3 half eggs to each person on a bed of mustard and cress, parsley or watercress; and with radishes if in season.

AN ANGLO-SPANISH OMELETTE

1 onion, sliced
bacon fat or lard or oil
2 boiled potatoes, peeled
2oz (56g) peeled shrimps
4 tinned sardines
4 eggs
pepper
nutmeg or mace
1oz (28g) cooked ham
parsley
butter

Preparation and cooking time: 35 minutes

Fry the onion gently in bacon fat, lard or oil. After 5 minutes, add the potatoes cut into cubes. Then add the shrimps and the quartered sardines. The pan should be rather full.

Stir the eggs and flavour them with pepper and nutmeg. Add the ham chopped very small. Add chopped parsley. Pour eggs over the onion and potato mixture. Mix all well together and cook over a medium heat for about 15 minutes. When the omelette is just beginning to set on the top but is still a bit wobbly if shaken, finish it under the grill with a little melted butter.

This can be eaten hot or cold. Makes an interesting picnic.

EGG AND BACON SALAD

4 hardboiled eggs
8 rashers streaky bacon
oil
3 different lettuces or the equivalent in leafy salad vegetables
fresh summer herbs, especially mint and chervil
vinegar
mustard
fried-bread croûtons

Preparation and cooking time: 15 minutes

Hardboil and cool the eggs.

Cut bacon across the grain in strips ⅜inch (1 cm) wide. Fry, slowly at first in bacon fat or oil. When fat begins to run from bacon increase the heat. Turn the bacon until it is crisp.

Assemble the salad vegetables and herbs in a bowl. It looks pretty if the colours and textures are as varied as possible. Toss the salad lightly in a mustardy vinaigrette. Then add the bacon and its fat. Then de-glaze the frying pan with a little more vinegar, cider vinegar for preference.

Put the salad on to individual plates and top these with chopped hardboiled egg. Triangles of fried bread or croûtons may also be added.

Admittedly this sort of salad, often made with raw spinach, has become rather a cliché, but the fashion will pass, the concept will be forgotten . . . so here it is for all time.

HOW TO EAT BOILED EGGS

By this method each mouthful is equally bright and the white is charmingly mingled with the yolk.

Softboil the eggs, let's say 4¼ minutes. Remove them from the water and allow them to lose heat for a minute. Then crack 1 or 2 into each person's cup, scooping out the contents with a large teaspoon. Add a teaspoon of butter to each cup. Let people help themselves to salt and pepper. Serve with fingers of bread and butter or toast.

The only snag is you do burn your fingers. A thin oven glove is the answer. Or let everybody cope with their own eggs.

COD'S ROE SCRAMBLE

5oz (140g) smoked cod's roe
3½oz (100g) unsalted, softened butter
cayenne pepper
4 slices wholemeal bread
6 eggs
butter for scrambling
white pepper
2½ tablespoons double cream
parsley, chervil or chives
4 wedges lemon

Preparation and cooking time: 20–5 minutes

Mash the cod's roe and the butter together, seasoning lightly with cayenne pepper. Chill.

Cut the bread into roundels or hexagons, removing all crust. Toast it.

Beat and (slowly) scramble the eggs, seasoning with a little white pepper. Remove the eggs from heat when they are just beginning to thicken, but before they have stopped being runny. Stir in the cream.

To serve: put a generous portion of cod's roe mixture on to each piece of toast; place an island of roe and toast in the centre of each – very warm – plate, and surround it by a sea of scrambled egg. Strew the egg lightly with chopped herbs (optional), and serve with wedges of lemon.

A lovely starter to the eye and to the palate.

6
MEAT & GAME

Beefeaters Still?

Yes, but mince-eaters and junk-eaters too. Meat remains central to the English concept of good eating, and meals without it often seem incomplete (even, as some admit, to vegetarians). Historically we have been so keen to get down to our meat that we haven't been too worried about how it was cooked. We have seasoned our dinners with half-truths – British beef is the best in the world; foreign stuff is inferior and has to be mucked around to make it edible . . . Such views are not wholly without foundation nor altogether negative in their effect. Much of the world, much of Europe, parts, even, of France put up with poor meat, or none, most of the time. Patriotic belief in the primacy of British materials produced a prudent policy of letting the meat speak for itself rather than disguising it by culinary sleights of hand. However the same policy has been practised without ill effect on South American beef and Antipodean lamb for generations. At the same time we turn a blind eye to such excellent creatures as the Charolais and such fine eating as very young lamb.

Relative to the cost of living, meat is now more expensive than it was (whereas chicken, of course, is cheaper). This alone is a powerful reason for upgrading our methods of cooking, presenting and exploiting it. Meat cooking, however, was overdue for renewal long before prices began to inflate. The very cheapness of beef, pork and mutton – together with the low status of kitchen staff in general – meant that concepts like bringing out the inherent qualities of each meat were all too often corrupted into the habit of letting it fend for itself within a perfunctory formula of roast or fry-up, pudding or pie. These strictures apply most to the urban middle – and upper – classes; farmhouse fare and working-class cookery retained many of their virtues until both submitted to Mother's Pride and the convenience food takeover. At about the same time, ironically, the now cookless – cook-emancipated? – classes were discovering the compensation of home-made French country cooking.

141

However, the new generation of continental cooks is not particularly interested in beef or pork. It prefers lamb on the whole, though only the best bits – and even these tend to be less popular than calves' liver, sweetbreads, veal and kidneys. Steak, even fillet, is somewhat obvious for the leaders of nouvelle cuisine; beef, generally, is too positive, perhaps, to be a good vehicle for chefs' magicianship. Similarly pork, though it continues to be respected as the prime source of charcuterie, and is still mandatory on the cheaper prix fixe menus in the form of côte de porc, seldom inspires the creation of new main dishes. One suspects, however, that some of the veal derives (venially enough) from the pigsty.

The meat cooking advocated in this book seeks to reform traditional British approaches rather than emulate the new French. It will help you to make more of your meat and produce dishes of tempting elegance within a no-nonsense style of cooking.

Fat – and the Taste of English Meat Cookery

Use natural fats in preference to butter, margarine or vegetable oils. Beef should be cooked with beef dripping, pork with pork lard, lamb with lamb or mutton fat. Most dishes can, of course, be cooked reasonably well with a neutral oil (like sunflower) but they taste more English – better – if meat and animal fat are correctly paired. Do not cook beef with lamb fat, or vice versa.

Good butchers supply lard, dripping and their mother fats at modest cost. These days some of them even find it hard to dispose of such culinary necessities. Keep the fats clearly marked and separate in the refrigerator; do not mix them. Fat bowls which mis-marry the greasy remains of several different joints give unhappy results, and are probably responsible for the fact that you may be dubious about the foregoing advice. Try it before resorting to characterless, tasteless, harmless oil.

Ham and bacon fat are also very good cooking media, particularly for dry meats such as hare and venison. Mutton fat, when available, is very compatible with venison. Veal, never very popular in Britain, may be basted with a mixture of lard and dripping as it is roasted, but is perhaps the one meat which is happier cooked with a mixture of oil and butter.

Animal fats are not recommended for fish, but are excellent for fried bread, roast potatoes, for onions, mushrooms, parsnips and tomatoes.

English meat dishes should never be greasy or swimming in fat, but some lubrication is usually essential. Diet, health and the polyunsaturated fat syndrome are discussed briefly but con brio on pages 6–7.

Fast-food Formula

As with fish, there is a simple formula for producing elegant and sophisticated meat dishes, as it were from scratch. This is a great standby for restaurant chefs, and is related to three-star fish (page 88), but more or less demands expensive cuts of meat (whereas its counterpart also works with the most unassuming of fish).

All that happens is that the meat – chop or fillet, mignon or medaillon, liver, kidney, sweetbread – is grilled or fried quickly. When just cooked, it is removed from the pan and kept warm, while a sauce is formulated with the juices left in the pan as its starting point. Some of the butter and oil may be poured off before the sauce-making begins. A member of the onion family is often introduced first, and cooked for a few minutes, then some alcohol or vinegar, which is bubbled down to a glaze, then stock – also reduced – followed by seasoning, other flavourings (such as herbs), sometimes fungi or a vegetable purée. The sauce may be finished with cream, especially for veal and chicken dishes, and sometimes with more butter. Any juices which seep from the meat being kept warm may also be incorporated.

Flavourings introduced towards the end of the 5–10 minute sauce-making process tend to occupy the foreground in terms of taste and influence – and to be the real test of the chef's originality (all the rest is formula). This is an area where one man has a good idea, hundreds follow the fashion, and somebody marketing red peppercorns or rambutans makes a fortune.

It will be appreciated that while the cooking formula is itself quick and easy, the preparatory work – trimming meat, poaching sweetbreads, peeling, washing, cutting up vegetables – may be

143

time-consuming and must obviously be done beforehand.

The five recipes which follow all apply a version of this formula to improve traditional English favourites.

STEAK AND ONIONS

4 good steaks
4 medium onions, chopped
beef dripping
¼pt (14cl) sweet stout (or brown ale)
2½ tablespoons cider vinegar
mushroom ketchup (optional)
⅓pt (20cl) meat cullis (page 26)
black pepper

Cooking time: about 20 minutes

Here the legitimate heartiness of an old favourite is enhanced by a sauce of tempting sophistication.

The steaks should be fried in good beef dripping – or grilled. Cooking time will depend on the quality and size of the steaks, and the diners' preferences as to rarity (see below). When cooked, they should be kept warm and their juices allowed to flow from them (tilt the dish slightly).

For the sauce, fry onions in dripping over a fairly high heat for 7 minutes. When they are nicely brown add the sweet stout and the vinegar. Mushroom ketchup may also be added, with advantage. Let stout and vinegar boil down to a thick, gooey syrup, before adding the strong stock. Simmer for a further 3 minutes, then add the meat juices and black pepper.

Notes on Steak Cooking

Thinly cut entrecôte steaks can be cooked for as little as 1 minute on each side; rump steak which is about ¾in (2cm) thick needs 4–5 minutes' grilling or frying on each side; steaks which are thicker may need as much as 15–18 minutes in all. When cooked, steaks may be rested in a warm place for 8–10 minutes. This improves taste and tenderness.

Steaks butchered in the traditional British way have their own fat adhering. A good tip is to trim most of this off the meat, cut it up small, and fry it over medium heat so that it greases the bottom of the pan. You can cook the steak in its own dripping; but discard the small pieces of fat as they brown.

LAMB AND GREEN PEAS

pea pods from peas (see below)
salt and pepper
3 spring onions
9oz (240g) shelled green peas
half a lemon
8 lamb chops (12 if chops are small or appetites large)
lamb fat (or clarified butter)
⅓pt (20cl) dry cider
3½oz (100g) young carrots, washed, scraped, thinly julienned
handful fresh mint
½oz (14g) butter

Cooking time: about 35 minutes

First make a green pea purée: simmer the pea pods in water or broth for 15 minutes, with salt and a spring onion. Discard pods and cook peas in same broth. As soon as they are cooked, blend them to a purée with some of the broth and a squeeze of lemon. Season with salt and pepper. Trim the fat from the chops.

Fry the well-seasoned chops for 1½ minutes on each side in very hot lamb or mutton fat. Then add the cider, reduce the heat slightly, cover the pan, and simmer for 6–7 minutes or until the chops are cooked, but still slightly pink in the middle.

Remove the chops and keep them hot. Add the remaining chopped spring onion and julienned carrots to juices in the pan. Cook for 1 minute then add the green-pea cullis. When this is simmering nicely, stir in first the mint, then the butter.

Serve sauce and chops separately.

LIVERS AND BACONS

Liver and bacon is one of the culinary marriages made in heaven, but also a liaison dangereuse, since it calls for critical timing. Overcook the liver, undercook – or render greasy – the bacon, and the dish is spoilt. And even if the timing is right, surely the dish needs at least a soupspoonful of sauce or lubrication? But what? In France, liver and bacon would have become a virtuoso piece with individual chefs providing their own cadenzas; in Britain, it has remained an unfinished symphony. Let's correct the score and devise a finale.

14 oz (400 g) calves' liver (or lambs')
milk
1 tablespoon seasoned flour
4 rashers back bacon
8 rashers streaky bacon, cut thin
ham, bacon or pork fat for frying
3½ oz (100 g) chicken livers
2 oz (56 g) mushrooms
5 tablespoons medium sherry
scant ½ pt (25 cl) meat cullis (page 26)

Preparation time: 70 minutes (if possible); cooking time: 20 minutes

Cut the liver into finger-thick slices and, if possible, soak it in milk for an hour, to draw out the blood. After soaking, the liver should be dried carefully, dusted with well-seasoned flour, and rolled between the palms into short chipolata shapes.

Fry the bacon first in ham, bacon or pork fat. Streaky bacon should be fried crisp but back bacon must not, though the fat part may be a little crisp. It is worth taking trouble over this, and fussing the bacon with a slice so that you get it just right. When removing it from the pan, shake each rasher free of fat.

To cook the liver, add a little more fat to the pan, if necessary. When it is very hot, fry the liver quickly for about 4 minutes, leaving the inside a soft, reddy-pink. Then remove it and keep it warm with the bacon.

The sauce is made by adding finely chopped chicken livers to the now floury fat in the pan, together with finely chopped raw mushrooms. Fry briskly for 2 minutes, stirring. Add sherry and reduce it, still stirring, to a glaze, then add the cullis, and simmer for 3 minutes (adding a knob of butter if you want to give the sauce extra gloss). This sauce intensifies the liver and bacon experience.

Good with mashed potato, grilled tomatoes and spinach.

SAUSAGES AND MASH

In the British pantheon, sausage is to mash as hope to glory, but far too often the dish is a national humiliation, with neither component worth eating.

8 good sausages, preferably 'pure pork' or 'Cumberland' (*not* continental)
lard for frying
1 large onion
salt and pepper
fresh or dried sage (to taste)
soft brown sugar
2 tablespoons wine vinegar
1 dessertspoon Worcestershire sauce
1 tablespoon tomato ketchup
⅓pt (20cl) strong stock (page 26)

Cooking time: about 30 minutes

Cook the sausages slowly. At home we sometimes start them in the oven and finish them in a frying pan. They should be well done right through and all but burnt on the outside. The best chance of achieving the 'knobbly bits' admired by H.G. Wells is to make small incisions at each end. This discourages a central explosion but allows minor eruptions at the ends.

When the sausages are cooked, keep them hot on a dish and make this simple version of frying-pan sauce (page 228): pour off some of the sausage fat but leave enough to fry a finely chopped onion, seasoning it with salt, pepper, sage and a little brown sugar. Fry till the onion is more brown than golden. Then add vinegar and Worcestershire sauce. Boil and stir these until they are reduced to a goo, at which point add tomato ketchup and, when this is bubbling nicely, the strong stock (which may be pre-heated). The sauce will be ready in a couple of minutes.

Grilled or fried tomatoes are probably the best vegetables to accompany the British banger; mushrooms are also compatible. The baked-bean option is not for me, but a few broad beans or peas incorporated into the mash make a pleasant change.

MASH

A potato ricer is the best implement for mash, mashed or puréed potato. It is a simple gadget by means of which peeled, boiled potato is extruded through very small holes, thereby emerging entirely free of lumps in threads which break up into rice-like lengths.

For stews and plentifully sauced dishes, potato is fine in the fluffy, aerated pile which falls from the ricer. No further ministration is necessary. A less austere version incorporates butter and milk.

Heat the milk and melt the butter – I tend to do this all at once in the same saucepan. Add them little by little to the riced potato, mashing and stirring with a large fork. The potato loses its fluffiness but acquires an equally enticing creaminess. For 4 people, use about ¼ pt (14 cl) of milk and 2–4 oz (56–112 g) of butter – but the proportions are not critical. It is in order to use very little butter, or to omit the milk and use butter only.

Mash should be strongly seasoned with salt and pepper. Nutmeg is sometimes a good seasoning, too, but not, I suggest, with sausages.

STEAK ET ROGNONS

Steak and kidney pudding is the top ancient monument of the English kitchen – a glorious, anachronistic way of fending off the north-east wind. We no longer need such filling fare, but many of us find it peculiarly and patriotically enjoyable, a challenge, an assertion of virility. Unfortunately, however, steak, kidneys and suet crust all take different times to cook, and this leads, far too often, to impenetrable steak, sodden crust or kidneys the texture of squash balls. Which in turn leads to compromise: the use of ox (least nice of all) kidneys; pie crust instead of suet; an arranged marriage of different elements which meet for the first time on one's plate. Yet the taste and texture of good beefsteak and properly prepared calves' kidneys are indeed complementary. That complementariness is the essence of our national dish – and of the new versions which follow.

2 shallots
3 oz (80 g) mushrooms
8 oz (226 g) veal kidney (or lamb's or pig's)
1 scant pt (50 cl) strong stock (page 26)
4 entrecôte steaks
beef dripping (clarified for preference)
5 tablespoons port
anchovy essence
pepper
arrowroot (optional)

Preparation time: 15 minutes; cooking time: 15 minutes

Preparation: chop shallots, mushrooms and one-third of the kidneys very small indeed. Make sure that the strong stock is really well reduced, as meaty as possible, and deepen its colour with gravy browning (unless you object in principle to such cosmetics). The remaining two-thirds of kidney should be de-cored and cut in pieces about ½ in (1¼ cm) thick.

Fry the steaks quickly, about 1 minute on each side assuming they are cut thin, in very hot dripping. Put them on a dish to keep warm. Fry the ½-inch kidneys in the same pan, 3–4 minutes in all. Add them to the steaks to keep warm. Keep to the same pan for the sauce, first frying the shallots for 2 minutes, then adding the mushrooms (2 minutes), then the remaining third of kidneys (2 minutes more, just long enough to seal them), then the port. Keep stirring all the time, allowing nothing to burn or stick. When the port has bubbled down to a syrup add a good dash of anchovy essence (in memory of the oysters of yesteryear), the strong stock (pre-heated but not quite boiling), and the juices which have exuded from the steak and kidneys keeping warm. Taste the sauce for seasoning; it should be salty enough if the stock is good, but may need pepper. Thicken with arrowroot if necessary (but, again, it should not be necessary if a good strong cullis is employed).

To serve steak et rognons, put 3 pieces of kidney on each entrecôte and top with the kidney and mushroom sauce. Accompany with roast potatoes, little dumplings (page 150) and a green vegetable.

By adjusting the initial cooking time, you can, of course, adapt steak et rognons to decent steaks of any degree of thickness. With thick fillet steaks, for instance, it can challenge tournedos Rossini on its own ground (tournedos Purcell?).

LITTLE DUMPLINGS

Preparation time: 5 minutes; cooking time: 12 minutes

Use suet and soft white breadcrumbs in equal proportions and mix
them with nearly as much chopped parsley. Commercial, shredded
suet is perfectly in order. As well as salt and pepper, the little
dumplings may be flavoured quite strongly with grated horseradish.

Mix all the ingredients together – for 4 people allow some 3 oz
(84 g) of crumbs and 3 oz (84 g) suet – in a mixing bowl, and bind
them with egg (a small egg is enough for these quantities).

Form the dumplings by rolling the mixture into little balls about
the size of chestnuts (only round) and simmer them gently in broth
or water for 12 minutes.

Little dumplings can be varied and embroidered by the addition of tiny pieces of bacon, liver or kidney; or enlivened by
a few dashes of anchovy essence. A suggestion of onion is also a

welcome addition, preferably in the form of chives. Further fresh, green herbs may be used in addition to parsley, but there should always be a strong element of parsley or the lightness and texture of the dumplings may be marred.

If submitting the dumplings to further cooking, as for rich rabbit pie (page 190), the initial simmering can be shortened to 9–10 minutes.

STEAK AND KIDNEY BARLEYCORN

1¼lbs (560g) fillet steak
½lb (225g) kidney (calves' or lambs')
beef dripping
1 tablespoon whisky
2 shallots (chopped)
4oz (112g) finely chopped mushrooms (or mushroom purée)
3½ tablespoons sweet stout
1 pickled walnut, finely chopped
5 tablespoons meat cullis (page 26)

Preparation time: 10 minutes; cooking time: 12–15 minutes

Cut both steak and kidney into thin (Stroganoff) strips. Fry them quickly in a little hot dripping. After 3–4 minutes, flare with warm whisky, then remove them and keep them warm.

Cook the shallot in remaining juices and as soon as it has begun to melt, add the mushrooms or mushroom purée. Cook together for 2 minutes then add the stout and pickled walnut. Bring to the boil and reduce slightly before adding the meat cullis. Test for seasoning.

Pour the steak and kidney mixture and its juices back into the sauce and transfer the whole to a serving dish when it is very hot but not quite boiling. (Boiling will make the kidneys toughen into rubber.)

STEAK AND KIDNEY STROGANOFF

Proceed as for steak and kidney barleycorn but use ¼pt (14cl) double cream instead of the meat cullis, and use rather less stout (or brown ale).

STEWED STEAK AND KIDNEY

1 lb 5 oz (600 g) lean stewing steak
beef dripping
1 large onion, peeled and sliced
2 large carrots, scraped and quartered
6 rashers streaky bacon
house broth (page 24)
7 oz (200 g) kidney (lambs' or calves')
2½ tablespoons port or sweet sherry
1 dessertspoon Urchfont-type or whole grain mustard

Preparation and braising time: 2½ hours; final cooking time: 10 minutes

The steak should be in 1 or 2 large pieces. Fry each side quickly in dripping to seal it.

Transfer steak to casserole with the onion, carrots and any other root vegetables you have to hand. Add broth to almost cover the meat. Lay rashers of bacon on top of the meat. Braise till the meat is tender.

Remove the meat and allow it to cool. Reduce juices in casserole by half, boiling fast. Strain the remaining cullis and throw away the vegetables. When the cullis is cold, remove all fat. Remove any fat, sinew or gristle from the meat.

That is the first operation – best done the day, or at least the morning, before the dish is required.

The second operation: cut the steak into 4 large pieces or 8 smaller ones if more convenient. Put the meat in a shallow, oven-proof dish and let it heat through in a medium oven, with half the reduced cooking juices.

Bisect and core the kidneys. Cook them very quickly in hot dripping, about 2 minutes on each side. Add the sherry or port and bubble for 1 minute. Add the mustard, then stir in the other half of the reserved cooking juices. Raise to simmering point, then pour over the steak. Serve with boiled potatoes.

The Roast

Purists maintain that ovens bake – whether bread, or pies or beef – rather than roast, and that roasting implies an open fire, probably with a spit. But let's accept the vernacular use of roast – the beef will taste just as good and we are spared the funereal overtones of 'baked meat'.

The ground rules for successful oven roasting need only be summarised. First, the oven should be pre-heated hot enough (gas regulo 7–9, 400–50°F, 250–300°C) immediately to sear the meat, and so conserve its juices. After 10–15 minutes, the heat may be reduced (gas regulo 6 or 7, 375–400°F, 225–50°C). Secondly, the meat should be basted with fat and cooking juices, possibly supplemented with water, wine, beer or cider. Fat joints require less basting and no extra fat, though a very thin coating of lard or oil can help exposed, lean surfaces. Lean, dry meats need a good supplement of dripping or lard, and frequent basting.

Beef should not be salted before being put into the oven, but pork skin should be, to help the crackling; lamb, up to you. All meats should be salted (or re-salted as the case may be) towards the end of the cooking process, just after a basting. Pepper them too. Pork skin crackles best if brushed with olive oil.

Various helpful things may be put into the roasting pan as well as the meat itself – bones, a chicken carcass (both of which help the eventual gravy), onion, garlic, a little water. Potatoes are best roasted separately but parsnips cook very well in the roasting juices.

Ducks, geese, belly of pork and anything which is very fat should be roasted on a rack above the baking dish so that they will not have to wallow in their own juices.

An important discovery of recent years is that roast meat benefits by being rested in a place warm enough to keep it hot but cool enough to prevent further cooking, for 10 minutes or more, depending on size, before being carved. This allows the juices which have been driven to the centre by the onslaught of heat from the outside, to seep back, redistribute themselves, and so make the cooking more even, the outside less dry.

Cooking times: 15 minutes per lb for good beef (ends up rare), 20 minutes for good lamb (slightly pink), 25–30 minutes per lb for pork (should always be well cooked). These timings are only a rough guide. Long thin joints obviously cook faster than short fat ones; many people like beef and lamb less undercooked than these timings afford. Certain comparatively cheap cuts such as brisket respond well to long, slow roasting, if they are reasonably fat.

Gravy

Resting the roast creates the ideal moment for making the gravy.

If there is a lot of fat in the roasting pan, most of it should be poured off. Keep a little and as much of the non-fat juices as possible. Use no flour! De-glaze the pan juices with a wine glass of vinegar, cider, beer-and-vinegar or sherry, cooking it over brisk heat so that it bubbles down to a syrupy consistency. Then add a generous allowance of meat cullis with a view to providing at least 2 tablespoons of gravy per person. The alternative is to use twice as much ordinary broth and reduce it by rapid boiling. If neither broth nor strong stock is available, plain water or the water in which vegetables have been cooked may be used instead, possibly in conjunction with a stock or Oxo cube. Salt may be added and a dribble or two of gravy browning will often improve the appearance (without affecting the taste). Rapid boiling should blend liquid and fat content, the result being slightly unctuous but free-flowing and in no way thick. Any bones or carcasses should be removed soon after the stock has been added, if not before. (All this, of course, best done in the original roasting pan.)

If the gravy remains obstinately thin, or if it retains unabsorbed fat, a teaspoon of arrowroot mixed to a thin paste with water, will give a better consistency.

Gravy should be a liquid extension of the meat rather than a sauce which provides a new, however complementary, taste or texture. It can happily accommodate a vegetable element, however, since it must also be a unifying link between the meat and its accompaniments. For this reason a spoonful of vegetable purée (mushrooms, say, or celeriac) is often a good idea.

IMPERIAL SWINE

This heroic dish is suitably inappropriate for the tropical climes of colonial man and altogether comforting in lands where winter can begin in August and last till July.

7oz (200g) pork sausage meat
3oz (80g) pig's liver, chopped
4 prunes (previously soaked in tea)
2oz (50g) bacon, chopped
juice of 1 orange
1 teaspoon crushed coriander
salt and pepper
1 egg
joint of pork boned and prepared for stuffing – about 4lbs (1¾kg)
oil
cider vinegar
2 large cooking apples, peeled and cored
scant 2oz (50g) soft brown sugar
2 slices brown bread
2 tablespoons cider vinegar
cayenne pepper
2½oz (70g) blue Stilton cheese
6 tablespoons port
gravy browning

Preparation time: 15 minutes; cooking time: about 2 hours

Make stuffing from sausage meat, liver, prunes, bacon, orange juice, coriander, salt, pepper and egg. Stuff and tie up the joint (which may be loin, leg, hand or blade and must have the skin well scored). Salt and oil the skin and roast for 30 minutes to the lb in a hot oven. The joint may be basted with its own juices from time to time, and with cider vinegar.

For the sauce, peeled cooking apples, brown sugar and crustless brown bread are simmered in water with a little cider vinegar and plenty of cayenne. When cooked down to a jammy consistency, the sauce is augmented by crumbled Stilton and port wine. 10 minutes' simmering will dissolve the cheese. Darken the sauce tactfully with gravy browning.

Meanwhile the roast pork should be transferred to a warm place to rest, while the roasting juices are added to the sauce. If the sauce is still too thick, add some strong stock.

155

LAMB DRESSED AS MUTTON

good lamb joint, at least 3 lb 4 oz (1½ kg)
scant 1 pt (50 cl) mild beer or brown ale
scant 1 pt (50 cl) sweet stout
5 tablespoons malt vinegar
2 bay leaves, crushed
2 teaspoons juniper berries, crushed
1 clove garlic, chopped
salt and black peppercorns
1 small onion
4 large onions
1 scant teaspoon powdered nutmeg
1 oz (28 g) soft brown sugar
Worcestershire sauce

Marinating time: 2 days; cooking time: about 1½ hours

Marinate the lamb for at least 2 days in beer, stout, vinegar, bay, juniper, garlic, salt, pepper and small onion (chopped). Pierce the meat in several places to encourage penetration of the marinade, and turn it once or twice a day.

Before cooking the meat, dry and salt it. Roast it in the usual way but with 4 large unpeeled onions around it. After 45 minutes remove the onions. Altogether allow the lamb 20 minutes to the lb in a fairly hot oven, then let it rest in a warm place for about 15 minutes.

Peel and chop the onions as soon as they are cool enough to handle, and throw them into a large saucepan with 2 tablespoons of fat from the roasting pan. Add salt and nutmeg; cook over gentle heat for 15 minutes, stirring occasionally, and raising the temperature towards the end just enough to brown them a little.

Pour surplus fat out of the roasting pan, but pour meat juices from it into the onion. Then add the brown sugar and a dash of Worcestershire sauce. Finally add enough of the strained marinade to give you a beautiful, brown, textured gravy. The gravy should be simmered for 10 minutes.

LAMB CRACKLING

While lamb has a much less obvious skin than pork, by the time it reaches the butcher, it does have a skinny membrane which, salted and basted, gives a crisp coating to roast leg, shoulder or saddle. Some like this, others leave it on the side of their plates.

For those who like lamb skin, a refinement is to remove (or have the butcher remove) the skin before cooking the meat, but to tie it back on for the roasting process. When the meat is cooked and ready to be rested, detach the skin and let it continue to roast, preferably on a rack above the pan. Meanwhile beat an egg white till stiff and stir into it some finely chopped mint. 7 minutes before serving, sprinkle the fat surface of the rested meat with mustard powder, then spread it with the egg-white mixture. Return it to the oven and roast for 5 minutes more or until the savoury meringue is set and beginning to change colour.

The skinless meat now has a delicious and appropriate non-fatty outside, and the crackling can be offered to those who like it as an optional bonus.

TOAD IN CRACKLING

1 lb 5 oz (600 g) pork sausage meat
3 tablespoons parsley
1 sage leaf, quartered
3½ oz (100 g) pig's liver, cut small
3½ oz (100 g) gammon, diced small
3½ oz (100 g) button mushrooms, chopped small
salt and pepper
1 large piece of pork skin from loin or belly
olive oil

Preparation time: 20 minutes; cooking time: 1½ hours

This is a cheap but interesting version of forcemeat crackle (page 158). It can be made without the liver, gammon and mushrooms at a pinch. If very pure sausage meat is used, breadcrumbs and an egg may be added.

Mix the forcemeat ingredients together in a bowl. Season them with salt and pepper. Stuff the pork skin with the sausage mixture and secure it with skewers or string. Brush the outside skin with olive oil, salt it. Roast in hot oven as described for forcemeat crackle.

Serve with a sharp sauce and plenty of mustard.

FORCEMEAT CRACKLE

14 oz (400 g) lean pork
14 oz (400 g) fattish pork (belly)
7 oz (200 g) lean gammon
black pepper
allspice
thyme or sage
3 pickled onions
3½ tablespoons medium sherry
saltpetre
1 egg
anchovy essence
large piece of pork skin, ideally from loin, scored to make crackling
oil
salt and pepper
caster sugar (optional)

Preparation time: 20 minutes; cooking time: 1½ hours

Make a forcemeat by mixing together finely chopped lean pork, minced fat pork, minced gammon, black pepper, allspice, thyme or sage, chopped pickled onion, sherry and a pinch of saltpetre if you have it. Bind with an egg and sharpen with anchovy essence – about 1 dessertspoonful.

Now the tricky part. The stuffing must be fitted into the pork skin and secured by skewers or string. When stuffed, the joint must be put on a very hot roasting pan with the joined part downwards so that any forcemeat which exudes quickly forms a crust. After 10 minutes in a hot oven insert a rack between meat and roasting pan. Lower the heat a little and roast for about 1½ hours, basting occasionally with water. The skin should be brushed with oil and salt-and-peppered before cooking, and re-salted at least once after basting. 10 minutes before the end a little caster sugar may be sprinkled over it too.

If served hot, make a gravy while the meat is resting, from the pan juices with excess fat poured off. Hot or cold this is quite a rich dish and calls for an astringent apple sauce such as the one on page 236, or pickles and strong mustard.

Essentially pork pie with crackling instead of pastry.

VEAL AND HAM ROAST

7 oz (200 g) chopped or coarsely minced ham (with some fat)
7 oz (200 g) sausage meat
2 shallots, chopped
juice of 1 small orange
1 egg
pepper
mace
2 lb 3 oz (1 kg) breast of veal or boned shoulder
1 scant pt (50 cl) cider
salt
thyme

Preparation time: 15 minutes; cooking time: 1¼ hours

Make a stuffing from the ham, sausage, shallots, orange juice and egg; season it with pepper and mace. Stuff and tie the veal. Roast in a very hot oven for 15 minutes. Reduce the heat and add dry cider so that it comes just under half-way up the side of the veal. Cook for a further hour in a medium oven. 15 minutes before the end sprinkle the basted surface of veal with salt and powdered thyme. Also add some thyme to the cidery gravy surrounding it.

The gravy does not need to be de-fatted if you have those French (gros et maigre) sauceboats, one of whose spouts draws from the top and one from the bottom.

Mince

'Isn't it lovely – no more mince,' said a friend of a friend on getting engaged to a rich man after an awkward few years as indigent divorcee and thrifty mama. For those less fortunate or less worldly, here are some alternatives to the shepherds' pie and spaghetti Bolognese which are recurring suppers elsewhere.

SCOTCH-POTCH

9 oz (250 g) pot (or pearl) barley
1 pt (56 cl) broth or water
1 lb (450 g) minced beef
2 onions
2½ tablespoons vinegar
carrot, turnip, celery as available
bay leaf
4 oz (112 g) mushrooms
black pepper
nutmeg
salt
Worcestershire sauce
2 oz (56 g) grated Cheddar cheese
cayenne pepper

Cooking time: 2½ hours

Cheap and filling but tempting and quite rich, this has overtones of haggis and of moussaka, but is superior to both, with mince and barley combining to provide a most distinctive texture.

Cook the barley in at least 3 times its own volume of broth or salted water; not a very fast boil but a sprightly simmer – for about 2 hours. Top up with extra liquid if necessary.

As soon as you have started off the barley, turn to the onions and mince. Peel and slice the onions and lay the slices on the bottom of a roasting pan. Spread the mince over the onions and cover it with greaseproof or butter paper. Roast in a hot oven for 15–20 minutes. Remove and drain off the copious fat through a fine sieve. Transfer the de-fatted mince and onion to a sauce or sauté pan, add the vinegar and boil till the latter has virtually evaporated, stirring occasionally. Then add just enough stock to cover the mince, together with any large pieces of carrot, celery or turnip you can spare, plus a bay leaf, and simmer till the mince is unquestionably cooked. Add the mushrooms, whole or halved, after 20 minutes. After some 30 minutes, strain off the cooking liquor and put it to one side.

When the barley is cooked, drain it reasonably dry. Remove bay leaf and any large pieces of root vegetable from the mince, but leave onion and mushroom. In a pie dish, layer the onion/mince mixture and the barley alternately, starting with barley, seasoning each layer with black pepper and nutmeg generously. A little salt may also be added with caution (and my family like a few dashes of Worcestershire sauce). Put a layer of mushrooms roughly in the middle. Finish with a layer of barley and moisten with a little of the cooking liquor. Scatter the top with grated cheese and cayenne. Bake in a hot oven till the cheese is golden-brown and bubbling.

BUDGET BAKED BEEF

1 lb (450 g) minced beef (raw)
3 carrots, grated
1 large onion, grated
3 tablespoons chopped parsley
1 egg
2 rashers lean bacon, diced
salt
pepper
Worcestershire sauce
3 tablespoons cider vinegar
leaf or two of spinach, chopped small
breadcrumbs

Preparation time: 30 minutes; cooking time: 35 minutes

Mix all the ingredients except the crumbs. Form them into a roll and allow them to stand for at least 20 minutes so that they can get to know each other.

About 45 minutes before you need to eat, coat the surface with breadcrumbs, put the roll on a rack and set rack in baking dish. Roast in hot oven for 35 minutes, then rest for 10 minutes.

Boiled or parboiled potatoes may be placed under the meat. So may a Yorkshire pudding mixture.

SHEPHERDS' JACKETS

1 onion, sliced
8 oz (226 g) butcher's mince or leftover meat
4 very large (or 8 medium) potatoes
salt and pepper
butter or margarine
piccalilli pickle

Cooking time: up to 1¾ hours

Another attractive but frugal dish – for mince or leftovers. If using the latter, chop it small or mince it, having removed sinew, fat and gristle.

For butcher's mince, start cooking the onion and mince as outlined in the third paragraph of previous recipe. After draining off the unwanted fat, return it to the oven with a little stock or water and cook for a further 15–20 minutes. Leftover meat should be mixed with onion, which has been precooked in a little dripping.

Start baking the potatoes before cooking the mince, however. Large, floury specimens will need at least 80 minutes in a hot oven if the outside is to become really crisp. I merely wash them first; you may also provide safety valves against (the very occasional) explosion by gashing them with knife or skewer; and some people roll them, wet, in salt before baking. That's up to you.

When cooked, the potatoes should be cut laterally so that two-thirds (or more) form potential containers and one-third (or less) potential lids. Scoop out most of the floury potato and put half of it in a bowl. Mash it up with salt, pepper, butter, meat and

pickle. Add a little more potato, if necessary, from the reserved second half. Heap each container overfull with the mixture and set its lid jauntily atop. Return to the oven for a further 10 minutes. (Eat with plenty of beer.)

A simple but effective dish which can be varied with herbs, horseradish, different chutneys, minced Brussels sprouts, spices, curry paste, and so on. It is very good for game leftovers. Meat jelly can be used instead of butter.

Boiled Meats

Boiled meats have played a vicious role in institutional cookery throughout recorded history. School, workhouse and prison have been run on the principle that boiled meats are part of the disciplinary process, and until recently the army regarded them as the foundation of good order and military training. Yet boiled meats also play a proud part in world cuisine – from pot au feu, bollito and olla podrida in Europe to mizutaki in the east and New England boiled dinner in the west. Modern French chefs have duly applied themselves to the tradition, refining, developing, synthesising: one new recipe – in which beef fillet and veal tenderloin are cooked together at table – derives from Japanese and Mongolian practice; another calls for five different meats, all cut from the foreleg of their respective animals; sometimes the broth is transformed into a blanquette with cream and eggs.

In Britain, boiled meats when not instruments of torture are characteristically uncomplicated: boiled beef and carrots (and/or dumplings), boiled mutton and caper or onion sauce, boiled gammon and pease pudding. Boiled mutton is now little more than a folk memory, and the process is seldom attempted with lamb, which is a shame. Another great shame is the invariable rule of serving boiled meat with ludicrously overboiled root vegetables.

If only we could all have an improved version of the music hall favourite: boiled meat in richly flavoursome broth, the original, waterlogged roots thrown away, and clean, bright, just-cooked vegetables instead . . .

The four boiled-meat dishes which follow all involve a few hours of simple, slow cooking followed by some relatively quick

163

finishing procedures. It is more convenient to carry out the initial stages on the day before the dish is wanted, but not essential. Among other conveniences this enables fat to be removed from the broth much more easily.

Dumplings

Originally dumplings were invented as a palatable way of taking plenty of fat on board in the form of suet, for comfort and protection in a hostile environment. They warmed as they filled as they nourished. Today we live in heated houses, have machines to do the taxing physical work, and may, if we wish, enjoy an infinitely better balanced and more varied diet than in the days when dumplings were so useful. The dumpling is therefore a bit of a dodo, but a dodo to which much of northern Europe, over the centuries, has become rather attached.

Nor is there anything in English ethnic cooking which insists that everything must be strictly utilitarian. The main function of dumplings may have been superseded, but they can still be fun, and they do not have to be very large or filling – see the recipe for little dumplings on page 150.

Great big balls of stodge should be kept in reserve as potential central heating in case of marked escalation in the energy crisis.

Salt – Friend or Foe?

The usual cut of boiling beef is silverside or brisket which has been salted for 7–10 days. Clearly the practice dates back to the time when salt was the main preservative, and most meats had to be brined for the fodderless winter. Salt prevented the meat from going putrid, but in doing so changed its nature. For example, it turned pork into ham or bacon – a very fair exchange, even an improvement. Few people would suggest that because preserving technology has now moved beyond the salt age, we should give up salting pig meat.

Salt worked less magic with other meats. Mutton 'hams' have some small following of nostalgic eccentrics and self-sufficiency nuts; salted lamb is exported from the Antipodes to protein-deficient Japan, but most people prefer chilled or frozen sheep, when fresh is too expensive. Although salt beef is nicer, it is not, like ham, a delicious meat in its own right, bearing comparison with fresh viands. If it were, we should salt the sirloin, as it is we only salt the cheaper cuts, and even this is declining, at least in non-Kosher butchers. Furthermore nutritionists are now telling us that we all eat too much salt anyway and that it's bad for our hearts.

Even those who adore salt beef and insist on eating it whatever the health hazards, have little use for the overwhelmingly salty broth which the boiling provides. It can be used to flavour certain rough soups, thereby saving real salt, and in a dire salt crisis it could presumably be sun-dried (providing there was a convenient heat-wave) in improvised salt pans, so that the original salt was recycled, but it would probably be tainted. By contrast the broth is an equal partner to meat and vegetables in pot au feu or mizutaki – or in the dish which follows – and that is a more practical economy.

165

BRISKET IN BROTH

2lb 3oz (1 kg) unsalted brisket, silverside, or topside – boned and rolled
7oz (200 g) lean gammon or salt pork in one piece
veal or beef bones
2 large onions
4 large carrots
peppercorns
cloves
bay leaf
8 young carrots
8 shallots or small onions, peeled
2 young turnips, peeled and quartered
selection of seasonable, non-root vegetables: peas, beans, broccoli,
  shredded cabbage
little dumplings (optional, see page 150)

Cooking time: 3½–4 hours

Meat and bones should be put into a very large pan with large
unpeeled onions and large carrots. Cover the whole with plenty of
cold water and bring to simmering point with the lid on. The meat
should barely simmer for 3 hours and the surface must be skimmed
carefully several times in the first 20–30 minutes. A teaspoon of
black peppercorns, 2–3 cloves and a bay leaf should be added when
most of the skimming has been done.

After 2½ hours add a fresh contribution of root vegetables:
young carrots, turnips, peeled shallots. Stage one ends when these
vegetables and the meats are cooked. They should be removed, but
the bones and the first, older vegetables left in the pot.

The next stage can begin right away or wait until later, maybe
the next day. Boil the broth fast and reduce by about half. Remove
bones, onions and carrots after that, reduce the heat, and poach
little dumplings in the broth for 12 minutes, if dumplings are
wanted. Finally strain the broth through a fine hair sieve into
another pan. Bring it back to the boil so that a final selection of
young seasonable vegetables can be cooked in it – peas, beans,
broccoli, shredded leek or cabbage. They need very little cooking –
5–10 minutes.

The meat (including the gammon if liked) should meanwhile
have been de-fatted and cut into large slices, moistened with a little
of the broth and heated through. Then it should be surrounded by

the second and third batches of vegetables, the dumplings (if included), and by separately boiled potatoes. Put the rest of the broth in a handsome tureen. Large soup plates are recommended, with spoons as well as knives and forks.

BRISKET IN BLANKET

ingredients as for brisket in broth plus:
½ pt (28 cl) double cream
2½ tablespoons single cream
2 eggs
parsley

Cooking time: about 4 hours

It is undeniable that boiled meats look less appetising than roast or grilled meats. Culinary cosmeticians try to remedy this by carving the vegetables into the shape of olives, but that is a fiddly business which momentarily attracts attention maybe, but has no effect on the palate, and often indicates a chef who pays more attention to appearance than taste.

Smothering the meat in a cream blanket, on the other hand, improves appearance and – potentially – taste. The procedure is the same as for brisket in broth until almost the end. When the third batch of vegetables has been cooked and removed from the broth, the blanket is made by liaising some of the broth with eggs and cream.

The double cream should be added to twice its volume of broth and brought back to the boil, while 2 egg yolks are mixed with 2½ tablespoons single cream. When thoroughly amalgamated, the cream and broth should be allowed to cool for 2 minutes before being merged with the eggs. No further boiling is now allowed and the sauce must be stirred until it thickens over very gentle heat. A generous handful of chopped parsley is stirred in just before the blanket is poured over the carved, boiled meat.

A rich, soothing, avuncular dish.

Mutton

As a small farmer's husband, I am married to an occasional source of mutton. While I work the muttons munch on the meadow within typewriter view, but sometimes, dissatisfied with a balanced diet of grass and charlock, nettle and thistle, they come through into the kitchen garden for a supplement of peas, cabbage or baby broccoli. No doubt this greatly improves the eventual taste; the more immediate benefit, however, is to local greengrocers and nurserypeople.

Other pens have lamented the substitution of elderly lamb for real mutton. I agree that sheep meat is best eaten at 3–4 months – or 3–4 years, yet I feel that it remains perfectly palatable between these optimum ages. 'Lamb'tton' may in practice be used successfully for most proper lamb or mutton recipes.

There is another option. Mutton can still be procured. Harrods do not stock it, nor do the multiples – but Asian butchers usually do. Cheaper and tastier than most lamb, it's a good buy – and, who knows, the ritual prayers of Halal butchers may prove useful insurance in the world to come . . .

IRISH STEW RENEWED

At its best Irish stew is a wonderful winter dish – particularly for those who affect the yeoman life-style. Watery, overcooked vegetables, however, are the normal by-product, while the stew liquor is often thin and grey, and the fattiness of scrag or breast not sufficiently countered. This recipe intensifies the best elements of the dish and corrects the hazards. It can be made in a few hours, but the first part of the process is best undertaken 24 hours before the stew is eaten.

2lb 3oz (1 kg) breast of mutton or lamb (scrag or neck) suitably prepared
   by the butcher
2 large onions
3 large carrots
1 turnip
⅓ pt (20 cl) Guinness
2–3 tablespoons pearl or pot barley
1lb 6oz (600 g) potatoes
salt and pepper
8 shallots
8 little carrots

Cooking time: about 3½ hours

Put meat, large onions, large carrots and turnip into saucepan and cover with cold water. Bring to the boil and remove scum. Simmer for 1½ hours, skimming from time to time. Then remove all the meat, but leave vegetables in the pan. Add the Guinness and boil fast till the liquor is reduced by at least one-third. At this stage the barley should be par-cooked for about 45 minutes, either in a steamer above the fast-boiling lamb broth, or in water of its own.

Strain the reduced broth and discard the vegetables. If possible, allow it to cool and then de-fat it. Trim the meat free of unwanted fat, but leave it on the bone. Here ends the first part of the process.

Finally, put a good layer of peeled, thickly sliced potatoes into a casserole. Put the meat on top of this and scatter it with par-cooked barley. Season with salt and pepper. Add small peeled shallots and carrots, cover with another layer of sliced potatoes and add enough reduced stock barely to cover the potatoes. Cook (covered) in a medium oven until the potatoes are well done and a good portion of the stock absorbed – about 1¼ hours. Remove lid for last 20 minutes – earlier if you decide the stew is too liquid.

BOILED MUTTON WITH CAPER SAUCE

1 leg of mutton or lamb weighing at least 4½lbs (2kg)
mutton or lamb bones
2 large onions
4 large carrots
peppercorns
bay leaf
16 small, young carrots
16 shallots, peeled
4 young turnips, peeled and quartered
10oz (280g) shelled or mangetout peas
1 medium onion, chopped
mutton fat (or butter) for frying
5 tablespoons port
scant ½pt (25cl) cream
2 egg yolks
2oz (56g) capers
chopped parsley

Cooking time: about 3 hours

This will feed eight.

The process is similar to brisket in broth (page 166). Put the leg into a very large pan together with lamb or mutton bones, large old onions, large old carrots, peppercorns and bay leaf; cover them all with plenty of cold water; slowly bring to the boil – and simmer, but only just, with the lid on, for 2–3 hours depending on weight. Frequent skimming is necessary at the beginning. (Lamb takes less time to cook than mutton and if required slightly pink needs only about 15 minutes per lb.)

Legs of lamb or mutton shrink however gently they are boiled, but they only toughen if they are cooked too fast.

Apart from the peas, the second batch of vegetables – those to be eaten as such – is added half an hour before full cooking time. When cooked, meat and second batch of vegetables are removed, while remaining broth, bones and original vegetables are boiled hard for a substantial reduction. The peas are best cooked during this reduction (in a muslin bag for about 8 minutes), and added to the other young vegetables. If tinned or frozen peas are used, they will require little more than a quick splash in the boiling broth.

Some of the reduced broth is needed for caper sauce, the rest can be kept for soup or Irish stew. In either case it must be de-fatted, preferably when cold. For the sauce, fry onion in mutton fat for 7 minutes without browning it. De-glaze with port; add ½pt (28cl) of broth and boil fast for 3 minutes; then add most of the cream and boil again for 1–2 minutes. Remove sauce from heat and beat the egg yolks with remaining cream. Then incorporate eggs into the sauce: no further boiling or simmering but place over gentle heat till the sauce thickens; then add the capers and chopped parsley. Pour the sauce over the thickly carved meat – and serve.

Boiled Gammon – and Problems

As with salt beef, the boiling of gammon, ham and bacon joints produces brine rather than broth. The brine can be used for certain soups but should be used with caution in sauces, if at all.

Conventional pease pudding is a 2–3-hour process. Though still revered in certain quarters, it belongs to the same generation as suet crust – the loyal retainer now deserving of well-earned retirement.

As to sauce for boiled gammon, parsleyed béchamel – old friend and club bore – is the usual choice, anchoring the dish in stolid worth and mediocrity. There is also Cumberland sauce, and its portly relatives – ambitious and creative, though better surely with cold than with hot ham?

The recipe for hot gammon which follows turns the prosaic into the lyrical without calling for undue bother or skill.

GAMMON AND SPINACH WITH PORTER SAUCE

2lb 3oz (1kg) middle gammon
10oz (300g) small red lentils
1 large onion
bacon or ham fat
8oz (226g) spinach leaves (no stalk)
3 eggs
scant 2oz (50g) black treacle
scant 2oz (50g) butter
4 pickled walnuts
black pepper
bay leaf
2 teaspoons bitter marmalade
⅓pt (20cl) milk stout
mustard powder
soft brown sugar

Cooking time: 1½ hours

A good piece of middle gammon is best, but hock or collar will do very well. The gammon should be de-salted in one or two changes of cold water for a couple of hours, and brought slowly to simmering point in fresh water. At a very gentle simmer, 2lbs will take about 1¼ hours.

After 45 minutes, remove some of the salty liquor and use it, with an equal quantity of unsalted water, to cook the red lentils. They will be soft, almost mushy, after 20 minutes of brisk boiling and will have absorbed most of the cooking liquor. Any excess should be drained off. Top up the gammon water meanwhile, if necessary.

When the lentils are nearly cooked, a large, finely chopped onion should be melted in bacon or ham fat for about 7 minutes. At the same time, cut the raw spinach into thin strips and stir them into a beaten mixture of 2 egg yolks and 1 whole egg. Beat the 2 egg whites stiff with a whisk.

Put the lentils into a buttered soufflé dish with the fried onions and bacon fat, followed by the eggs and spinach mixture and some black pepper. After a good stir, add the beaten egg whites, and bake the whole thing in the oven for 20 minutes. You are not attempting a soufflé, but the egg white will lighten the lentils and make them fluffy.

172

For the sauce, melt treacle and butter over lowish heat, add chopped pickled walnuts and black pepper, a bay leaf and marmalade. When this is well mixed and just beginning to seethe, add milk stout. Let the sauce work for most of the time the lentils are in the oven, and salt it to taste with gammon water.

The gammon, having been skinned, should be glazed in the oven (also while the lentils are there). To glaze: rub the outside, particularly the fat, with mustard powder, brown sugar and a little of the porter sauce.

PORTER SAUCE (alternative recipe)

1 onion, chopped
½oz (14g) butter
2 tablespoons vinegar
1 tablespoon sweet chutney
1 tablespoon black treacle
⅓pt (20cl) sweet stout (or sweet, dark beer)
bay leaf
1 tablespoon marmalade
black pepper
tabasco

Cooking time: 30 minutes

Fry the onion in butter till golden. Add vinegar and de-glaze. Stir in chutney and treacle and when these are amalgamated with the onion, add the stout, bay leaf, marmalade, pepper and tabasco. Simmer for 20 minutes.

Casseroles – Two Observations

Stews and casseroles are soups posing as main dishes. While not playing a star role in new English cooking, they remain a practical way of cooking the cheaper cuts of meat and the older sort of bird. How can they be improved?

Most recipes begin by telling you to 'brown the meat on all sides'. In a frying pan this is impossible if the meat is at all bony or irregular in shape and jolly difficult even if it is geometrically cubed. Fat-injection rather than meat-sealing is the usual result. The only effective way of browning on all sides is by deep-frying. My advice is don't fry at all. Frying may partially seal the meat but also impregnates it with unwanted oil or fat – doubly so if the meat, as usually suggested, is first floured. Secondly, in so far as the sealing is effective, it inhibits the subsequent cooking-by-exchange which is the whole essence of your stew or casserole. After all, what you are trying to do is suffuse the meat with vegetable, herb, stock and maybe alcoholic flavours and at the same time enhance the cooking liquor by extracting flavour from the meat.

So why fry at all (unless merely to darken the colour)? It is just not true that pre-frying will make tough meat more tender or that failure to pre-fry will make tender meat tough. If you gently raise all the casserole ingredients from cold together, the only disadvantage as compared with the fry-first method is that rather more scum will rise to the top. Conscientious skimming is recommended during the first quarter of an hour after the stew has reached sub-simmering point. Long slow cooking follows.

The other way of improving casseroles is to finish them sensibly. By the time the meat is cooked, the original vegetables will probably be overcooked. The best plan is to remove the meat to a dish, discard the now sodden vegetables and herbs, de-fat, as necessary, meat and broth, and reduce the broth by fast boiling till there is barely enough to cover the meat. Introduction of a fresh batch of carrot and onion at this stage is a further improvement, as is thickening the broth with arrowroot and water (see page 27).

These suggestions add at least 30 minutes to the overall cooking time. If possible, casseroles should be begun 12 hours or more in advance. They improve with keeping and are more easily de-fatted if allowed to get cold.

N.B. Very fat meats, such as breast of lamb, should be roasted in a hot oven for 15–25 minutes. The fat is poured off before the casseroling begins.

Devilling

We seem to have cast the devil more effectively from our kitchens than, say, our bedrooms. It is possible that welcoming him back to the former would help expel him from the latter, since good dinners make for good marriages.

Devilling, the Hell Fire Club's answer to curry, may have gone out of fashion because Indian and Anglo-Indian food have come in; and also because, in its later years, it was usually given the menial and thankless task of resuscitating meats well past their prime, the scruffy leftovers from much exploited joints. It survives in various guises – Worcestershire sauce is a proprietary devil, for example, and steak au poivre has plenty of the diable about it; best of all is the piri piri cooking of South Africa (out of Mozambique out of Portugal).

What is devilling? How is it distinguished from curry and curry-related cooking processes? Devilling involves the use of mustard, red pepper and melted butter. It may also be supported by anchovy, vinegar, black pepper, chutney and cream. Curries, on the other hand, use several tropical spices fused so as to form a more or less homogeneous brown, spicy taste. Turmeric, cumin, coriander, ginger, fenugreek, cardamom, cinnamon, nutmeg, cloves, for example, are all constituents of curries but have no place in devils.

The result is that curries have more variety than devils (if not quite as much variety as some of their apologists claim) and, at their best, more subtlety and refinement, but the number of spices used makes for tastes and aromas which are exceedingly complex (even when they are also crudely hot). Devils, on the other hand, produce clean and simple tastes, however hot and mustardy.

The difference is worth labouring here since it follows that the devil-eater can fully appreciate good wine, whereas the curry-eater cannot. The curry-eater has too much on his palate (and in his nostrils) to cope with another equally complex, taste experience. It is possible to read Proust while listening to Ravi Shankar but

175

impossible to give both the attention they deserve at the same time – nor can good wine and curry be appreciated simultaneously. It is no coincidence that devils were invented by – and for – a claret-besotted (sic) age.

DEVIL PEPPER

cayenne pepper or dried chillies
freshly ground black pepper
salt

Grind equal weights of these 3 ingredients together in a mortar. Transfer to an airtight jar. If you like devils, make fairly large batches of this pepper so that you always have some handy, e.g. 6 oz (160 g) at a time.

DEVIL BUTTER

8 oz (226 g) butter
6 anchovy fillets
1–2 cloves garlic
2 tablespoons made English mustard
6 dashes of tabasco

Soften but do not melt the butter. Chop the anchovies and the garlic. Work the 3 together with fork or pestle; then work in the mustard and tabasco. Refrigerate before use.

These mixtures provide the basic form of devilling. Apply the devil pepper quite generously to both sides of the meat and rub it in. Leave for at least 15 minutes. Before cooking, brush the meat with melted fat, dripping or butter and then lightly re-devil-butter it. Then grill or fry the meat.

When cooked, serve the meat with a good pat of devil butter.

This treatment is suitable for steaks, chops and chicken joints – anything, indeed, which can be fried or grilled successfully. It is very effective providing you throw caution to the wind.

The reliability, excellence and simplicity of the basic devil should not deter anyone from trying some of the variations which follow.

DEVILLED KIDNEYS

The breakfast favourite of Edwardians with hangovers, devilled kidneys also make an excellent main course or savoury at the more sober and sombre end of the century.

¼pt (14cl) double cream
1 dessertspoon dry English mustard powder
Worcestershire sauce or tabasco
1¼lbs (570g) veal kidney
salt and black pepper
butter and oil for frying
4 shallots, chopped
1 dried chilli (more, if you can take more)
5 tablespoons chilli vinegar (or cider vinegar pepped up with tabasco)
5 tablespoons port or Madeira
8 rashers streaky bacon
4 slices white crustless bread (quite thick)

Preparation time: 15 minutes; cooking time: 20 minutes

Use half the cream, the dry mustard and Worcestershire sauce or tabasco to make mustard-cream (page 232).

Cut the kidneys into roundels, de-coring as necessary. Season well with salt and black pepper, then sear on both sides in very hot oil and butter – about 3 minutes in all. Lift them from pan and keep warm in a dish. Warning: do not attempt to fry all the kidneys at once – or the fat temperature will fall and the kidneys will first exude a juice and then stew in it. Fry a few at a time, quite fiercely.

In the same butter and oil now fry the chopped shallots and the dried chilli. When the shallots are beginning to change colour, add the chilli vinegar and let it all but evaporate, then add the port and let it all but evaporate too. The remaining cream should be added next and bubbled for 1–2 minutes. Then reduce the heat and stir in the kidneys together with their juices. If the sauce now boils, the kidneys may get rubbery. Heat them through for 2 minutes, then stir in the mustard-cream and serve.

The best accompaniments are grilled streaky bacon and fried bread. If served as a savoury, 2 or 3 symbolic triangular-shaped croûtons are more appropriate than fried bread as such.

177

DEVILLED LAMB CHOPS

English mustard made with 3 parts water, 1 part Worcestershire sauce
8 lamb chops
black pepper
salt
2 shallots
¼ pt (14 cl) cider vinegar
2–3 dried chillies
1 teaspoon soft brown sugar
2 large tablespoons redcurrant jelly (or similar)

Preparation time: 30 minutes; cooking time: 20 minutes

Spread mustard on chops and sprinkle liberally with black pepper and a little salt. Leave to soak in the flavours for at least 30 minutes.

Chop the shallots finely and boil them in the cider vinegar with the chillies, coarsely crushed, and sugar. When this has reduced to a syrupy consistency, add the redcurrant jelly. Let the jelly dissolve and hold it at a sub-simmer for 15 minutes or so.

Grill or fry the chops and serve with the strained chilli and redcurrant sauce.

DEVILLED STEAKS

4 steaks (for grilling or frying)
black peppercorns
English mustard made rather thick
tin of anchovies
cider vinegar
beef dripping or oil
1 onion
sweet chutney (green tomato if possible)
tabasco
½ pt (28 cl) meat cullis

Preparation time: 35 minutes; cooking time: 25 minutes

Black-pepper the steaks. Dilute the mustard with oil from the tin of anchovies and a teaspoonful or so of vinegar. Add 2 anchovy fillets chopped very small. Spread each steak with this mixture and leave them for at least 30 minutes.

Fry the onion, chopped very small, in dripping or oil. Add 1 tea-spoonful (or more) of crushed black peppercorns per person. After 5–6 minutes de-glaze with 2 tablespoonsful of cider vinegar, then add

178

1 scant tablespoonful of chutney for every 2 people, with any large lumps cut small, and a few dashes of tabasco. Stir, bubble and amalgamate this basis of the sauce before adding the meat cullis (strong stock) and bringing it all to a brief simmer.

Meanwhile grill or fry the steaks in beef dripping for as long as they need according to their size and the underdone/overdone preferences of those eating (see page 144 for some general guidance). When cooked, transfer them to a warm serving dish.

Pour the sauce over the steaks and serve with roast potatoes or fried bread. If fried bread is chosen, let each steak be placed on a slice in the serving dish, so that the bread absorbs the steak juices. Mushrooms and tomatoes are suitable accompaniments to devilled steak. Watercress provides further bite which is not strictly necessary but will be enjoyed by a good many people.

DEVILLED STEAKS, ANOTHER WAY

4 hardboiled egg yolks
an equal amount of softened butter
1 oz (28 g or a little more) grated horseradish
salt
devil pepper (page 176)
vinegar
dripping
4 steaks
¼ pt (14 cl) single cream

Preparation time: 65 minutes; cooking time: 15 minutes

Mix the egg yolks, butter and horseradish. Add a little salt. Divide into 4 portions and refrigerate.

Mix 1 tablespoonful of devil pepper with just over 1 tablespoonful of vinegar. Brush the steaks with this mixture on both sides. Leave them for 1 hour.

Before cooking, brush the steaks with melted dripping and give them a further thin coating of devil pepper. Then fry the steaks in a little more, very hot dripping. Timing will depend on thickness, quality and rarity required. When cooked, keep the steaks hot. De-glaze pan with vinegar, adding a teaspoonful of devil pepper. Then add the cream, bring to the boil, and pour over the steaks. The cream now mixes with the juices which have seeped from the meat, and a pat of the horseradish mixture is put on each steak.

179

DEVILLED PORK CHOPS

4 pork chops
½pt (28 cl) British medium sherry
4 dried chillies
1 clove garlic
cayenne pepper
1 oz (28 g) lard
2 shallots
⅓pt (20 cl) single cream
salt
parsley or watercress (optional)

Preparation and marinating time: at least 6 hours; cooking time: 20–5 minutes

Put the chops in a polythene bag or other container which fits them closely and cover them with the sherry. Add chopped chillies and a halved clove of garlic. Marinate for 6–12 hours. Then remove the chops, dry them and sprinkle with cayenne. Discard the garlic. Pour remainder of marinade into saucepan.

Grill or fry the chops using lard or lard and butter mixed. If you grill, baste the chops with the fat to prevent drying out. Don't cook too fast. After about 12–14 minutes the chops should be virtually cooked. Remove them to a low oven which will allow a little further cooking.

Meanwhile reduce the marinade and the chillies by at least 50 per cent by fast boiling.

Fry the chopped shallots in the fat left over from the chops for 5 minutes. Strain in the reduced sherry and bubble it down to a glaze. Add the cream and boil it briefly. Season with a little salt and some chopped parsley or watercress. Pour the sauce over the chops.

PANDEMONIUM

'Pandemonium' today conveys little more than the amiable confusion of situation comedies – a mild chaos far removed from the city and proud seat of Lucifer, high capital of Hell. Milton lost. This new dish goes a little way towards pandemonium regained. It is a very hot hotpot, fiery enough for the common run of demons.

2lb 3oz (1kg) belly of pork
½oz (14g) lard
8oz (226g) lean gammon, cubed
2 onions, sliced
2 teaspoons cayenne pepper
1 teaspoon black pepper, coarsely ground
3 tablespoons cider vinegar
2 dried chillies
2 tablespoons grated horseradish
1 clove garlic
1–1½pts (56–84cl) dry cider
8oz (226g) pig's kidney
8oz (226g) pig's liver
3 tablespoons medium sherry
1 teaspoon Worcestershire sauce

Preparation time: 10 minutes; cooking time: 70 minutes

Remove the skin in one piece from the pork and separate the ribs (or ask the butcher to do it for you). Discarding excess fat, sear the ribs in a very hot pan, using a very little lard. Toss the gammon in the pan too. Transfer all to a large casserole. Fry onions in the fat produced by first frying (add a little lard if need be) with 2 teaspoonsful of cayenne and 1 of ground black pepper. After 6 minutes de-glaze with vinegar and transfer to casserole, together with 2 dried chillies, 1 tablespoonful of horseradish and 1 clove of garlic. Add dry cider barely to cover and braise in a hot oven for 45 minutes, without a lid.

At the same time roast the pork skin, scored, oiled and salted, on a wire grid above a roasting pan – to make a crackling lid for the hotpot.

After some 30 minutes, cut the kidney and liver into very small pieces. Fry these in fat from under the crackling (or bacon fat) for 3 minutes, shaking the pan vigorously. De-glaze with sherry and Worcestershire sauce.

Add the liver and kidney (still very underdone) to the braise in

181

the casserole. Put the crackling on top of the braise – the liquor of which is now greatly reduced – and continue to bake for a further 10 minutes but reducing the oven temperature to medium. Just before serving, stir in the second tablespoonful of grated horseradish.

Red cabbage and plain boiled potatoes go well with pandemonium.

VEAL SAGACITY

8 oz (226 g) gammon, diced
1½ oz (42 g) butter
6 sage leaves
4 veal cutlets
8 shallots or small onions, peeled
⅓ pt (20 cl) dry cider
house broth, preferably chicken (page 24)
made English mustard diluted by lemon juice

Cooking time: 1¼ hours

Gently fry the gammon in one-third of the (seasoned) butter, adding 2 of the sage leaves, shredded. After 3 minutes remove the gammon to plate and seal the cutlets in the same butter on both sides, without browning. Remove them to braising pan and put 1 sage leaf under each. Add the gammon. Toss the shallots in same butter and de-glaze with half the cider. Reduce the cider to a thin syrup and add contents of frying pan to the cutlets. Add remaining cider and enough chicken broth just to cover the meat. Put lid on braising dish and cook in a low to medium oven for an hour.

To serve: put cutlets on to plates or platter, sprinkle with gammon and allow 2 shallots per person. Keep hot. Reduce the sauce by rapid boiling till you have a generous serving for each person. Then finish the sauce with a butter-and-mustard mixture from the refrigerator, made as follows.

Mash together 1 oz (28 g) soft butter and 3 teaspoons of English mustard which after being made (rather stiff) with water and left for 20 minutes, has been diluted with lemon juice (to be rather runny). Refrigerate the mixture.

This procedure also works very well with pork chops, provided most of the fat is removed.

On Game in General

Blessed with game – and gamekeepers – cold-climate countries have been perverse in culinary exploitation of their wild resources. On the one hand they have decided to hang most of their game. Opinions vary as to the boundary between the well-hung state and the putrescent, but there is little doubt that hanging reduces dryness (the biggest single problem in game cookery) while deepening the taste and gastronomic individuality of the creature concerned. On the other hand, our cooking of game is unimaginative: if it's young, we roast it; if not we put it in a casserole and hope for the best. The only dish which has any pretensions beyond good, plain cooking is jugged hare; game pies can be satisfying in an obvious sort of way, but often aren't.

Unfair? Unfair especially to the sporting wives who do most of the plucking, gutting and skinning while their menfolk blaze away? No doubt individual cooks are creative or innovatory (though Julia Drysdale's resourceful and disarming *Game Cookery Book* shows that grouse widows, in general, are repetitious or plagiaristic in the kitchen), but surely it must stand as an indictment of British game cooking that the official way of dealing with blackcock, grouse, partridge, pheasant, pigeon, snipe and woodcock (to say nothing of ptarmigan, plover,* ortolan* and teal) is essentially the same, viz. roast it on a piece of toasted bread, serve it with toasted bread-crumbs, and – daring breakthrough – accompany it with bread sauce . . . The roasting, of course, further dries out the already dry flesh, and the juices which are meant to be collected by the toast evaporate en route to plate.

Some of the other traditional accompaniments – the use of fruit jellies or port wine, for instance – are laudably delicious.

The central difficulty in devising game recipes is that a sequence of operations which works with one bird won't work with another, seemingly similar, bird. As Mrs Drysdale points out, two hen pheasants from the same rearing pen cleanly shot on the same day will often cook differently. Today's subsidies and farm practice tend to standardisation in domestic animals, but game remains wild, even in the most over-organised shoots, and each example fulfils its own genes without sparing a thought for the cook; quite

* Now protected from both guns and cooks.

right too. That said, young birds usually do roast satisfactorily provided their natural dryness and lack of fat is allowed for in trussing and cooking/basting.

Sauces and Gravies for Roast Game

Gravy, as noted already, should be a liquid extension of the roast. The dryness of game, however, means that normal roasting yields precious little in the way of gustful juices, and none at all if the bird is perched conventionally on a piece of toast or fried bread. A partial answer is no toast but frequent, almost excessive, basting – if possible with both a fatty element (good lard or dripping, clarified butter) and a liquid element (broth, cider, British sherry diluted with water, red wine). For venison, Julia Drysdale recommends gin and water because of the juniper flavouring.

Another answer is a plentiful supply of game broth or game cullis – ideally made from the same species as the one which is sizzling away in the oven, e.g. use casseroled grouse as the base for a strong stock which, with port wine or rowan jelly, becomes a gravy for roast grouse. However, this is impractical and far too expensive for most households. A compromise is to 'gamify' ordinary stock by working it into game and chicken livers, sautéed and mashed.

Tinned game soup usually tastes like – tinned game soup, but discreetly mixed with stock and cheap sherry, it makes a passable sauce or gravy when one is in a hurry.

The alternative is to forget about gravy and go for an independent sauce – but in this case the conventional piece of toast under the bird to catch any inherent juices is quite a good idea. The following sauces are recommended: marmalade sauce (page 230), Crabbie sauce (page 233), no-bread sauce (page 231) and sauce X (page 229).

Game Suprême

People who live far from shoots and for whom pheasants are very occasional treats, will continue to roast them, but there is a way of making even more of your game . . .

First, with a filleting knife remove and skin the breasts; the thighs too if they are tender and meaty. Break up or chop the rest of the bird and, with the skin and some unpeeled onion, roast it in a hot oven for 20–30 minutes. Lubricate this process with some fat bacon. When the carcass has turned nicely brown, throw in a glass of dry cider, wine or vinegar, and let it bubble down to a gooey

glaze. Then fill up with water or broth till the bird is completely submerged. Simmer it with the lid on for 2 hours; then reduce it with the lid off by rapid boiling until you have a rich, concentrated game cullis, the very essence of the bird. Strain this through a conical sieve, pressing every last drop out of drumsticks, carcass and meat fragments.

The breasts are cooked separately, for example in butter or bacon fat, and the cullis is used to make a sauce.

This procedure is very flexible and although superficially it may seem wasteful to eat only the breasts, in fact it is thrifty since you get much more out of the bird than if you roast and carve it conventionally. In effect, you eat everything. Moreover it is very simple, although the cullis production takes a long time. The method was devised for birds, but can be adapted to saddles of rabbit or hare, and, I suppose, venison.

A few of the possible variations are indicated in the succeeding pages, but the important thing is to understand the grammar of game suprême.

185

PHEASANT AND BLACKBERRIES SUPRÊME

2 hen pheasants
1 large onion
⅓pt (20cl) cider vinegar
4oz (112g) blackberries
1oz (28g) white sugar
½oz (14g) butter
¼pt (14cl) double cream

Preparation and cooking time: 3 hours

Remove pheasant breasts. Break up legs and carcasses; roast them for 20 minutes in a hot oven, adding a quartered but unpeeled onion. De-glaze with a wineglassful of cider vinegar, then add water to cover the bird and simmer for 2 hours with the lid on. Later remove the lid and reduce by rapid boiling. During this reduction you might like to break up the carcass further with a potato masher.

Meanwhile simmer blackberries (but keep 6–8 aside) in the remaining vinegar and an equal quantity of water plus a little sugar. Reduce them to a jammy consistency. If you have any, you may also add a nip of cassis or its blackberry equivalent, crème de mûres (Murelle).

Cook the pheasant breasts very gently in butter, covering the pan or cocotte. Turn them over at least once – and don't let them go brown or even golden.

When it is greatly reduced, add the pheasant broth to the blackberries and strain the resulting sauce through a hair sieve. Return sauce to pan and add cream. When the cream is simmering, add buttery juices from the cocotte. Carve the pheasant breasts thinly into about 4 slices each. Put the pheasant on a hot platter and surround it by sauce. Decorate with 6 or 8 blackberries which have been blanched (if that is the word) in boiling water for 2 minutes.

PIGEON AND PARSNIP SUPRÊME

4 pigeons
2 onions
4 rashers fat bacon
¼pt (14cl) sweet beer plus 1 tablespoon vinegar
9oz (250g) parsnips
bacon fat or lard

Preparation and cooking time: about 2¼ hours

Remove breasts from pigeons. Hack up carcasses and roast with the onions and bacon for 15 minutes. De-glaze with the beer and when latter has stopped sizzling, submerge the carcasses in water. Simmer for 1½ hours with lid on.

Wash, peel and quarter the parsnips. Simmer them in water till soft. Add peel to the simmering pigeon broth. When the parsnips are soft (about 25 minutes) whizz them to a purée with a ladleful of pigeon broth.

Remove lid from pigeon broth and reduce it by fast boiling to a concentrated pigeon cullis. Strain it into another saucepan.

Fry pigeon breasts in lard or bacon fat, quickly searing them on each side. Remove them to kitchen paper and dab off the fat. Poach them in the (de-fatted) cullis for about 7 minutes, then remove to a warm platter and slice them in half laterally. They should be pink in the middle. If they aren't, continue poaching for 2–3 minutes. Finally add cullis to parsnip purée and use as sauce.

GAME WITH MUSHROOMS

The game suprême technique works very well with mushrooms as the principal aide. A fungous element should be included with the carcass for the broth-making stage – dried fungi are excellent for this – and a mushroom purée (page 32) should be made separately, with fresh mushrooms. After being blended, the purée should be fortified by port or brown sherry and simmered. While the suprêmes are cooking, concentrated game broth is added to saucify the purée.

Cultivated white mushrooms are suitable for pheasant or partridge; real field mushrooms are preferable for darker-fleshed game, such as wild duck.

187

GAME WITH APPLES AND CIDER

Apples and game share the same season and, frequently, the same pot. By extension cider has become a beguilingly game-compatible cooking medium. There are many recipes and variations, but, again, the game suprême procedure makes the most of all ingredients.

After roasting the (de-breasted) carcass, de-glaze with cider vinegar; then cover the bird with water and cider half-and-half. Simmer and reduce in the usual way.

Using peeled but not cored apples, make a sharp purée by melting the fruit in a little butter, sugar and cider, with a generous sharpening of lemon juice. When the apples are quite soft blend them, pips and all, in a blender.

Reduce the game cullis as much as you dare; add it to the apple purée, and finish the sauce with cream. After being cooked in butter (and perhaps a little cullis), the suprêmes themselves may be flared in whisky or gin (in France it would be Calvados, of course). Finally their cooking juices too should be added to the sauce.

SMOTHERED GAME

This is a most satisfying way of flattering old birds and recalcitrant rabbits. You need plenty of onions and a pot or casserole which fits the game to be smothered without too much space to spare.

Put a generous layer of sliced onions in the bottom of the (buttered) pot. Place the game on the onions, whole or cut in large pieces. Surround it with more onion slices plus a few pieces of carrot, celery, apple, turnip, fungus, and so on, if you have some handy (but let onion predominate), so that game is quite tightly embedded in vegetables. Season with salt and pepper; moisten with a glass of broth or cider; surmount with a knob of butter and some rashers of fat bacon. Bake in a low oven for up to 3 hours.

To serve: discard the bacon. Whizz vegetables and cooking juices to a purée. Enrich purée with cream and more butter (if you like) and re-heat.

BAY-BRAISED VENISON

8 bay leaves
4 teaspoons black peppercorns, crushed
dripping, mutton fat, or oil (for frying, marinading)
lovage
4 large venison cutlets or steaks
2 large onions, chopped
5 tablespoons vinegar
½pt (28cl) old ale (or brown ale or sweet stout)
½pt (28cl) meat or game cullis
black treacle
8 rashers streaky bacon
4 tangerines (or small tin mandarin oranges)

Preparation and cooking time: up to 4 hours

Crush bay leaves and peppercorns and mix them with melted
dripping or mutton fat, or warm oil. Add lovage – frozen or dried
assuming it's autumn or winter. Paint this marinade as thickly as
possible on both sides of the meat, and leave to steep for 2 hours. If
using animal fat, a second or third coating may be added.

In a large pan, fry onions gently, using same spiced fat as for
marinade. When the onions are translucent, push them to perimeter
of pan, raise the temperature, and fry the venison briefly but quite
fiercely on both sides. De-glaze pan with vinegar. Add equal quantities of old ale and meat cullis plus a tablespoonful of treacle
(and more lovage if available). The liquid should come about
three-quarters up the sides of the meat but not over the top. Cover
the venison with fat bacon and surround it with pigs of tangerine.
Raise to simmering point and transfer to low oven. Braise for 1
hour with lid on, then remove lid. Cook for a further 30 minutes,
or until the meat is tender (test with skewer).

When the meat is cooked, remove it to a hot dish. Boil the
remaining juices fast for 5 minutes. Taste for salt. Strain juices
through a fine sieve, rubbing some of the pulp through with a
wooden spoon. Re-boil in smaller pan. The sauce should need no
further thickening, but use arrowroot if it does. Pour a little of the
sauce over the venison and serve the rest separately. Everything
should be as hot as possible, including the plates.

RICH RABBIT PIE

I once asked the chief restaurant inspector of Michelin if English food such as rabbit pie could ever hope to earn three stars in his respected guide. 'Certainement pas.' This version consequently emerged.

2 young rabbits
oil
thyme
8 rashers fat bacon
2 large onions
¼ pt (14 cl) cider vinegar
½ pt (28 cl) rough, dry cider
1 pt (56 cl) chicken broth or water
2 large carrots
8 little dumplings (page 150)
8 shallots
2 oz (56 g) button mushrooms
butter
1 apple, peeled and diced
5 tablespoons double cream
salt and pepper
1 tablespoon made English mustard
shortcrust pastry

Preparation and cooking time: up to 3 hours

Joint the rabbits and remove fillets whole from the saddles. Halve the fillets lengthways; cut hind legs in half and put upper half with the fillets in a dish with a little oil and thyme. Turn them over in the oil once or twice while preparing the rabbit cullis.

Break up the rib cages. Put them with the rest of the rabbit, including heart and kidneys but not liver, in a large pan. Cover with bacon and roast in a hot oven. After 10 minutes add the onions, quartered but not peeled. After a further 10 minutes add the cider vinegar and let it bubble down till it has nearly evaporated. Transfer pan to top of stove and add the cider. Bring it to the boil. Add the broth or water, carrots and more thyme. Bring it up to a gentle simmer – with lid on. After 45 minutes remove lid and turn up heat a little. Skim as necessary.

Meanwhile prepare (but do not cook) little dumplings, but also include very finely chopped rabbit liver in them.

190

After a further 30–45 minutes cooking, strain the rabbit broth into a smaller pan. Return it to a simmer. Poach the shallots and mushrooms in it for 5 minutes. Remove them to a pie dish. Poach the dumplings in same liquor for 5 minutes. Remove to pie dish. De-fat the rabbit liquor (off the heat, with tablespoon, not worrying too much if you take a little of the juice too). Then reduce the remaining broth by rapid boiling.

Fry rabbit fillets and upper legs in butter gently for 2 minutes on each side. Remove to pie dish. Fry apple in same pan for 2 minutes. Remove to pie dish. Add cream to boiling cullis. Taste for seasoning, especially for pepper.

Spread made English mustard on the rabbit in pie dish. Pour in the creamy cullis. Cover with shortcrust or puff pastry (decorating it appropriately) and bake in a moderate oven for 30 minutes.

Shortcrust Pastry

4 oz (112 g) butter, margarine, or lard
8 oz (226 g) plain flour
3 tablespoons cold water
pinch of salt

Rub the fat into the sifted flour. Add enough water to form a firm dough, incorporating a little salt. Roll to ¼-in (½-cm) thickness on floured board.

Flaky, rough puff or puff pastry may also be used for rich rabbit pie. If rough puff is preferred, the fat content should be half butter or margarine (say 3 oz/84 g) and half lard.

Jugged Hare

In practice, hare is seldom *jugged* these days, that is to say packed and sealed in a jug without water, the jug then put in a pan of boiling water so that the hare is cooked slowly and indirectly, the juices which issue from the meat ultimately being thickened by the animal's blood . . . Usually it is merely casseroled with some wine and some redcurrant jelly, and if this is done carefully the result is a very palatable, flour-thickened, hare stew. There are dozens of different recipes (many of them suggesting forcemeat balls) for this kind of jugging.

Cooked until it falls off the bone, hare retains much of its taste and character – but saddles certainly and the hind legs arguably are better eaten rare, like good lamb or beef, if the animal is anything like worth eating. Below are two versions of a dish which keeps the best meat pink but enjoys a richly traditional sauce. The first is somewhat extravagant.

As to the use of blood as a thickening agent, I am open-minded about it (well, a bit squeamish actually). It isn't essential to a good rich sauce, and it curdles given half a chance – but traditionalists may want to incorporate it at the end of the process.

TAWNY HARE

legs of 1 or 2 hares
3½ tablespoons British medium sherry
2 onions
8oz (226g) streaky bacon
1¾pts (100cl) meat or chicken broth (page 26)
livers of 2 hares
2 shallots
2 saddles of hare
2½ tablespoons port
2 tablespoons redcurrant jelly
2 Seville oranges
mace or nutmeg
cayenne pepper

Preparation and cooking time: 2¼ hours

With the hind and forelegs make a cullis by the game suprême method outlined on page 184, using British sherry (or a fortified red wine such as Tarragona) to de-glaze after the initial roasting.

Include the onions and a third of the bacon in the cullis, but not the liver or shallots, and use good meat or chicken broth if possible.

Chop the livers and shallots. Put these on rashers of bacon on a greased roasting pan and put the convex saddles over them. Cover the meaty part of the saddles with more bacon, and roast in a hot oven for 15 minutes or a little more. When each saddle is barely cooked, remove it and let it cool. Also reserve all bacon from roasting dish, while transferring liver and shallots plus fat and roasting juices such as they are to a sauce-making pan. Re-heat liver, etc., and add the port, bubbling it fast for a minute; then add the redcurrant jelly and the juice of the oranges – and bubble again for 2–3 minutes, stirring well. Add a pinch of mace or nutmeg and season with pepper. The embryo sauce can now be left till the cullis is ready.

When the saddles are cool, carve them in long fillets parallel with the backbone. (Or, if you like, carve off each fillet whole leaving a nice clean rib cage, and cut the fillets into long slices later.) Chop up the remaining ribs and throw them into the simmering hare broth.

After the broth has been simmering some 1½ hours in all, remove the lid and complete the cullis by very rapid boiling till it has been reduced to not more than a generous ½ pt (30 cl). Strain it.

To finish: warm the carved hare, taking care not to cook it further or dry it out; crispen the reserved bacon in frying pan or hot oven. Add hare cullis to embryo sauce and bring to a simmer, stirring well. Taste for seasoning. (Thicken with arrowroot and water if necessary – or with blood from hare.) Strain sauce over and round the hare pieces; float crisp bacon on sauce.

TAWNY HARE (Family Version)

1 whole hare
4 rashers streaky bacon
2 onions
2 carrots
bay leaf
4 tablespoons red wine
liver of the hare (plus another, if easily obtained)
2½ tablespoons British sherry or cheap fortified wine
2 dessertspoons redcurrant jelly
cayenne pepper
nutmeg or mace
2½ tablespoons unsweetened orange juice (commercial or real)

Preparation and cooking time: 2½ hours

Cut hare into 4 pieces – saddle, hind legs (in one), front legs (separate). Cover saddle and hind legs with bacon. Put front legs into a well-larded roasting pan with the saddle over them and the hind legs beside the saddle. Roast in a hot oven for 20 minutes. Remove from oven and put hind legs and saddle to cool. Put front legs in saucepan with bacon, onions, carrots and bay leaf. De-glaze juices in roasting pan with red wine and add to saucepan. Do this again with water to get everything out of roasting pan. Add to the saucepan and raise to a gentle boil.

When it is cool, carve the saddle into nice fillets parallel with the backbone. And carve slices off the legs as elegantly as you can. Put the carved (pink) meat in a dish and cover with foil or film to keep it moist. Break up remaining bones and add to simmering hare broth in saucepan. Cook the broth for at least another hour with the lid on, skimming as necessary, and for a further half hour with the lid off, boiling more briskly. When the hare meat comes away from legs easily, strain the stock into a jug, and set it to cool. Remove all worthwhile meat from bones and, when cool enough, chop it up small. All this is best done the day or the morning before the meal is to be eaten. The final stages are quick.

Fry the hare liver(s) in bacon fat, lard or dripping until it can be mashed with a fork. Add the chopped-up meat. Gradually add the British sherry allowing it to bubble and amalgamate with liver and meat, then add the jelly, cayenne, nutmeg or mace, and orange juice. Amalgamate and simmer before adding the reduced (and

194

de-fatted) hare stock. Meanwhile warm the pink meat through in medium oven. Thicken the sauce with arrowroot (or blood) should it need thickening and pour it over the pink meat.

HARE AND BEETROOT

An autumn coupling at once sturdy and stylish.

1 hare and its liver
2 onions
2 large carrots
1 beetroot, peeled and diced (raw)
2 large sweet oranges
1 pt (56 cl) cider vinegar
2 tablespoons hazelnut oil
4 rashers bacon, rinded and diced
2 beetroots, unpeeled (raw)
2½ tablespoons grated horseradish

Preparation time: 12–24 hours; cooking time: 3 hours

Cut or chop the hare into very small pieces, season them strongly with salt and pepper, and pack tightly into an earthenware pot or casserole together with the onions and carrots quartered, and the diced beetroot. Add the juice of two oranges and 1 tablespoonful hazelnut oil; cover with cider vinegar and marinate overnight, retaining the hare's liver and the peel of one orange for future use.

Next day pare the rind off orange, cut it into strips, and blanch these in boiling water for one minute. Add peel and diced bacon to hare and mix well. Cover the pot and put it into a hot oven; also put the 2 unpeeled beetroots into the oven (on a small roasting pan). After 20–30 minutes, reduce the oven temperature to medium-low (gas mark 3). The hare will need about 2½ more hours – if anything err on the side of long, slow cooking – depending on its age. After about 2 hours, remove the unpeeled beetroots and poke skewer into them to make sure they are cooked through. If still not quite cooked, cut them in half and boil for 10 minutes. Otherwise peel them, cut them into cubes, and purée them in blender with a little liquor from the cooking pot. Transfer purée to large saucepan, adding the liver cut into 4 or 8 pieces, and the orange strips. Simmer for 1–2 minutes.

195

Meanwhile remove cooked pieces of hare to deep, warm serving dish and strain the liquor through a fine sieve into the beetroot purée. Taste for seasoning, bring to the boil, and add further scant tablespoonful of hazelnut oil. After 2 minutes remove sauce from heat and stir in 2 tablespoonsful of horseradish. Pour sauce over hare and sprinkle remaining horseradish on top.

Serve with boiled or mashed (or scrambled) potatoes and some bright green vegetables.

Game Casserole Technique

'Brown on all sides' begin the casserole recipes, repeating each other slavishly. No one seems to have noticed that it is impossible to brown a pigeon or partridge all over in a frying pan, and almost as difficult to brown quarters of, say, pheasant or hare. As with meat casseroles, preliminary browning is not strictly necessary, but those who maintain that it provides a better texture or colour should resort to deep-frying: lightly flour the game and plunge it in boiling oil (or whatever you use for deep fat) for about half a minute (not more than one minute). While you are about it, deep-fry the onions and giblets too, for a few seconds. Then proceed as for any normal casserole – using cider, broth, carrots, celery, bacon, mushrooms, herbs – until the game is cooked. You then have dozens of options, of which the simplest are:

1) to remove giblets, but otherwise take the stew straight to table as it is;

2) to strain off broth, fortify it with sherry, port or ginger wine and reduce it by rapid boiling, perhaps thickening it with a paste of arrowroot and water;

3) to blend the vegetables and liver to a purée and return this to the cooking liquor (minus remaining giblets).

N.B. Game and poultry livers are particularly good for game sauces. Three-star restaurants, for example, use pâté de foie gras almost as a matter of course with pheasant, woodcock and partridge. Without going to such expense, it is practicable to keep tubs of chicken liver in the deep freeze and use these instead, suitably fried and minced (or mashed).

7
VEGETABLES & SALADS

Vegetables

With a few exceptions – asparagus or cauliflower cheese, for example – vegetables have always been treated in English cooking as accompaniments rather than individual dishes or courses in their own right. Let them remain so: it is not the intention here to preach vegetarianism nor to advocate the – in its place enjoyable – continental practice of serving vegetables separately from the meat or fish. However, a few mainly vegetable starters are included in the appropriate section on pages 58–61.

Another tradition is to overcook or otherwise maltreat most vegetables. A good deal has been written on this subject over the years, and reform has long been in the air. The idea now is that cooking should bring out the natural taste and texture of each vegetable. Currently Chinese techniques and equipment are popular in reformist kitchens. For many reader-cooks the ensuing remarks will be reminders rather than new concepts, but general change, like general cooking of cabbage, is slow, slow.

Vegetables grown above ground (most of which are green) should be cooked quickly and briefly, either in a great deal of fiercely boiling water, or in a very small amount of some less scalding medium, be it water, broth or butter. The former method seals in the vegetable flavour and preserves its texture; the latter may extract some of the flavour but only to transfer it to the cooking liquor which is going to be kept and consumed along with the vegetable, usually on its own, sometimes as part of a mini-sauce.

Steaming, when skilfully done, is a refinement of the fast-boiling technique, but I hardly ever use it; it makes me think of invalid cooking.

There are leading authorities who insist that the vegetable pan should never be covered, since uncovered boiling produces a brighter-looking, brighter-tasting end-product, while re-circulated steam in lidded saucepans has some kind of chemical effect which causes discoloration. Uncovered pans, however, exaggerate the

199

difficulty of making up for the heat loss which occurs when cold, raw vegetables are thrown into boiling water, while covered pans give a quicker, hotter, cooking process. So both methods have advantages and snags. The gastronomic gains of uncovered cooking seem real but marginal; the benefits of covered cooking normally balance the losses. A counsel of perfection is to cook your vegetables batch by tiny batch in a gigantic uncovered cauldron.

Quite a mystique has grown up about 'refreshing' vegetables by plunging them into cold or icy water to stop them cooking. This is due to an unlikely alliance between home-freezer buffs and restaurateur-writers. Blanch-then-refresh-then-dry-then-freeze gives fair results with kitchen-garden gluts (the best reason for freezing being to avoid waste); but there are no gastronomic reasons for doing this if the vegetables are going to be eaten straight away. Blanch-then-refresh suits restaurants which prepare their vegetables well in advance for last-minute re-heating and finishing when customers place their orders – but in the home kitchen refreshment often represents an unnecessary extra step. If the vegetables only take a few minutes to cook, they can usually be done last thing before the meal. The cutting up, of course, can be done earlier. Refreshing prevents vegetables from going to sleep after being cooked, but doesn't improve them. It is essentially a technique for times when as much work as possible must be done in advance – or for the freezer.

These notes also apply to young root vegetables such as carrots and turnips, though not to potatoes.

Many vegetables are best if shredded or julienned before being cooked. The initial process is fiddly, though satisfying – and one becomes faster at it with a little practice. For normal home cooking it is not essential to achieve the geometrical precision expected of the student commis as he learns his craft. Short cuts are to use the shredding attachment of a food processor, a mandolin, or the coarse serrations of an ordinary hand grater. I have a rooted dislike for the Mouli-légumes type of contraption, but it is supposed to do the job well (and is useful for purées where you want to exclude coarse fibres).

Vegetables which respond happily to being shredded or julienned (the two terms are used synonymously here) include carrot, leek, cabbage, sprouts, turnip, French beans, runner beans and even beetroot.

Blanching

Originally blanching was the act of pouring boiling water on to the vegetable (or dropping the vegetable into boiling water), with no further application of external heat. By extension it can now include a short period of rapid cooking after the initial immersion, but not more than, 5 minutes. To say 'blanch for 20 minutes' would be exactly the same as to say 'boil for 20 minutes'. After blanching, vegetables are only par-cooked.

Vegetables which have been cut to matchstick widths need very little cooking; young ones can be enjoyed raw. The best way to prepare them for eating hot, is to blanch them for 2–3 minutes, then drain them (and, of course, refresh them if they are not wanted immediately). To finish, toss them for 2 minutes in hot butter – or stir-fry them.

For accompanying a dish with which a buttery or stir-fried finish would be wrong, for example a braise or casserole, slightly lengthen the initial blanching process, unless you like the vegetables very crunchy.

Stir-frying

This is an oriental technique, usually carried out in a wok. As far as we are concerned here, it is quite legitimate to borrow the method for renewing English vegetable cookery, but not permissible to emulate the Chinese by spiking with soya sauce, ginger, star anise, and so on. And while the wok is a useful, permissible appliance, stir-frying of shredded vegetables can perfectly well be done in a large frying or saucepan.

Keen as I am on natural animal fats (in their proper place and correct quantities), I think that a mixture of butter and oil, seasoned with salt and pepper, is best for stir-frying. The oil should be as neutral and tasteless as possible – sunflower or rape-seed rather than corn or olive oil. Comparatively little is necessary but it does need to be very hot, just short of smoking. The vegetables must be kept in motion with a wooden spoon or specially made spatula to prevent them frying brown or colouring, as in normal frying. If using an ordinary frying pan, re-heat the julienned vegetables in smallish batches, fussing with spoon till each wisp or shred glistens, having had contact with pan and cooking medium, and repeat the process until all the vegetables are cooked, adding extra butter and oil as necessary, with seasoning and (as always) circumspection.

VEGETABLE JULIENNES

6 carrots
3 turnips (or small parsnips)
4 leeks
1 cabbage (bright green if possible)
1 oz (28 g) butter

Preparation and cooking time: 15 minutes

Cut the vegetables to matchstick juliennes of approximately the same length. It does not matter exactly what vegetables you use but if possible one of them should be white, one red, one green.

Blanch them in boiling water for 2 minutes. Drain (and, if not wanted immediately, refresh in icy water).

Before serving, toss them for 2 minutes in hot butter.

Alternatively, serve them as a salad with a light vinaigrette.

They can also be served tepid, as a starter, with marinated haddock julienne (page 38), or with fried chicken livers.

As far as possible keep the vegetables apart in the cooking. If you have time, cook them separately.

VEGETABLE TERRINES

Terrines make excellent contributions both to vegetarian meals and as starters or meat accompaniments.

The starting point is any vegetable purée or cullis. Beat raw egg

into the purée in a ratio of approximately 1 egg to ½pt (28 cl) purée. Cream or cream cheese may also be added, as may herbs, spices or grated cheese.

Terrines may be cooked in individual, buttered ramekins or in larger dishes such as those used for soufflés. Either way the cooking pot(s) should be placed in a bain-marie – for example, a deep-sided roasting pan half-filled with cold water – and baked in a medium oven for 15 minutes (ramekins) to 20–5 minutes. Enjoyable hot or cold – mild sophistication for little effort.

See also watercress terrine (page 58).

TREGUNTER CABBAGE

My late uncle Alan never ate his evening meal before the theatres (or pubs) had closed. He was a good cook and when he returned to his Tregunter Road flat between eleven and midnight, it was normally to find a complex and well-considered casserole in the oven. In 5 minutes his favourite cabbage dish was ready as an accompaniment or hot salad.

cabbage (any kind)
onion
butter
Worcestershire sauce

Preparation and cooking time: 10 minutes

Shred as much cabbage as you require and chop up about half a smallish onion per person. Bring 1 in (2½ cm, no more) of salted water to the boil in a very large saucepan. Throw in the onion, first, then a knob of butter, then the cabbage, then a dash of Worcestershire sauce. Put the lid on the pan and boil over the highest possible heat for 2 minutes (no more). Then drain the cabbage and eat immediately, adding a little more butter if you are eating it with something dry but none if you are having a sauce or gravy as well.

This technique works equally well with sprouts, spring greens and most other members of the brassica family.

(Admittedly this recipe is not wholly consistent with the general instructions given above, but it is how Uncle Alan made it, and it works very well.)

CABBAGE CRUMBLE

1 cabbage, preferably Savoy
1 large shallot
1 tablespoon oil
1 oz (28 g) butter
salt and pepper
2 oz (56 g) grated cheese (Double Gloucester or Cheddar)
1 egg yolk
breadcrumbs (soft)

Preparation and cooking time: 25 minutes

Shred the cabbage coarsely, discarding thick stalk. Blanch cabbage in boiling water for 1 minute; drain it.

Fry the shallot using the oil and butter, preferably in a wok. After 2 minutes add the cabbage and stir-fry for 2–3 minutes. Then put cabbage and shallot into a hot pie dish, draining away surplus butter and oil. Season with pepper and salt.

Grate the cheese. Stir half of it into the cabbage. When the vegetables are no longer so hot that they will instantly cook it, add the egg yolk and mix it in well. Mix the remaining grated cheese with its own volume of breadcrumbs and sprinkle the mixture on top of the cabbage. Cover with buttered paper and bake in a medium to hottish oven for 10 minutes. Remove paper and brown the crumbs under the grill, taking care not to over-toast them.

Extraordinarily fresh and good, this will convert cabbage despisers. The dish can be adapted to sprouts or broccoli and can be augmented by other vegetables. As I write this, we have just finished a cabbage crumble which included the season's first baby broad beans, pod and all, cut into half-inch lengths, then blanched and stir-fried along with the cabbage. Peas, French beans and runners all make excellent additions.

Though most satisfactory as an accompaniment to meat, this makes a particularly fine starter before, say, cold salmon, ham or a hot fish dish.

SUFFOLK SPROUTS

12 oz (340 g) Brussels sprouts
1 shallot
½ oz (14 g) butter
salt and black pepper
1 heaped tablespoon breadcrumbs
2 tablespoons single cream
¼ lemon
1 tablespoon grated horseradish

Preparation and cooking time: 10–12 minutes

Remove outer and discoloured sprout leaves. Finely chop remainder of sprouts. Blanch the shredded sprouts for 2 minutes in boiling water, then drain them.

While the sprouts are draining, melt a chopped shallot in butter (or the fat from a roast); add salt and black pepper; add the sprouts and cook 4–5 minutes, stir-frying. Towards the end of this process add the breadcrumbs, followed by the cream and a squeeze of lemon. As you take sprouts off the heat, stir in the grated horseradish.

205

CAULIFLOWER CHEESE CUSTARD

1 cauliflower
1 pt (56 cl) milk
¼ pt (14 cl) double cream
2 oz (56 g) grated Cheddar cheese or Double Gloucester
salt
pepper
cayenne pepper
made English mustard
3 eggs

Preparation and cooking time: 45 minutes

Break or cut the cauliflower into individual florets (if that's really what they are called), retaining all but the thickest pieces of stalk.

Simmer the cauliflower in milk, watching to see that it doesn't boil over. Allow 10 minutes, then strain the milk into a bowl and put the par-cooked cauliflower into a Pyrex or pie dish. Add half the cream to the hot milk and three-quarters of the grated cheese. Stir till amalgamated and melted. Season with salt, pepper, cayenne and, if liked, made English mustard which has been diluted till runny with milk.

Whisk together the eggs and remaining cream. Add a little of the hot, seasoned milk, then pour the egg mixture back into the bowl and stir. The bowl now contains a cheesy, seasoned custard mixture. Pour it over the cauliflower.

Put the cauliflower dish into a deep roasting pan and fill the pan with warm water – to form a bain-marie. Strew the pie dish with the remaining grated cheese, cover it with greaseproof paper and bake in a low to medium oven until it sets, about 30 minutes.

This is a cauliflower cheese without the flour-thickened white sauce. It will achieve a custardy consistency with only 2 eggs, and it gels more firmly as it gets colder. Good cold or hot, but better hot.

Spinach

Marxist doctrine states that it would be 'a better world for children if the parents had to eat spinach',[*] and this has always been tacitly

[*] G. Marx, *Animal Crackers* (MGM, 1930).

accepted by young people even when the spinach lobby in capitalist America invented a nautical superman whose power and strength were spinach-dependent. Popeye's popularity was always greater than his credibility, possibly because, though iron-rich, spinach has such a high oxalic-acid content that, when cooked, its minerals form insoluble oxalates and become 'effectively unavailable'.* It's poor washing, slow cooking and the dreary, dubious theory that it is good for us which make spinach unattractive.

Spinach must be washed very carefully, if possible leaf by leaf under running water. Hot water is more effective than cold – and marginally reduces cooking time.

Almost the best way of cooking it is to stir-fry it a few leaves at a time as in the following recipe. Another very good way is to blanch it in a great deal of boiling salted water for about 2 minutes in an uncovered pan. Cooking more slowly by the conservation method – that is, using the spinach's own water content – involves covering the pan and carries the risk of overcooking the spinach to limp khaki, but can be useful if it is watched carefully and given not more than 10 minutes over medium to low heat. A fourth method, also good, is to sweat the spinach in butter, observing the same general procedures and precautions as in the third.

FRIED SPINACH

young spinach, 5 or 6 leaves for each person
butter with a little oil

Preparation and cooking time: 10 minutes

Remove the coarse stalks from spinach leaves, and wash the leaves well. Dry them on kitchen paper.

Heat the butter and oil in a large frying pan; not fiercely hot. Stir-fry the leaves one portion at a time, if possible while dinner is being served. They will be cooked in 2 minutes and should be transferred to a hot serving dish or straight on to plates – with a pinch of nutmeg if you want to be slightly traditional. A drop or two of lemon juice is also a help.

This is a lovely way to cook young spinach.

* T. Stobart, *The Cook's Encyclopaedia* (Batsford, 1980).

FRIED SORREL

The culinary establishment has a thing about sorrel. I regard it as a pleasantly tangy weed to chew on a country walk (it grows everywhere round us and knows no season) or to add to a salad, but a bore to harvest in sufficient quantity to feed other people.

The cultivated variety makes heavy demands on the soil and stunts the development of vegetables growing in parallel rows nearby.

As soon as sorrel is cooked, in fact virtually on contact with any heat, it changes from a nice Bentley green to unappetising khaki, at the same time it becomes unexpectedly limp and flaccid.

Last but not least, the larger forms of sorrel are easily confused with another arrow-eared, but poisonous leaf, known as lords and ladies. I put some of this in a sorrel soup one Saturday morning and set fire to a merchant banker and his American wife. Happily we discovered the antidote (red Rioja) in time, and they lived to tell the tale – which they do at every opportunity.

These reservations apart, sorrel does have a special taste. Apply the recipe on page 207 for spinach, omitting the lemon juice. Or eat it with eggs – scrambled, in an omelette, baked.

BUTTERED TURNIPS
(or Carrots or Parsnips)

8 young turnips
1½oz (42g) butter
1 shallot
¾pt (42cl) house broth (page 24)
1 small lemon

Preparation and cooking time: about 20 minutes

Peel the turnips and cut them into slim chips (or small cubes). Melt half the butter in a saucepan. Add the turnips and the shallot whole or halved. Barely cover with the broth and cook over a brisk heat till virtually all the broth has evaporated – no lid. But shortly before, when say three-quarters of the broth has gone, add the juice of a small lemon or half lemon, and the rest of the butter.

GLAZED TURNIPS

Proceed as for buttered turnips but instead of adding second knob of butter, sprinkle in a tablespoon of caster sugar. Shake the pan while the final evaporation is taking place.

Glazed turnips may be cooked in ordinary water rather than broth.

If you have to use middle-aged or elderly vegetables for this recipe or for buttered turnips, blanch the chips or cubes for 5 minutes before carrying out the above procedures.

MULLED ARTICHOKES

8 Jerusalem artichokes
½pt (28cl) brown ale
¼pt (14cl) vinegar
1 clove garlic, chopped
2 teaspoons salt
1 teaspoon black peppercorns
1 scant teaspoon cayenne pepper
1 tablespoon black treacle
1 small onion, peeled and chopped
butter
soft brown sugar
lemon juice

Preparation and cooking time: 30 minutes

Simmer all the ingredients except the artichokes, butter, sugar and lemon juice for 10 minutes.

Wash the artichokes. Cut them into roundels about ½in (1cm) thick but do not try to peel them unless you need to acquire special merit. Blanch the artichokes in boiling water for 2 minutes, then drain and return them to the same saucepan.

Strain the boiling mull over the artichokes. Boil fast for 5 minutes. Turn off the heat and leave for another 10 minutes. Strain off the mull.

To serve: fry the artichokes briefly in butter, sprinkle lightly with brown sugar, and de-glaze with a squeeze of lemon.

Turnips, parsnips and elderly carrots are all good mulled in this way.

MULLED RED CABBAGE

small red cabbage (or half a large one)
2½ tablespoons lemon juice
⅓ pt (20 cl) dry cider
⅓ pt (20 cl) cider vinegar
salt and pepper
1 tablespoon honey (or black treacle)
2 cloves
1 scant teaspoon mixed spice
1 onion, peeled and sliced
1 apple, peeled, sliced, but not cored
butter and oil

Preparation time: up to 24 hours; cooking time: 10 minutes

Heat all the ingredients except the cabbage, onion, apple, butter and
oil to blood temperature or a little hotter, making sure the honey is
fully dissolved.

Shred the cabbage and put it in a large mixing bowl. Add the
apple and the onion. Pour the warm mull over the cabbage and
leave this to marinate as long as possible, up to 24 hours.

Drain the cabbage, retaining the mull.

Stir-fry the cabbage in a wok or braising pan, using a mixture of
butter and oil. Meanwhile re-boil the mull. After the cabbage has
been cooking for 3–4 minutes, pour in the boiling mull. Cook fast
for a further 5 minutes, or longer if you like the cabbage fairly soft.
Serve the cabbage in its by now scant mull.

ANOTHER MULL

2 teaspoons Worcestershire sauce
½ bottle British sweet sherry (or very cheap fortified wine)
juice of 2 lemons
2 bay leaves
1 teaspoon black pepper
1 tablespoon soft brown sugar
mixed dry herbs

Simmer the ingredients for 10 minutes before using as in either of
the recipes above.

Suitable for parsnips, turnips, artichokes, elderly carrots, swedes;

or leafed vegetables such as cabbage (red or green) and sprouts, leeks or celery. Cooking time is not critical and should be adjusted according to how well cooked or al dente you like them. Mulling is a flexible and challenging new treatment for vegetables.

Seven Ages of the Broad Bean

At first the infant . . . When very young they are delicious eaten in the pod, like French beans or mangetouts. The pods may be boiled whole or chopped into short lengths and braised in water and butter.

At the next age, just when the pods are becoming coarse, and the beans inside are the size of flattened peas, they are lovely to eat raw, with salt.

A little larger and they are better cooked again – with water (not much), sugar and salt, parsley and butter. Sweet as peas, but the flavour improves with maturity.

When the skins begin to turn from green to grey, though still intensely edible, there is much to be said for blending them (after boiling) into a whole bean purée. The purée may be eaten as such, turned into a vegetable terrine (see page 202), or mixed with egg, chives, parsley – and fried in very hot oil: beancakes.

But in time (a day or two) the skins really toughen. Never mind, they can be discarded when cooked and the bean meat inside, still bright, sieved or minced to a verdant flour, for eating hot with melted butter or using as a purée for thickening sauces, stuffing vegetables . . .

Older still, they can be dried, for subsequent reconstruction by long, slow cooking as one of the more unusual and rewarding dried pulses . . .

Or for planting the following spring. (Dried broad beans can be bought at health shops and delicatessens.)

And nowadays broad beans have an eighth form: they freeze better than almost any other vegetable. Freeze them at the third stage, if possible, at latest the fourth.

Hurray for broad beans, oldest, truest friend – and commiseration to those who can't stand them.

Stuffed Vegetables

Stuffed giant marrows ('vegetable ducks') are a familiar, if reluctantly welcome, alternative in the autumn to shepherds' pie for using up leftover meat or mince. Small vegetables are more rewarding. They can be served either as first courses in their own right or as accompaniments to a main course. Those with meaty, fishy, or cheesy stuffings are, on the whole, better as first courses; when supporting a main course the stuffed vegetable is either a blend of two or more complementary plants or, in effect, a single vegetable with a self-contained sauce. For stuffed starters see pages 58–60.

STUFFED TOMATOES

6 medium to large tomatoes
6 tablespoons onion or leek cullis (purée)
1 egg yolk
salt and pepper
3 tablespoons chopped parsley
1 tablespoon basil
dry croûtons
butter
broth

Preparation and cooking time: 25 minutes

Slice the tops off tomatoes; scoop out (and keep) the seeds but leave most of the flesh intact.

Mix the cullis with egg, seasoning and herbs. Cut 2 slices of crustless white bread into very small cubes and fry these in a pan without fat till they are golden and crisp but not at all burnt (in short, toast them). Add half the croûtons to the cullis stuffing.

Fill the tomatoes with stuffing. Top them with the rest of the croûtons. Put them in a baking dish, and pour round them a little melted butter, a few tablespoonsful of broth, and the reserved tomato seeds. Bake in a medium oven for 15–20 minutes. Before serving, spoon juices from bottom of baking dish on to the tomatoes.

STUFFED MARROW

Vegetable marrows have lately been ousted by upstart, omnipresent courgettes. They deserve a better fate. Watery they may be, but their delicate flavour is a late summer blessing, so long as it is not boiled away or drowned in flour-thick sauce. Use medium-sized, middle-aged (vis-à-vis courgettes) marrows, rather than ancient, fibrous, armour-plated senior citizens (whose experience is best converted into marrow rum). Let the unassertive stuffing be relatively dry since it will be steamed internally as the marrow is cooked. Here are two stuffings:

1) cooked rice, julienned runner beans blanched for 1 minute, peeled not over-ripe tomatoes, mint and chopped, blanched onion;

2) breadcrumbs, ground hazelnuts, blanched and julienned carrots, blanched and julienned leeks, an egg to bind, parsley and thyme.

Cut the end off marrow and scoop out seeds. Fill cavity with stuffing. Put the end back and fasten it with cocktail sticks or skewers – as tightly as possible since it is much easier to cook the marrow on its side than trying to balance it vertically. Paint it with melted butter and bake it in a medium oven for about 50 minutes (well, as long as it needs depending on its size), basting it with more butter or bacon fat and the juices which gradually seep.

STUFFED ONIONS

4 well-grown onions
4 tablespoons spinach purée
1 oz (28 g) grated Cheddar cheese, or milder hard cheese, or cream/cottage
   cheese
5 tablespoons cream
salt and pepper
melted butter

Cooking time: 1½ hours

Bake the onions without peeling them in a medium to hot oven for 50 minutes. Allow them to cool until you can remove their skins without too much risk. Cut off their tops, that is counting the roots as the onions' bottoms. Scoop the middle of the onions into a bowl, leaving 2 or 3 thicknesses. Mash the onions, spinach, cheese and cream together. Season vigorously. Fill the onion shells with the stuffing. Cover with the removed tops. Paint the onions with melted butter and bake in a medium oven for 15 minutes.

Beetroot

This most English-tasting vegetable was apparently developed only in the nineteenth century – though there were earlier forms of beet – by a Frenchman (Vilmorin), dammit.

A few elementary points: eat or harvest them when they are relatively young; buy them raw; cook them unskinned in the oven – baking them in their jackets – in so far as you cook them at all; young beets, sliced wafer thin, are excellent raw. The cooked beetroot which you sometimes see steaming in the shop has had a lot of its taste boiled away, its blood dispersed in the greengrocer's cauldron – and often has a horribly slimy texture. Supermarket beetroot, encased in film and polystyrene, are equally slimy and hardly worth buying.

Beetroot are positively greedy about garlic.

BAKED BEETS

Allow one small to medium beetroot per person. Bake the beetroot for 50–60 minutes in a medium-hot oven. Test them with a skewer at 45 minutes to make sure they are not already cooked; it's better to undercook than overcook them, unless they are ancient.

Remove the skins as soon as they are cool enough to handle. Using a knife and fork, cut the flesh into slices or cubes. It doesn't matter if the heart resists cutting more than the periphery.

Here are three ways of finishing beetroot as a hot dish:

1) fry butter, heavily seasoned with salt and pepper, till it goes brown. Turn down the heat and add lemon juice. When the lemon juice has bubbled for no more than a minute, pour it all over the still hot beetroot, and sprinkle with plenty of grated horseradish;

2) make mustard-cream (page 232). Season it with extra salt and pepper; heat but do not boil the cream. Pour it over the hot beetroot (which, I feel, should be cubed rather than sliced);

3) fry shallots in a small amount of butter. De-glaze the pan with sloe gin or an orange liqueur. Let this bubble for 1–2 minutes, then add 2½ tablespoonsful of fresh orange juice, a generous dash of tabasco and salt. Simmer for a moment and pour over the beetroot.

BEETROOT SALADS

Bake, peel and slice the beetroot, as above. Then either:

1) pour a generous glass of orange juice over it, while the slices are still hot or at least warm. When cold, dress the salad with oil and chopped spring onion or chives.

2) Pound garlic, cardamom pods, and fresh grated horseradish together in a mortar; slowly add oil and vinegar in the ratio of 3

parts oil to 1 part vinegar, and season with salt. Pour dressing over the tepid beetroot. Toss the salad thoroughly but gingerly to avoid hurting the beets. It cannot be pretended that any dish relying for its effect on garlic and cardamom is particularly English, but this salad is so good, and has been so popular in our house since we first discovered it (in the *Penguin Book of Herbs and Spices*) that we have granted it a special dispensation.

3) Alternatively, peel and grate raw young beetroot and mix it with grated raw carrot – in the company of a decent oil and vinegar dressing.

Barley

Barley is a splendid and very historical alternative to rice, potatoes or pasta. With pleasantly 'real' taste and most distinctive texture, it contains masses of fibre, vitamins, minerals and protein, and so is awfully good for you. Don't let this put you off, it is by no means aggressive in its healthiness. The only snag is it takes a long time to cook, over 1½ hours.

Two forms are available commercially, pot barley and pearl barley. The former is the more natural, less refined product, but pearl barley is by no means over-refined, and is probably easier to buy. Both give considerable satisfaction plain boiled, in salted water or broth, with stews, casseroles or braises. Allow a scant 2 oz (say 50 g) per person. The individual grains absorb liquid and expand in the cooking.

Barley is also the best indigenous cereal for substantial cassoulet-type dishes such as stretched duck (page 132) or Scotch-potch (page 160).

To reduce the cooking time, blanch the barley in 3 successive kettles of boiling water; allow it to soak 3 minutes in each water before being drained ready for the next. 10 minutes spent on this operation saves 20–30 minutes' cooking. Presumably a pressure cooker would save even more time.

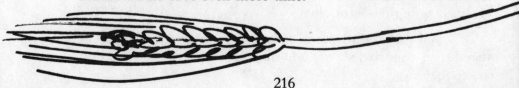

BARLEY SALAD

7 oz (200 g) pot barley
4 tablespoons olive oil
4 tablespoons sunflower oil
black pepper and salt
4 tablespoons chopped parsley
4 spring onions (or equivalent in shallots)
lemon juice to taste

Preparation and cooking time: 3 hours

Boil the barley in salted water (not broth). Take it off the heat when it is yielding but still slightly al dente. Drain it patiently, removing as much water as the absorbent cereal will allow.

Put the barley in a salad bowl or large, deep dish. While it is still hot, add the oils, pepper and a little salt. Mix well. When it has cooled down to tepid, add the parsley and chopped spring onion. Mix them in thoroughly. When it is cold, add the lemon juice gradually, tasting till you have the right acidity.

Much nicer than boring old rice salad, this stands comparison with the cracked wheat salads of Levantine cooking.

FRIED BARLEY

1 oz (28 g) bacon fat, lard or dripping
2 onions, chopped
8 oz (226 g) barley, boiled and well drained
seasonings
parsley (optional)

Cooking time: 15 minutes

This can be made effectively with any frying medium, but is perhaps best with bacon fat or bacon fat mixed with beef dripping or pork lard.

Fry the onions first in the fat, over medium heat. Let them turn just the golden side of translucent, then add the barley and fry, stirring, till all the fat has been taken up, and the barley, glistening, has itself turned one or two shades darker. At the same time, season with salt and pepper – and sprinkle in some parsley.

Delicious with chops, steaks, sausages.

BARLOTTO

Cooking time: 25 minutes

Make fried barley as page 217.

Separately fry cubed bacon, diced chicken liver and (not essential) small pieces of kidney. Add leftover chicken or pork if available. After a few minutes' cooking, stir in 2–3 tablespoonsful of home-made tomato cullis. Heat the cullis through then add it and the meats to the fried barley.

Commercial tomato purée or tomato juice may be used, but not tomato ketchup.

Potatoes

The potato has taken more than its share of blame for the pear-shaped figure of Mr and Mrs Average Briton. It is usually the first item dropped by slimmers. Properly cooked, however, it is nutritious and healthy; it can be eaten every day, in moderation, without being fattening, so long as the rest of the menu isn't too sugared with sugars or saturated with saturates.

Chips with everything, on the other hand, and soggy, salty chips at that, no doubt fatten, as they threaten, as they infect. Good chips know their place in renewed English food, and it's definitely below roast, scrambled or mashed potatoes.

ROAST POTATOES

Roast potatoes should be quite small, crisp, golden-to-dark brown on at least two sides, dry and floury inside. Like that they are the king of all potatoes; infinitely superior to fried, sautéed, chipped, boiled or rösti'd. They should be eaten with grills and other meat dishes as often as possible, rather than be confined monogamously to roast joints.

It is best to start with large, mature potatoes at least 1½ hours before dinner time. After they have been peeled, they should be cut into (necessarily) irregular cubes, so that they occupy about the same air space as hens' eggs, and boiled for 7 minutes.

Potatoes may be roasted in dripping, lard, lamb fat (according to the meat being served), oil or oil and butter mixed. Comparatively little fat is needed, just enough to put a very thin coat on each piece of potato. Whatever roasting medium is chosen, it should be heated first, to facilitate the coating operation, and before being put into a hot oven, the potatoes should be salted. After roasting for some 40 minutes, they should be turned over with a slice, re-salted, and roasted for a further half hour at least. They will not get as crisp as they should in less than 65 minutes, and will happily go on improving if cooked up to 90 or 100 minutes.

Thus the traditional practice of roasting potatoes round the joint has several potential drawbacks: some joints produce much more fat than the potatoes need, others not enough; some joints need basting with water, cider or wine, potatoes never; small joints need less cooking time than their potatoes; and if the rest period (page 153) is used for further potato cooking, the roasting pan cannot at the same time be used for gravy . . . In short, it is often better to roast the potatoes separately, timing them to be ready when the joint has finished resting, and with joints or birds large enough to need more time in the oven than the potatoes need, borrowing fat from the meat produced by the prior cooking.

New potatoes, incidentally, are not as useless for roasting as is sometimes suggested. Try roasting Arran Pilot, for example. Of the maincrop varieties commonly available in shops, Desirée, King Edward and Maris Piper all roast well.

With properly roasted potatoes, and masterly gravy, even the most carnivorous eat less meat.

SCRAMBLED POTATOES

mashed potato
1 or 1½ eggs per person
butter – about ½oz (14g) per person
salt and pepper
1 dessertspoon single cream per person
parsley or chives, chopped (optional)

Cooking time: 25 minutes

These are particularly good as a luncheon or supper dish, with bacon, sausages, fish – or vegetables with differentiated textures. The potatoes emerge runny enough to require no sauce or gravy but too creamily rich, perhaps, to be the neutral accompaniment to an elaborate main dish.

Peel, halve or quarter, and boil the potatoes. Mash them, if possible using a potato ricer. Add no milk or butter at this stage.

Crack the eggs into a pan in which the butter has already melted. Stir them over a low heat, adding salt and plenty of ground white pepper, and a little cream. When they begin to thicken but not to set, amalgamate them with the hot potato. Chopped parsley or chives may also be added.

Ideally to be eaten straight away, but will keep, covered in butter papers, in a low oven for 10 minutes or more without spoiling.

BUBBLE AND SQUEAK

Preparation and cooking time: up to 30 minutes

One of my earliest gastronomic memories: leftover cabbage and potatoes were mashed together, floured and fried like fish cakes – and how much everyone preferred bubble and squeak to the day before's healthy boiled vegetables. Here is a better method.

Boil the peeled potatoes and put them through a potato ricer (or otherwise render them lump-free). Shred the cabbage and blanch it for 5 minutes in boiling water.

After draining the cabbage, chop it even smaller, and dry it in a clean cloth. Mix with the potato: two-thirds potato, one-third cabbage is a suitable ratio. Bind the mixture with beaten egg. Season with salt, pepper, chives.

Fry a teaspoonful of mustard seed in very hot dripping. As soon as it pops, transfer the seeds with as little of the fat as possible to the potato mixture. Mash all together thoroughly and add a dash or two of Worcestershire sauce.

Form the mixture into balls; flatten the balls into thickish cakes; flour the cakes very lightly, and fry them on both sides to a rich, nutty brown in the very hot dripping. Allow at least one per person. Young people of all ages require more. Alternatively cook the mixture in one big cake, filling the whole pan. However, you may find it difficult to turn it over (to brown on the second side) cleanly.

Blanched, shredded sprouts are just as welcome as cabbage in this robust partner to chops, steak or gammon.

Potato Salads

A few generalisations . . .

Waxy potatoes are commonly considered better for salad, but floury ones are serviceable provided they are not overcooked.

Potato salads are not really improved by mayonnaise, cream or sour cream. What they need by way of dressing is oil – at least one-third of it olive – and lemon juice (much better than vinegar in this context) and salt. The oil should be introduced while the potatoes are still hot, but not the lemon.

An onion element is more or less essential, and spring onions, including plenty of green, are best. Herbs are very welcome and changes should be rung: mixed sweet herbs one day, dill only another, or chervil. (For once let's side with Ogden Nash and exhibit our gumption by declaring that any potato salad which can be improved by the addition of parsley is, ipso facto, a salad unfit for human consumption.)

Normally a potato salad's status is that of side dish or subsidiary element in a cold collation. However, if you add to it meat or fish or hardboiled eggs or chicken or, indeed, beans, lentils or cheese, the salad becomes a main course in itself. Equally it can be a substantial first course to be followed by something light and frivolous. Cold beef, cold pork, sardines and tunny fish are particularly recommended.

POTATO SALAD

1 lb (450 g) potatoes, new or waxy, if possible
2 tablespoons olive oil
4 tablespoons sunflower oil
salt and pepper
juice of 1 large or 2 small lemons
1 dessertspoon made English mustard

Preparation, cooking and cooling time: 1 hour

Peel (or scrub) and boil the potatoes. Remove from water as soon as cooked, and cut each into chunky cubes. Put these in salad bowl and while they are still hot add oil, salt and pepper. (The proportion of olive oil to sunflower is up to you.) Turn the potatoes carefully to distribute oil evenly.

When the potatoes are cold, add lemon juice previously mixed with made English mustard, and toss carefully.

8
SAUCES & CONDIMENTS

Sauce theory has changed radically since 1970 when the late Ambrose Heath[*] propounded six 'mother' sauces and divided them into two families – roux-based sauces and emulsions (usually egg-thickened). New English cooking rejects the use of flour and fat combined into a roux and largely excludes eggs. Its sauces are lighter, less thick but often stronger, more defined, more relevant to the dish itself. In fact, if there are two sauce categories now, they are specific sauces, those which derive from the preparation of the dish they adorn, and multi-purpose sauces, those which are made independently. In many ways the former category, where each sauce is intrinsic to its purpose, is more satisfactory – and examples occur frequently throughout this book. However this chapter is concerned mainly with extrinsic, versatile sauces, the English cousins of mayonnaise and hollandaise.

Sauces are important but the idea that sauce-making is a separate and higher art than ordinary cooking can lead to the absurd situation of chefs demonstrating their skills by loading each plate with a repertoire of sauces almost irrespective of what's underneath. This is like larding a Mozart symphony with Schubert songs and Chopin mazurkas. Hollandaise with everything is as stultifying as HP, ketchup or chips with everything. One sauce per course is usually just right.

[*] Ambrose Heath, *The Penguin Book of Sauces* (1970).

225

Usually Reliable Sauces

In new English cooking, most sauces are made by one of the following routes:

1) copious broths concentrated and saucefied by simple reduction (sometimes thickened with arrowroot);

2) combinations of broth and vegetable cullis (purée);

3) a reduction of alcohol or vinegar, saucefied by butter, cream, broth, cullis (or some combination of these);

4) cooking fats de-glazed by alcohol or vinegar, and saucefied by broth, cullis or cream (or some combination);

5) scant cooking juices saucefied by cream and/or butter, or cullis.

In each case, materials which are inessential to the sauce's chemistry or structure – herbs, spices, fungi, and so on – may be essential to its character.

Butter Sauces

The eggless 'beurre blanc' has the sweet taste of success. Restaurant chefs reduce white wine, add butter, maybe a little cream, maybe a truffle, crayfish tail or exotic fruit – and call it nouvelle cuisine. More than a century before, English butter sauce was fulfilling a similar role, though it used water or milk rather than wine, and a little flour. The English method was marred by a tendency to 'oil' and the taste of uncooked flour. No such problems pertain to today's . . .

WHITE BUTTER SAUCE

1 shallot
5 tablespoons dry cider (or cider and cider vinegar mixed)
4oz (112g) butter (or Flora-type margarine)
1 tablespoon double cream

Cooking time: up to 15 minutes

Mainly for fish.

Peel and chop the shallot. Boil it in the cider (or cider and vinegar) mixed with an equal quantity of water for 10 minutes uncovered – until the liquid has reduced to a scant tablespoonful. Reduce the heat and, stirring with wooden spoon, add one-fifth of the (cold) butter. As it melts, add the cream, and then – still stirring of course – another portion of butter, and when that emulsifies another, and another. Don't hurry the process; allow 5 or 6 minutes from the first addition of butter, and enjoy your occupation. Taste, and season if necessary. Think about other little things you could slip into the sauce . . .

Even in its simplest form this key sauce is smooth, elegant, appetising. It can be elaborated or varied in numberless ways: with the addition of fish-cooking juices; with shrimps or other shellfish; with smoked fish; with lemon or lime juice instead of vinegar; or orange juice; with celery instead of shallot; with all manner of herbs (or just one); with mustard, horseradish, anchovy, tabasco, Angostura bitters . . . Over to you.

This sauce is essentially for fish and shellfish, but also enhances salsify, sweetbreads, chicken, and so on.

BAY LEAF SAUCE (for Fish)

2 shallots, chopped
2 crushed bay leaves
1 oz (28 g) butter
1 tablespoon warm gin
2 tablespoons Rose's lime juice
¼ pt (14 cl) double cream
salt and white pepper
Angostura bitters

Cooking time: 12 minutes

Fry the shallots and bay leaves gently in half of the butter. When the shallots are cooked but no more than slightly golden, flare them with gin. As the flames die down add the lime juice. The gin and the lime together de-glaze the pan. Now add the cream, stirring with a wooden spoon. Let the sauce simmer for 2–3 minutes. Season with salt and white pepper but not too vigorously. Finish with a good knob of butter and a dash of Angostura.

227

BAY LEAF SAUCE (for Meat or Game)

1 onion
dripping for frying
4 bay leaves
3½ tablespoons cider vinegar
1 pt (56 cl) meat broth
2 tablespoons tomato cullis (home-made) or 1 tablespoon bought tomato purée
1 teaspoon arrowroot
salt and pepper

Cooking time: 40 minutes

Fry the onion to a golden brown in the dripping together with the bay leaves. De-glaze with the vinegar. Add the meat broth and tomato. Simmer briskly for 30 minutes, reducing by about 50 per cent. Thicken with arrowroot. Season with salt and pepper, and perhaps something sweet like redcurrant jelly, if you are having it with lamb or venison.

FRYING-PAN SAUCE

A versatile, meal-enhancing sauce for chops, steaks, mixed grills, liver and bacon, sausages, even (if you must) hamburgers.

oil or fat left from frying or grilling meat
1 onion, finely chopped
salt and pepper
bay leaf
2 tablespoons vinegar
3 tablespoons brown ale
1 scant pt (50 cl) broth
arrowroot

Cooking time: 15–30 minutes

First cook the meat(s). Retain sufficient fat to fry the onion – until it is fairly brown. Season with salt, pepper and bay leaf. De-glaze with vinegar and beer. Boil till the liquids have all but evaporated. Add the stock (and for dark meats a drop of gravy browning). The sauce can be used as a thinnish gravy but is better if boiled down to a seductively lubricious consistency. Encourage it with a little arrowroot if time presses. Before serving (strained or unstrained), pour in any juices which have emanated from the meat itself.

Frying-pan sauce can speak with – and to – many tongues. The beer element may be omitted, or replaced by cider or cheap sherry; piquancy may be added in the form of red pepper, chilli vinegar, Worcestershire sauce, anchovy; fresh or dried herbs may be introduced, as may fungi or vegetable purées; butter can be stirred in during the final reduction to give a smoother finish.

The basic procedure is very simple but creates a surprisingly sophisticated, unashamedly insular sauce.

SAUCE X

2oz (56g) chicken livers
3 shallots
bacon fat, lard, or butter for frying
5 tablespoons cider vinegar
½pt (28cl) British medium sherry or ruby wine
⅓pt (20cl) house broth (page 24)
1 tablespoon dried mushrooms or other dried fungi
Worcestershire sauce
black pepper
1 teaspoon arrowroot

Cooking time: 20 minutes

Chop the chicken livers and shallots very small. Fry them, in bacon fat if possible. After 5–6 minutes, de-glaze with cider vinegar. Boil the vinegar nearly dry, stirring with a wooden spoon. Add British sherry, broth, dried mushrooms and a good injection of Worcestershire sauce. Bring to the boil. Reduce in volume by rapid boiling, and season with plenty of black pepper. Thicken sauce with a teaspoonful of arrowroot dissolved in cold water. Strain before use.

Sweet but piquant, this sauce is good with roast game or mutton. You may find it needs extra salt (depending on how salty the meat broth is).

GREEN PEA SAUCE

3 shallots
½pt (28 cl) meat cullis (page 26)
scant 1 oz (25 g) butter (or duck fat)
½lb (226 g) shelled peas
1½ tablespoons dry sherry
salt and pepper
¼pt (14 cl) double cream
mint leaves
a few sorrel leaves (optional)

Cooking time: 20–5 minutes

Yes, this is best made with fresh peas. Outside the pea season it can be made with canned garden peas from France or Belgium, or – less satisfactorily – with frozen or 'surprise' peas.

Peel the shallots and boil them for 10 minutes in the cullis. Remove them from the cullis, chop them up, and fry them gently in butter (or duck fat). At the same time cook the peas in the original cullis.

When onions are beginning to go golden, de-glaze the pan with sherry. Blend the onion and peas to a purée, using enough cullis as is necessary. Return purée to saucepan and re-heat. Add salt and pepper to taste and stir in the cream. Add a few snipped mint leaves.

The taste is sharpened if a few sorrel leaves are boiled with the peas and included in the purée.

Particularly good with lamb or duck.

MARMALADE SAUCE

3 shallots, peeled
½pt (28 cl) meat cullis (page 26)
butter or duck fat for frying
1½ tablespoons cider vinegar
1 tablespoon bitter marmalade
1 teaspoon arrowroot (optional)

Cooking time: 20–5 minutes

As for green pea sauce, cook the shallots in cullis. Strain shallots, retaining cullis, then chop and fry them in butter or duck fat.

De-glaze with the cider vinegar when shallots have reached a good, golden colour. Add the marmalade.

When the vinegar has largely evaporated, add the cullis in which the shallots were originally cooked. Bring to the boil and thicken the sauce with arrowroot if necessary.

For duck or wild duck.

NO-BREAD SAUCE

⅓ pt (20 cl) double cream
5 tablespoons chicken or meat cullis (page 26)
1 small onion, peeled and halved
2 cloves
2 egg yolks
1 tablespoon single cream
salt and white pepper

Cooking time: about 45 minutes

Put cream and cullis into saucepan. Add onion halves stuck with cloves. Heat slowly with the lid on, stirring occasionally until the mixture is suffused with the scent of onion and clove – about half an hour of not quite boiling.

Put egg yolks into double saucepan and stir a tablespoonful of single cream into them. Half fill lower saucepan with hot water. Removing the onion and cloves, add the cream mixture to the eggs, stirring. Sharpen with salt and white pepper. Put the double pan over a low heat and stir until the sauce thickens to a custardy consistency. (The hot water must neither boil nor touch the pan above.)

Hot or cold, this is excellent with chicken, turkey, pheasant and in other contexts where bread sauce is the norm. (Conventional bread sauce, incidentally, remains one of the minor glories of our ethnic cookery.)

DEVIL SAUCE

1 onion, peeled and chopped
4 dried chillies (or more)
1 teaspoon crushed black peppercorns
5 tablespoons vinegar
3½oz (100g) butter
1 tablespoon single cream
1 tablespoon piccalilli juice

Cooking time: 20 minutes

Boil onion, chillies (broken in half) and black pepper in vinegar and the same amount of water. Continue till there is a scant tablespoonful of liquid left. Add one-fifth of butter, stirring. As it melts, add the cream. Then add the rest of the butter, fifth by fifth, stirring all the time. Strain the mixture into a pre-heated sauce boat. Stir in the piccalilli juice.

For grilled meats, herrings, mackerel.

MUSTARD-CREAM

This can be used as a sauce in its own right or as a key constituent of other sauces and dishes. Incorporated at the end of a cooking process, it bestows the full mustardy tang, so easily destroyed by heat.

1 tablespoon dry English mustard powder
3½ tablespoons single cream
¼pt (14cl) double cream
Worcestershire sauce or tabasco (optional)

Preparation time: 30 minutes

Make a smooth paste using mustard powder and single cream. Leave for 30 minutes. Then treble its volume by stirring in double cream and mixing it well. A dash or two of Worcestershire sauce or tabasco may also be included.

Mustard-cream may be heated gently or added to already hot sauces, but should not be subjected to prolonged boiling.

CRABBIE SAUCE

When my great-aunt, Edie Gordon-Brown, married an affluent young officer in the Scots Greys, she shrugged off his connection with trade, and persuaded her husband to do likewise. Sure enough, as soon as the Boer War was over, Captain Crabbie dropped the 'i' from his name to dissociate himself from the delicious green ginger wine which had made his father's fortune. Thus spake the Edinburgh wits: 'Jack Crabbe lost his eye in the war'; and the Manse had its own version of the same joke – 'Crabbe has complied with the Biblical injunction, "If thine eye offend thee, cast it out".'

Today one is only too pleased to have connections with trade, and I think that even Aunt Edie would approve the use of ginger wine in the kitchen. Why it has never been used before remains a mystery. Crabbie sauce is excellent with grouse, wild duck, lamb chops, venison, and can also be used with steaks and roasts.

2 shallots, peeled and chopped
1 stick celery, chopped
1 oz (28 g) butter
3½ tablespoons ginger wine
1 teaspoon cayenne and black pepper mixed
scant ½ pt (25 cl) meat cullis (page 26)
arrowroot (optional)

Cooking time: 12–15 minutes

Fry shallots and celery gently in butter for 6–7 minutes. Add the ginger wine and let it bubble down to a sticky glaze, seasoning with cayenne and black pepper. Then add the meat cullis and cook for about 5 minutes. Thicken with arrowroot and darken with browning if necessary.

If you only have a light meat or chicken broth, strengthen it by rapid boiling before you use it for the sauce.

SARDINE SAUCE

1 tin sardines
1 onion
juice of 1 lemon
⅓ pt (20 cl) single cream mixed with 4 tablespoons fish stock
arrowroot
cayenne pepper
chopped parsley

Cooking time: 15–20 minutes

Drain the sardines, retaining oil. Chop the onion and sardines. Fry them, starting with the onion, in the oil from the sardine tin. When the onion is cooked but not burnt, de-glaze with lemon juice (or cider vinegar). Add the cream and fish stock slowly. Thicken with 1 teaspoonful of arrowroot mixed with water. Season with cayenne. Add parsley just before decanting to the sauce boat.

Delicious with haddock or cod or poured over boiled potatoes.

LOST SAUCE

Mayonnaise is one of history's more important chemical discoveries but is essentially Mediterranean. It cannot be made without oil and the oil should be olive or at least partly olive, so it cannot be claimed as an English sauce. There is an almost forgotten English sauce, however, which can be updated and extended instead. It's just about as good as mayonnaise for most purposes.

3 hardboiled egg yolks
1 raw yolk
scant ½ pt (25 cl) double cream
1 lemon
salt and white pepper

Preparation time: 12 minutes; refrigeration time: at least 1 hour

Mash all the yolks together. Stir in the cream slowly but not quite as slowly as the oil for mayonnaise. Add the juice of the lemon last. Season with salt and white pepper. Before being used, the sauce must be refrigerated for at least an hour (in which time it stiffens appreciably in consistency).

Lost sauce can be accentuated one way or another by the addition of herbs, anchovy, chopped spring onion, or mustard. Mustard should be added to the egg yolks before the cream. It's particularly good with shellfish if sharpened by tabasco or cayenne pepper.

N.B. Do not use UHT cream.

SIMPLE CREAM SAUCE FOR BAKED OR POACHED FISH

¼pt (14cl) whipping cream
1–2 teaspoons anchovy essence
2 dashes Angostura bitters
lemon juice
fish liquor (from the poaching or baking)

Cooking time: about 10 minutes

Raise the cream to near simmering point. Add anchovy essence, Angostura and a few drops of lemon juice.

Bring fish liquor to boil and, if more than about 3 tablespoonsful, reduce it to that volume by rapid simmering. When it is reduced sufficiently, add the cream.

In addition, shrimps, mussels, cockles or mushrooms may be added with the cream. Taste for seasoning, then pour over the fish.

Alternatively the savoury cream may be flavoured with a mild curry paste, with mustard or with horseradish.

SIMPLE BUTTER SAUCE FOR BAKED OR POACHED FISH

Preparation and cooking time: 10–12 minutes

Reduce the fish-cooking liquors as above but take them down to about 1½ tablespoons. Stir into these some 2oz (50g) of savoury butter, that is to say butter mashed up with anchovy, herbs, smoked fish, the brown meat of crab or mild curry paste.

GREEN SUMMER SAUCE

2 lettuce hearts, shredded
6 spring onions, chopped
⅓ pt (20 cl) chicken stock
3½ tablespoons cider
½ oz (14 g) butter
2 teaspoons caster sugar
7 oz (200 g) shelled peas
salt
3½ tablespoons double cream
mint
chives

Cooking time: 15 minutes

Braise lettuce and spring onions in chicken stock, cider and butter, sprinkle with the sugar. After 5 minutes, add the peas. When the peas are cooked, blend all 3 vegetables to a purée using only as much of the cooking liquor as you need. Re-heat and season with salt. Add cream. Flavour with chopped mint and (for appearance rather than taste) chopped chives.

Excellent with salmon, trout, and all poached fish.

This sauce is also good cold, but should then be made with oil instead of butter.

SHARP APPLE SAUCE

1 lb (450 g) cooking apples
¼ pt (14 cl) cider vinegar
2 oz (56 g) soft brown sugar
1 clove
1 dried chilli
lemon rind

Cooking time: 25–30 minutes

Peel the apples and chop them small; exclude core and pips. Simmer gently with vinegar, sugar, clove, chilli and a few parings of lemon rind free of all pith. Cook with the lid on for about 10 minutes, then half remove the lid (tilt it so that steam can escape but some of it condenses on the lid and falls back into the apple), and continue cooking slowly till you have a rich, brown, marmalady pulp. Stir to prevent it burning or sticking to the bottom of the pan.

When it is nearly ready, taste it, and add a little more brown sugar or a squeeze of lemon if it needs sharpening or sweetening.

Serve hot, tepid or cold.

For a change use cinnamon in place of clove; include a chopped shallot; or use orange instead of lemon.

Zests and Gustos

These sibling sauces derive from the fresh chutneys of Indian cooking and are particularly good with deep-fried food such as fish and chips. They will keep a few days but are easy to make and might as well be prepared at some convenient moment on the day they are required.

The gusto is a cooked relish served hot or warm, while zests are composed of cold ingredients: both should be thick as jam. With fried fish they are a vast improvement on vinegar, tomato ketchup or sauce tartare. It is usually a mistake to serve anything rich or unctuous with fried food – forceful astringency should be the rule. (In this connection, pommes frites with mayonnaise – as served in skiing resorts and as advertised on television – seem the ultimate barbarity; readers who can think of something even more disgusting should keep it to themselves.)

237

WATERCRESS GUSTO

1 bunch watercress
¾oz (20g) butter
juice of 1 lemon
2 egg yolks
1 teaspoon dry mustard powder

Preparation and cooking time: 15 minutes

Chop the watercress, discarding very coarse stalks. Cook very slowly in butter and lemon juice till the cress is soft enough to purée. Liquidise it in blender.

Mix egg yolks with dry mustard powder. Return purée to pan and re-heat. Remove it from the heat and stir in the egg yolks. Taste and season with salt and more lemon if necessary.

TOMATO AND THYME GUSTO

1 small onion or equivalent in shallots
oil for frying
5 tablespoons cider vinegar
1oz (28g) tomato purée (tinned or tubed will do)
1oz (28g) tomato ketchup (bottled will do)
salt
pepper
cayenne pepper
thyme
¼pt (14cl) dry cider

Cooking time: 20 minutes

Fry the onion in oil till golden. De-glaze with cider vinegar. Add equal quantities of tomato purée and tomato ketchup, giving them a good stir as they bubble. Season with salt, the peppers and thyme. Add dry cider and boil fast till it reduces to a jammy consistency. An extra spoonful of thyme can be stirred in shortly before the gusto is served.

When fresh tomatoes are abundant and cheap, they can be used instead of the purée and ketchup. The vinegar element should be increased, and either the tomatoes must be peeled or the gusto, after being cooked, strained. Fry onion; de-glaze with vinegar; add 12oz (350g) chopped tomatoes and seasonings; add cider; reduce by rapid boiling.

ANCHOVY GUSTO

7 oz (200 g) turnips (young if possible)
1 scant pt (50 cl) fish stock (or water)
1 shallot, chopped
1 tin anchovies
2 tablespoons lemon juice or cider vinegar
parsley

Cooking time: 20 minutes

The vehicle for this sauce is a root vegetable purée, preferably turnip. Peel, quarter and boil the turnips till they are soft enough to blend with a little of their cooking liquor. For the boiling use fish stock if this is easy, but water will do.

Fry the shallot in oil from the anchovy tin. When it is golden, add 3 or more anchovy fillets, chopped small. When the fillets have begun to cook, de-glaze the pan with lemon juice or cider vinegar. Add the turnip purée when the acid element has all but evaporated. Just before serving, stir in plenty of chopped parsley.

Purées of carrot, leek or salsify are further options for this gusto. A purée of garlic would represent a trespass into foreign territory and I cannot possibly recommend it in a book such as this, except to say that it would be delicious.

LEMON GUSTO

2 medium lemons
1 oz (28 g) soft brown sugar
⅓ pt (20 cl) water
½ teaspoon mustard powder
1½ tablespoons brown rum

Preparation and cooking time: 30 minutes

Use whole lemons, discarding only the pips. Cut them into sixteenths and simmer in water and ¾ oz (20 g) sugar for 20–5 minutes. Transfer them to blender and mix to a purée, using all their cooking liquor. Then add the remaining ¼ oz (8 g) brown sugar and the mustard powder to the purée and blend again for a few seconds. Transfer purée to saucepan, add the rum and simmer for a couple of minutes.

Excellent with chicken, duck and pork, as well as fried fish.

SCOTCH GUSTO

2 shallots, chopped
1 tin anchovies
2½oz (70g) soft herring roes
2 tablespoons whisky
juice of 1 lemon
3 teaspoons made English mustard
black pepper
2 egg yolks

Cooking time: 15 minutes

Gently fry the shallots in some of the oil from the anchovy tin. When the shallots are translucent, add the herring roes and cook for 3 minutes.

Mix whisky, 1–2 anchovy fillets finely chopped, lemon juice, mustard, black pepper and a few more drops of anchovy oil. Add this mixture to the roes, increase the heat slightly, and cook for a further 3–4 minutes, stirring and mixing.

Remove gusto from the heat and stir in the egg yolks. Keep hottish but do not scramble the eggs.

Excellent with herrings and mackerel as well as fried fish.

FRUIT GUSTO

Or 'Dad's sauce', according to Toby.

½pt (28cl) cider vinegar
⅓pt (20cl) cheap sherry or ruby wine
1oz (30g) raisins
4 prunes
1 bay leaf
1 heaped teaspoon crushed black peppercorns
½ cucumber, peeled and chopped
3 teaspoons salt
1 heaped teaspoon cayenne pepper (or 4 dried chillies)
1 apple, peeled but not cored, quartered
1 clove garlic
2 onions
8oz (224g) blackberries, loganberries or other soft fruit as available
1 heaped teaspoon mustard seed
oil

Cooking time: 1 hour

240

Boil all the ingredients together for 45 minutes, except mustard seed and oil. Fry mustard seed in a little very hot oil till it pops. Add seed without much oil to the other ingredients. When fruits are easily soft enough to blend, remove prune stones and liquidise to thick purée. Return to saucepan. Simmer for another 15 minutes very gently with lid on (without the lid the mixture plops and splashes the cooker surround).

Eat hot or cold. Keeps well. The exact composition of fruit ingredients is not critical.

PICKLE ZEST

Preparation time: 5 minutes

This depends on what you have on your pickle shelf. A good mixture is gherkins, capers, sweet chutney, a (chilli) hot pickle and fresh dill. Mix them together in roughly equal quantities. Add chopped spring onions and a little fresh orange juice. Chopped fresh tomato may be added too, but it must be cut small and peeled beforehand.

Make a similar zest using a lot of very fresh mint instead of dill.

APPLE ZEST

2 cooking apples, peeled and cored
1 small onion
2oz (56g) soft brown sugar
1 dessertspoon mustard powder
2 teaspoons salt
1 teaspoon black peppercorns, freshly ground
juice of 1 lemon

Preparation time: 7 minutes

Dice the apples small. Chop the onion finely. Mix together. Mix all the other ingredients except the lemon juice. Combine apple mixture with sugar mixture and mix well. Sprinkle with lemon juice.

Fresh mint is a pleasant addition but changes the nature of this zest and makes it more like an alternative to mint sauce.

HORSERADISH ZEST

1½oz (40g) grated horseradish
3oz (84g) turnip purée
juice of 1 large lemon
½ teaspoon salt
1 teaspoon white sugar
1 tablespoon whipped cream
chopped chives

Preparation and cooking time: 1½ hours

Mix horseradish with turnip purée. Add lemon juice, salt and sugar. Leave for 1 hour. Add whipped cream and chives.

HORSERADISH HAZE

Preparation time: 10 minutes

Similar to the above but is lightened by beaten egg white; the turnip may be omitted. Whip cream. Add lemon juice, horseradish, salt and sugar. Then fold in one stiffly beaten egg white.

CAYENNE ZEST

The sting for this sauce comes from onion and chilli, the body from hardboiled egg yolks, the lubrication from sherry. It is unsuitable for young persons.

1 medium onion
2 teaspoons cayenne pepper (or fresh or dried chillies)
¼pt (14cl) amontillado (or cheap sherry)
2 teaspoons salt
1 teaspoon white sugar
3 hardboiled eggs
½oz (14g) soft white breadcrumbs

Preparation time: 1 hour 10 minutes

Mince the onion and put it in a bowl with the cayenne or chopped chillies. Cover with sherry, add salt and sugar, and marinate for at least 1 hour, preferably several.

Hardboil the eggs. Cool them. Remove yolks.

Strain the sherry out of the onion with a fine sieve. Press out as much juice as possible. Mash sherry and egg yolks together. Add onion. Thicken with white breadcrumbs, mix all together thoroughly.

ONION ZEST

large onion(s)
1 teaspoon mustard seed per onion
oil
salt and pepper   .
juice of 1 small lemon or orange per onion
1 teaspoon soft brown sugar per onion

Preparation and cooking time: 10 minutes

Peel the onion(s) and chop very small. Blanch for 2 minutes in plenty of boiling water. Drain well and pat dry with kitchen paper.

Fry mustard seed in a little very hot oil until the seeds pop. Add oil and seed to onion. Season with salt, pepper, lemon or orange juice and brown sugar. If using very sweet orange, reduce the quantity of sugar slightly.

Can be made with bottled lime juice, in which case add 1 dessertspoonful per onion.

TOMATO ZEST

6 ripe tomatoes
2 pickled onions
1 tablespoon grated horseradish
1 teaspoon salt
tabasco

Preparation time: 10 minutes

Peel the tomatoes. Cut them small. Chop the pickled onions. Mix onions, tomatoes, horseradish and salt. Season with tabasco to taste. Add whatever herb you fancy.

9
SAVOURIES & CHEESE

Uniquely English, the savoury has all but disappeared from our tables. If it had been a French creation, it would have been preserved, nurtured and elaborated. The reason for its decline is that the people who used to serve savouries at the end of their dinners, now have to do the cooking themselves. Savouries belong to the days of kitchen staff, and were prepared downstairs just as pudding was being eaten upstairs. Most of them are horrid if conveniently made hours in advance: old, re-heated Welsh rabbit (however spelt) is terribly indigestible, for example, and Scotch woodcock (scrambled egg and anchovy) moults in minutes.

Savouries only justify their place in the menu if they provide a dramatic climax to the meal, a clash of cymbals. The finale is for brazen sapidity rather than delicacy or restraint. Cold, salady dishes in this spot tend only to provide anti-climax – at a time when the palate needs heat and pungency. Most of the classic savouries, accordingly, are strong in salt or pepper: bacon, anchovy, Worcestershire sauce and Parmesan being typical ingredients.

For those ready to make last-minute efforts, there follow two or three recipes which observe the right precepts. Old favourites such as angels on horseback, devils on horseback, chicken livers on toast, mushrooms with Parmesan, and Welsh rabbit are too well known to need repetition here. Among dishes suggested as starters earlier in this book, the following also make good finishers, if seasoned enthusiastically: curried fish custards (page 44); savoury syllabubs (page 45); tomato cavaliers (page 60); crab crumble (page 55); devilled kidneys (page 177).

Incidentally, the logistical problems of serving savouries in peak condition, do not apply to restaurants. It is strange that so few of them bother about savouries.

N.B. All savouries should be small. At this stage of the game appetites have long since been assuaged. If served on toast, as is usual, the toast should measure not more than 2–2½ ins (5–6 cm) across.

247

SARDINES SATANIC

4 plump tinned sardines
devil pepper (page 176)
4 pieces of toast cut to accommodate one sardine each
butter
anchovy butter (optional)
Gentlemen's Relish (optional)

Cooking time: 10 minutes

Roll the sardines in devil pepper. Grill them briefly but fiercely on each side. Put them on crustless hot-buttered toast and serve immediately with onion zest (page 243).

A variant is to spread the hot toast with anchovy butter or Gentlemen's Relish (with butter). Using devil butter (page 176) is even more infernal.

BEETROOT AND ANCHOVY

This is an exception to the rule that cold savouries are anti-climactic.

1 large beetroot
4 eggs
1 tin anchovies
1 lemon
grated horseradish or made English mustard
red pepper

Preparation time: 15 minutes

Skin the beetroot and cut from it 4 slices of maximum diameter rather less than ⅓in (1 cm) thick. Boil these in salted water for 5 minutes only.

Hardboil the eggs. Plunge both eggs and beetroot in cold water after the appropriate time of boiling. Dry the beetroot slices.

Remove the egg yolks and mash them with oil from the anchovy tin, a squeeze of lemon juice, and mustard or horseradish. Arrange one or more anchovy fillet on each piece of beetroot, cutting the fillet as necessary. Surmount with the egg-yolk mixture. Sprinkle with paprika or cayenne pepper.

VEGETABLE TERRINES

Piquant vegetable terrines also provide climactic savouries. The basic method of making them is outlined on pages 202–3. Particularly recommended are watercress, sorrel and spinach. Spinach terrine should be boosted by curry paste, and all of them should be manfully peppered.

KIDNEYS AND BACON

4 rashers streaky bacon
4 small portions of veal kidney (or lamb's)
devil pepper (page 176)
4 small pieces white bread
butter
made English mustard

Cooking time: 10 minutes

Sprinkle bacon and kidney with devil pepper. Wrap each kidney portion in a roll of bacon and secure it with thread or cocktail stick.

Fry the portions of bread, using clarified butter if at all possible. When cooked, spread them on one side with made English mustard.

Grill the bacon and kidneys on both sides, about 5 minutes in all, allowing the bacon to begin crispening.

Fry a scant teaspoonful of devil pepper in a little more butter.

Put bacon and kidney on to fried bread. Dribble a teaspoonful of devilled butter on top of each. Serve immediately.

Kidneys and Bacon (Roasted)

An alternative method is to prepare kidneys and bacon as above, but to roast them on small pieces of bread and butter while you are eating pudding. About 10 minutes in a hottish oven. Serve with devilled butter as above.

BEST SAVOURY OF ALL?

A roast snipe on a morsel of fried bread.

DEVILLED CHEESE

1 shallot
3½ tablespoons port (or British ruby wine)
2oz (56g) Stilton (or other English blue cheese)
2oz (56g) farmhouse Cheddar
½ teaspoon cayenne pepper
½ teaspoon black pepper
1 tablespoon mustard pickle
2 pickled walnuts
4 slices dry, crisp toast

Cooking time: 15–20 minutes

Peel and chop the shallot. Boil it in the port together with an equal quantity of water. When the liquid has evaporated to less than 2 tablespoonsful, reduce heat and crumble in both cheeses. Season with both peppers, the black coarsely ground.

Melt the cheeses slowly, stirring the while. When they have merged and seethed for 2 minutes, fold in the mustard pickle and chopped walnuts.

Serve very hot on thin, crisp, unbuttered toast – with port or claret – if possible in a room lit by cosily dim candles. Devilled cheese tastes sensational at the end of a good dinner, but looks a mess.

The Cheese Board

The decline of savouries has been matched by the rise of cheese boards. Many of the best savouries were cheesy anyhow, and it's both simple and effective to provide cheese in good condition. The best time to offer cheese is after the main course and before the sweet. Another alternative is to serve cheese and fruit together and dispense with pudding as such. It always seems retrogressive to have cheese after pudding.

Which English cheeses? Basically there are only two – Cheddar and Stilton. The other hard cheeses, Leicester, Gloucester, Caerphilly, Cheshire, and so on, are close cousins of Cheddar with slightly different accents. Blue cheeses are a separate family, and it is these which are best at the end of dinner: Stilton itself, blue Cheshire, blue Wensleydale (best of the lot?).

As suggested in the introductory section, Cheddar, a most satisfying meal in its own right, is redundant after two or three other courses. Filling and fairly mild, all the hard English cheeses are fine for lunch, high tea, supper, as snacks, in sandwiches, but lack the bite which makes a perfect after-dinner (or after-multi-coursed lunch) cheese. If you must put Cheddar on a cheese board, let it be as mature and piquant a farmhouse variety as you can find.

In a sense, there is now a third form of English cheese – the ordinary types flavoured with herbs, beer, garlic, spices, etc., and sometimes sandwiched together or processed in some other way. It is tempting to be snobbish about these parvenus, but sage Derby – surely their progenitor – is a fabrication of pedigree. Ilchester cheese was probably the first of the new generation and I would rather find Ilchester on the board than ordinary Cheddar (in the end of dinner context). If you discover any cheese concoctions you like, which have individuality and punch, put them on your cheese board and hope for the best.

It is, of course, absolutely right to be snobbish about most forms of processed, packeted, plastic-wrapped, supermarket, factory cheese. Canadian Cheddar is a possible exception.

Cooking with Cheese

Though Italian and, perhaps, American cooks might not agree, cheese tends to camouflage or compete with meat and to over-whelm fish. Sauce mornay is a classic, it's true, but arguably it is better at covering up mediocre or boring fish than at bringing out the best in sole or turbot.

In cooking, cheese has an affinity with eggs and to a less extent with ham and bacon. It complements most vegetables, too, though in England for some reason cauliflower seems to monopolise its attention. Cheese and apple – including cheese and apple pie – are gastronomically a most satisfying tradition, on both sides of the Atlantic.

The English hard cheeses cook well even if the range of taste is limited. None is as sharp as Parmesan nor as sweet as Gruyère. France, incidentally, has a much wider range of cheeses but uses relatively few of them for culinary purposes. It seems likely that in England, too, most cheese will continue to be eaten – as cheese, with bread or biscuits.

SLOW CHEESE OMELETTE

4 eggs
2 tablespoons single cream
3–4 tablespoons grated cheese (e.g. Cheddar)
chives (optional)
butter

Preparation and cooking time: 25–30 minutes

Beat eggs and cream together. Add grated cheese, salt and pepper, and chives if liked.

Melt butter in large omelette or non-stick frying pan over low heat. Pour in the egg and cheese mixture and cook very slowly without turning the omelette for 20 minutes. When the egg has just about set but is still wobbly, pour a little melted butter over the top and put the pan under a hot grill for 2 minutes.

Toasted Cheese

Calling for white sauce or beer, some Welsh rabbit recipes are quite complex and time-consuming. A simpler procedure is to grill slices of Cheddar (or grated cheese) on buttered toast. The whole process takes about 6 minutes, and the seething, goldy-brown result is so superior to the average pizza that one is baffled by the latter's commercial success worldwide.

Cheddar may be the best English cheese for toasting, but most of the others toast pretty well too.

As with pizza, toasted cheese can be seasoned or augmented in innumerable ways. Black pepper, cayenne pepper, English mustard, Worcestershire sauce and/or powdered sage can be spread or sprinkled on the cheese; chutney or mustard pickle can be spread on the toast under the cheese. Toasted cheese goes well with bacon or, indeed, bacon and eggs. Little slivers of anchovy provide attractively dangerous bite. Mixing blue cheese with Cheddar provides a different – better – bite. The onion family has a special affinity with cheese: spread the toast with gently fried shallot, for example, or sprinkle the finished dish with freshly chopped chives.

CHEESE TARTLETS

white bread
butter
tomatoes
ham
mild English cheese (Cheshire?)

Preparation and cooking time: 15 minutes

Cut circles of fresh white bread so that their diameter is slightly larger than that of the recesses in your tart tray. Butter each circle of bread on one side and liberally butter the tart recesses. Push the bread down into the recesses, butter side up, and bake in a very hot oven for 5 minutes.

You now have tartlets made of fried bread instead of pastry. Into each put a thin slice of tomato, covered by a matching slice of ham covered by a slice of cheese about ⅓ in (1 cm) thick. Grill under high heat until the cheese melts and bubbles.

CHEESE AND APPLE TARTLETS

Proceed as above to prepare fried-bread tartlets.

When the bread cases are ready, put a slice of apple in each (instead of tomato), spread it with made English mustard, and surmount it with a layer of Lancashire or Double Gloucester. Grill till bubbling.

CHEESE SAUCE

1 shallot
5 tablespoons brown ale
5 tablespoons vinegar
2 oz (56 g) butter
3½ tablespoons single cream
3½ oz (100 g) grated English hard cheese
salt and pepper

Cooking time: 15–20 minutes

Peel and chop the shallot. Boil it in beer and vinegar till the liquid has reduced to about 1 tablespoonful. Stir in one-quarter of the (cold) butter, then the cream, then some more butter – keep stirring. Reserving the final quarter of butter, add the grated cheese. Stir till it has dissolved and coalesced. Finally stir in the remaining butter, and season with pepper and salt.

A rich and powerful sauce for eating with boiled potatoes, boiled barley or potatoes baked in their jackets. This works well as a substantial first course to be followed by a light main course.

ANOTHER CHEESE SAUCE

6 leeks
1 oz (28 g) butter
3 oz (84 g) grated English hard cheese
⅓ pt (20 cl) meat cullis (page 26)
red pepper

Cooking time: 30 minutes

Make a leek (or onion) purée by sweating the finely chopped vegetables in butter for 20 minutes, then blending them in a

254

liquidiser. Return purée to saucepan and add the grated cheese. Stir till cheese melts. Add the meat cullis, bring back to simmering point, and cook for 3 minutes. Season with pepper.

A good sauce for chicken or leftover turkey; also for Jerusalem artichokes.

VEGETABLE TERRINES WITH CHEESE

Grated cheese or cream cheese can be added, with the egg, in the preparation of vegetable terrines (page 202–3). These make delicious first courses or light lunches. Spinach is particularly recommended.

CHEESE STUFFING FOR VEGETABLE MARROW

1 onion
2 oz (56 g) grated cheese
2 oz (56 g) breadcrumbs (soft)
fresh or powdered sage to taste
1 tablespoon chopped parsley
2 slices ham, diced (optional)
1 egg

Cooking time: 15–20 minutes

Peel and finely chop the onion. Mix it with the other dry ingredients in a bowl and bind with egg.

Put the stuffing in marrow which has been halved lengthways, de-seeded and blanched for 5 minutes in boiling water.

Put the marrow in a baking dish and pour a tumbler of water into the bottom. Bake in a medium to hot oven until the marrow is cooked and the stuffing is crisply brown on the outside.

For a large marrow, increase the quantities as necessary.

The same stuffing can be used for field mushrooms.

CHEESE MUNCHES

A delectable improvement on cheese straws.

3½oz (100g) grated Cheddar (or other hard cheese)
3½oz (100g) plain flour
3½oz (100g) softened butter
mustard powder
cayenne pepper
salt

Preparation and cooking time: 15 minutes

Mix the Cheddar, flour and butter and knead them well. Roll out the resulting dough so that it is not much more than ¼in (5mm) thick. Cut it into appropriate biscuit shapes, roughly the size of an old penny. (Triangles or squares are just as suitable as circles.)

Bake the biscuits in a medium oven for about 7 minutes – until they are a very light brown and slightly risen. There is no need to grease the baking tin.

They crispen up as they cool, and should be served cold.

A word about seasoning and fat content. If using a very mild cheese, season with cayenne pepper and mustard powder. A piquant cheese needs very little cayenne and no mustard. With a very soft cheese, the butter content can be reduced. If using a dry cheese like Parmesan, the butter content can be slightly increased. Also take into account how salty a cheese you are using, before adding any extra.

PUDDINGS & FRUIT

For many people, pudding is the chief glory – and point – of British food. Usually male, they get hooked on roly-poly, apple pie or treacle tart in childhood and take their passion through life, from nursery to nursing home. I am not an addict myself but agree that more love and genius have been lavished on the creation of our sweet dishes than on anything else; accordingly, modernisation and improvement are less necessary here than in other departments. At the risk of infuriating traditionalists, however, and all those who declare stoutly, 'I'm not hungry but thank God I'm greedy', I do make a few suggestions for lightening the pudding load.

The Role of Pudding

In times gone by, appetites were larger than now, energy needs greater, houses colder. This inspired a demand for puddings which were filling, warming and very sweet. The pre-conditions for such puddings no longer apply with such force – even children are salt-toothed as well as sweet-toothed today.

Coming at the end or nearly the end of a meal, the pudding's role on any occasion largely depends on what has gone before. After fish or some comparatively light main dish, it may well have a hunger-assuaging job. At the conclusion of a banquet, pudding's function is to please sweetly rather than nourish. Between the two, conventional menus can easily be balanced so as to leave a few genuine corners for the sweet course to fill; on the whole, however, the puddings of new English cooking are charmers rather than fillers.

Contrast

The progress of a meal from savoury to sweet normally supplies contrast enough. To follow a rich main course with a rich pudding is fine so long as key constituents like pastry or cream are not too prominent in both – ideally they shouldn't duplicate each other at all. It is important to remember that a pudding can be rich without being heavy. Personally I lean towards small helpings of flour-free confections which are beguilingly sweet, creamily rich and astringently alcoholic.

A minor problem in devising indigenously English desserts is the almost complete absence of English liqueurs and brandies. Sloe gin qualifies, but oh for a native applejack. Pears, cherries, blackcurrants, raspberries and virtually all the fruit we grow here are, on the continent, converted into delicious, pudding-enhancing potions . . . Why not here?

English Tastes and Treatments

While lacking cordials, we do have cider, and cider features quite frequently in the recipes which follow. Other well-used materials which have a particular, though not exclusive, Englishness of taste include blackberries, honey, gooseberries, rhubarb, prunes, golden syrup and black treacle. Imported ingredients which can be classed as naturalised British include raisins, sultanas, oranges, lemons, candied peel and sherry.

Loathed or loved, junket is the British answer to yogurt and crème fraîche. It is also the answer when you want something light, luxurious and soothing at the end of an indulgent meal. So even if you have held junket (nursery junket) in utter contempt for years, please try one or other of the grown-up versions suggested on pages 268–70.

Lighter – but Richer

Flour, fat, crumbs, sugar and eggs in various combinations dominate hundreds of British puddings. A vast extended family stretches from suet pud itself through batters and fritters, bread- and cake-based puddings, pies and tarts and crumbles, to the lightest of sponges. Most are 'satisfying', 'filling' or 'stodgy' according to how much or how little you like them, but many can be made lighter and/or richer by simple alterations in the balance of ingredients. In practice, traditional character can usually be retained while traditional function is shifted hedonistically from energy-giving, warmth-promoting nourishment towards gastronomic gratification pure and simple. This may sound immoral, but is there anything terribly uplifting about old-fashioned spotted Dick?

Suet mixtures, for example, are lighter if made with breadcrumbs as well as, or even instead of, flour. At least 50 per cent of the normal flour content should be crumbs, but I have made excellent dumplings (page 150) with no flour at all.

Arrowroot can also be used instead of flour – for suet crusts, pastry and crumbles. It is lighter and more digestible. At least one-quarter of the flour content in traditional recipes can with advantage be arrowroot.

A flour-free recipe for tart pastry is given. This uses ground almonds. Ground hazelnuts make most intriguing cakes, also without the help of flour. Fruit 'pies' topped with meringue mixture instead of pastry are often more welcome at the end of a meal than fruit incarcerated in short-crust.

Egg yolk or whole eggs make a suet crust richer and more interesting without making it heavier. The effect is to raise it several rungs up the social scale. Similarly suet is less bother and quicker to cook if baked rather than steamed or boiled. To my mind it is also much nicer – crisp outside and gooey inside, instead of soggy all through. This view may be anathema to pudding purists.

In new English pudding-making, considerable use is also made of fruit cullises (purées, see page 34). These are essentially single or mixed fruits blended in a liquidiser with or without syrup. If frozen, the fruit cullis becomes a simple sorbet or water ice.

APPLE CHEESE PIE

6 apples, peeled, cored, quartered
6 tablespoons brown sugar (less if apples sweet)
5 tablespoons sweet cider
2 lemons
clove
1 egg white
1 tablespoon caster sugar

Preparation and cooking time: 2½ hours

Simmer apples, brown sugar, cider and lemon juice over a very low heat for 2 hours until you have what is essentially apple cheese. Stir it from time to time and make sure it doesn't burn at the bottom. Season with a clove if you like. Sharpen with more lemon juice or sweeten with more brown sugar as you think fit. You must end up with an almost toffee-like purée.

Beat egg whites as for meringue, adding caster sugar. It should not be a very sweet meringue mixture.

Put the apple cheese in a flattish pie dish. Spread meringue mixture over the apple. Bake in medium oven till the meringue is the lightest of browns.

Serve with cream – or real custard.

ANOTHER APPLE PIE

Hands off apple pie – some things are sacred? Americans as well as Britons claim apple pie as their own. There are already scores of alternative recipes and only a brave or foolish cook would claim that he has found a better way. Here is a variation which calls for no pastry and provides a good excuse for getting out the sloe gin.

1 lb (450 g) eating apples
1 scant oz (25 g) butter
juice of ½ lemon
1½ tablespoons sloe gin
meringue mixture of 2 egg whites and 1 oz (28 g) caster sugar

Preparation and cooking time: 25–30 minutes

Peel and core the apples; cut them into wedges about the size of lemon segments.

Fry them gently in butter for 3 minutes, turning once. Add the lemon juice and sloe gin. Cook for 1 more minute.

Remove contents of frying pan to shallow pie dish. Whip egg whites to stiff peaks and fold in sugar. Cover apples with meringue mixture and bake in a low to medium oven for 20 minutes or until the meringue is set.

SUET PUDDING RENEWED

4oz (112g) soft breadcrumbs
½oz (14g) arrowroot
1oz (28g) ground almonds
3oz (84g) suet
2oz (56g) soft brown sugar
1 egg
2 tablespoons milk

Preparation time: 10 minutes; cooking time: 20 minutes

Mix the dry ingredients and make a well in the middle. Beat the egg in a little milk and pour into the well. Knead into a dough (on a floured surface in the usual way).

Still on floured surface, roll the dough into an oblong shape about ½in (1cm) thick. Spread the filling lengthwise along the centre. Pinch the edges together, forming a pasty shape. Bake in a hot oven for 20 minutes.

The filling may be jam, marmalade, fruit cullis, golden syrup or black treacle. If using golden syrup or treacle, include a few slices of lemon or orange. Here is a particularly good filling:

1oz (28g) raisins
2 tablespoons sweet sherry
redcurrant (or other soft fruit) cullis (or redcurrant jelly)
double cream
sugar or lemon juice

Marinating time: 6–12 hours

Steep the raisins in sherry overnight, or for as long as possible. Drain them, reserving sherry. Spread cullis or jelly nearly to the edges of the rolled-out suet dough. Strew jelly with raisins. Pinch the dough into pasty-shape. Bake till golden, about 20 minutes.

Whip the cream. Add the sherry marinade to form a simple syllabub. Add sugar or lemon juice after tasting. Serve the syllabub with the baked pudding.

TART LOUISE

1½oz (42g) ground almonds
2oz (56g) butter (softened)
½oz (14g) arrowroot
2oz (56g) white sugar

Preparation and cooking time: 25–30 minutes

Mix the ingredients well. Put a good teaspoon of the mixture in a round blob into each individual recess of a tart tray. (These quantities will make 10 little tarts, or 8 big ones.) Bake in a hot oven for 15–20 minutes. The blobs will flatten out and then take on the contour of the tart recesses.

When they are slightly darker than golden, remove the tray from the oven. Allow the tartlets to cool for about 7 minutes before easing them out. When they are quite cold, fill them with soft fruit, fruit cullis or jam. If making lots, have 2 or 3 different fruity fillings. Fresh fruits will look better with a little syrup to glaze them. Cullis or jam fillings can be judiciously laced with orange gin or other fruity alcohol.

Unless feeling poor, parsimonious or ascetic, top the tarts with whipped cream or syllabub.

CHRISTMAS PIE

Christmas pudding and mince pies are very much the same in their active ingredients except that one is held together by a casing of pastry while the other has the pastry as it were inherent, in the form of flour or breadcrumbs mixed with the fruit and suet which are common to both. Therefore it has always seemed strangely supererogatory to serve both at the same meal. It is also odd to serve such a heavy pudding after what is usually the richest main course of the year – roast turkey or roast goose with an exaggerated (if sacrosanct) number of trimmings . . .

Here is a lighter form of Christmas pudding or mince pie, for those who reject the grossness but like the taste and remain traditionalists. Stirring the Christmas pudding was my own earliest culinary experience. This one can be stirred too, by all members of the family.

4 lemons
7 oz (200 g) raisins
7 oz (200 g) sultanas
7 oz (200 g) currants
3½ oz (100 g) candied peel
2 teaspoons mixed spice
9 oz (254 g) marmalade (not bitter)
3½ oz (100 g) blanched almonds, chopped
4 apples
3½ oz (100 g) suet
7 oz (200 g) dark brown sugar
5 tablespoons brandy or rum
4 carrots (grated)

Preparation time: about 1 hour of a late autumn evening

Squeeze the lemons and reserve juice. Pare 2 of them and blanch the rind in boiling water. Then cut it very fine.

Mix the dried fruits, candied peel and mixed spice in large bowl. Add lemon juice, marmalade and almonds. Peel, core and chop the apples. Add them to mixture. Stir well. Add the suet and the brown sugar. Continue stirring. Add the brandy. Stir on. Add grated carrot and blanched rind. Now get everyone in the house to have a stir.

Put the mixture in jars, excluding all the air. Leave for as long as possible, at least a week.

To serve, make tartlets as for tart Louise. Remove them from the oven when golden. Leave them in tray. Fill each with the mixture and return to oven for 10 minutes.

A CHRISTMAS FRUIT SALAD

4 apples
4 tangerines
1 grapefruit
2 oz (56 g) raisins
2 oz (56 g) sultanas
2 oz (56 g) currants
2 oz (56 g) candied peel
2 oz (56 g) chopped dried figs
2 oz (56 g) almonds
½ pt (28 cl) sweet cider
6 oz (168 g) caster sugar
juice of 1 lemon
2 tablespoons brown rum

Preparation time: 15–30 minutes

Peel the first 3 ingredients. Cut the apples into segments; divide tangerines and grapefruit into pigs. Mix the fresh fruit with the dried fruit and the nuts. Moisten with a sugar syrup made with 4 oz (112 g) caster sugar and cider instead of water, well laced with lemon juice. Don't add too much syrup – each item in the salad needs to be glistening with syrup but not swimming. Stir in the rum. Sprinkle quite liberally with remaining caster sugar, mixing it well so that every mouthful has an element of crunch.

This dish is greatly improved if you remove the skin or membrane which encloses each citrus segment.

BREAD AND BUTTER PUDDING RENEWED

¾ pt (42 cl) milk
¼ pt (14 cl) cream
2 tablespoons honey
3 eggs
4 tablespoons soft white breadcrumbs
4 tablespoons raisins
1 oz (28 g) butter
juice and rind of 1 lemon
icing sugar
3 tablespoons jam
4 tablespoons sweet sherry

Preparation and cooking time: 30 minutes

266

Prepare a custard mixture with milk, cream, honey and eggs. Raise it to blood temperature or a little higher. Add the breadcrumbs, raisins and melted butter. Stir all well together. Add a few slivers of blanched lemon rind. Pour the mixture into a buttered dish and bake in a bain-marie in a moderate to low oven for 25 minutes. Sprinkle surface of custard with icing sugar 5 minutes before removing from oven.

Serve with a jam sauce made by simmering jam in a mixture of lemon juice and sweet sherry.

Note: do not cover the custard as it bakes, as you want it to form a skin.

NUTS IN MAY

hazelnut cake (page 268)
rowan jelly
home-made or bought marzipan
whipped cream
macaroons

Preparation time: at least 1 hour

You will allow that rowan is botanically close enough to may (hawthorn) to justify the name?

Make a sufficient quantity of hazelnut cake, baking it in a shallow tin. It will rise to about 1–1½ins (3–4cm) thick.

While it is still hot, spread it with rowan jelly. Alternatively spread the cold cake with melted jelly. The jelly should permeate the upper part of the cake but not saturate the whole.

Spread a thickish layer of marzipan on the cake and another layer of – cold – jelly on the marzipan. Dollop the jelly thickly with whipped cream. Chill.

Before serving, sprinkle the chilled pudding with crushed macaroons.

This delicious confection works perfectly well with other jellies or jams.

HAZELNUT CAKE

6oz (168g) sugar, preferably vanilla sugar
4 eggs
8oz (226g) ground hazelnuts
N.B. No flour!

Preparation time: 10 minutes; cooking time: 30 minutes

Mix the sugar and the egg yolks. Beat till fluffy. Beat the egg whites till stiff.

Add the hazelnuts to egg-yolk mixture. Fold in the whites. Bake in a fairly hot oven for 30 minutes or until the cake rises. It won't rise very much.

This is an interesting cake to eat as cake or to use as the base of a trifle. It goes particularly well with a coffee-flavoured filling.

The ground hazelnuts must be reasonably fresh. I once made it with stale nuts and the result was inedible.

NOT JUNK – BUT JUNKET

The rehabilitation of junket is overdue. What was once a creamy, rum-flavoured curd has become nursery junk food, and even in the nursery it is being drowned in a tidal wave of commercial yogurt.

Real junket, made with plain rennet, is highly digestible, extremely 'minceur' and indubitably British. Use it for cool summer soups instead of jellied consommé or for light, all-weather puddings. Even if you do not care for ordinary curds and whey made with plain milk, you should enjoy junket fortified by cream, rum or brandy, and honey.

¾pt (42cl) milk
¼pt (14cl) single cream
1 tablespoon rum
2 tablespoons honey
1 teaspoon rennet
nutmeg or cinnamon

Preparation and cooking time: 10 minutes; cooling time: 45 minutes or longer

Heat milk and cream to 98·4°F, adding the honey and rum. Make sure honey is fully dissolved, if necessary heat milk a little higher.

Remove milk from heat and add rennet. Put it in a cool place to set but not the refrigerator. Sprinkle with nutmeg or cinnamon.

EVENING JUNKET

This can be made with virtually any soft fruit, single or mixed. If large strawberries are used, halve or quarter them; frozen fruit may be used too, thawed and dried. Red, white and blackcurrants all freeze well, as do raspberries and loganberries. Strawberries freeze but change their character in doing so, and not for the better.

8 oz (226 g) soft fruit (red)
juice of 2 oranges
1½ tablespoons sloe gin
2 tablespoons sugar
½ pt (28 cl) milk
½ pt (28 cl) single cream
1 teaspoon rennet
Alpine strawberries or sugared redcurrants (for decoration)

Preparation time: at least 2 hours

Marinate fruit in orange juice, sloe gin and sugar for 1 hour. Without damaging the fruit, strain off the juices and put them to one side. Put the fruit in a glass serving dish with sides high enough to contain just over a pint of milk.

Add the orange and sloe gin mixtures strained from the fruit to the milk and the cream in a saucepan. Raise to blood heat and take off stove at once. Add the rennet. Pour over the fruit and leave to set in a cool place outside the fridge. Before serving the junket, decorate with Alpine strawberries or sugared redcurrants.

The sloe gin may be omitted or another liqueur substituted.

MIDNIGHT JUNKET

Evening junket made with blackberries or blackcurrants.

269

JUNKET TRIFLE

sponge cake or macaroons
strawberry jam (or raspberry)
1 egg
1 tablespoon brandy
¾pt (42cl) milk
¼pt (14cl) cream
2 tablespoons caster sugar
1 teaspoon rennet
angelica or Alpine strawberries (for decoration)

Preparation time: at least 1 hour

In the bottom of a pudding bowl or cut-glass junket bowl, put sponge cake or coarsely broken macaroons. Do not sprinkle with sherry. Instead, spread thickly with dollops of jam.

Beat the egg with the brandy and a tablespoonful of milk. Add this to the rest of the milk and the cream and heat to blood temperature in a saucepan, together with the sugar.

Remove milk mixture from heat and add a teaspoonful of rennet. Pour over the jam and cake. Leave junket to set – not in the refrigerator.

Before serving, decorate with angelica or Alpine strawberries.

CHOCOLATE PEPPERMINT CREAM

½pt (28cl) double cream
1½ tablespoons crème de menthe
2½ tablespoons cider
1 lemon
3oz (84g) caster sugar
2½oz (70g) plain, bitter chocolate, grated
4 peppermint (or mint) leaves

Preparation time: 20 minutes; refrigeration time: 40 minutes or more

Whip the cream stiff. Mix crème de menthe with lemon juice and cider. Add sugar to cream, then incorporate the crème de menthe mixture, stirring. Also stir in half the grated chocolate. Transfer to large wine glasses. Sprinkle each glass with more grated chocolate and refrigerate.

Before serving decorate each glass with a peppermint leaf.

This will make 6 or 8 servings.

270

GOOSEBERRY COCKTAIL

7 oz (200 g) green gooseberries
¾ pt (40 cl) sweet cider
3½ oz (100 g) white sugar
2 oz (56 g) ripe redcurrants
2½ tablespoons sloe gin (or fruit liqueur such as Cointreau)

Preparation and cooking time: 1 hour

Simmer gooseberries in a syrup made from sweet cider and sugar, taking care not to overcook them. They should be green, cooking gooseberries, not the enormous sweet variety.

When cooked, remove and drain the fruit, retaining the syrup. When the fruit are cold, put them into individual wine or custard glasses and dot them with redcurrants.

Meanwhile boil the syrup for 5 minutes and taste it to make sure that the gooseberries have not made it too tart. If they have add more sugar.

Allowing about 1½ tablespoonsful of syrup per person, pour it into a jug to cool and stir in the sloe gin (or other cordial).

When it is down to about blood temperature, trickle it over the gooseberries and redcurrants. Serve cold but not necessarily re-frigerated.

This is a nice clean way of concluding a rich meal. Since gooseberries and redcurrants both freeze much better than some other fruit, it is really an all-the-year-round dish.

ICED SUMMER PUDDING

6 slices crustless white bread
10 oz (300 g) redcurrants
3½ oz (100 g) icing sugar (or caster)
2 tablespoons sloe gin (or other liqueur)
3½ oz (100 g) raspberries and redcurrants mixed
¼ pt (14 cl) sweet cider
2 oz (56 g) caster sugar

Preparation and freezing time: 3 hours

Line a pudding basin with bread, as for summer pudding.

In a blender, whizz uncooked redcurrants, or other soft fruit, to a fine purée. Mix the purée with sugar and enrich it with a little sloe gin, or other liqueur. You now have a delicious fruit cullis. Strain out the pips, using a fine sieve.

Pour cullis into pudding basin and put basin in freezer. In the course of the freezing process,* mash the water ice as it forms 2 or 3 times, to break down the crystals. This also helps to diffuse colour through the bread. After the final mashing, cover the exposed fruit with white bread, first coloured as follows.

Boil the raspberries and currants in cider, adding the sugar (and a little more sloe gin if you feel that way inclined). After 2–3 minutes, strain some of the red juice on to the bread. Simmer remaining syrup down to a runny but jammy consistency, suitable for use as a sweet sauce.

Freeze the pudding for at least 1 hour.

To serve: lower the pudding basin into a bowl of very hot water and keep it there for 1 minute. Turn the pudding itself out on to a plate. Leave it for 15 minutes or so. Then dribble the warm sauce over the top of the pudding, guiding it to any patches of bread which need extra colour.

This dish can easily be adapted to strawberries, loganberries or blackberries.

---

* The process can be speeded up, of course, if you have a sorbetière or ice-cream machine. In that case, make the sauce first, rather more of it; colour all the bread; line the basin; add the cullis already frozen.

ORANGES AND LIME

½pt (28cl) sweet cider
½pt (28cl) water
2½ tablespoons Rose's lime juice
7oz (200g) sugar
orange-based liqueur (optional)
6 oranges
1 fresh lime or lemon

Preparation and cooking time: 40 minutes

Simmer the cider, water, lime juice and sugar for about 20 minutes, to make a cider syrup. Cool it to blood temperature and stir in orange liqueur if used.

Meanwhile peel oranges, removing as much of the pith as possible. Cut them horizontally into discs or – ideally – divide them into pigs, *peeling each pig*.

Put them into a cut-glass dish and pour in the syrup. Chill before serving with fresh lime wedges if possible.

PEARS IN CIDER

¾pt (42cl) sweet cider
3½oz (100g) white sugar
1 tablespoon bitter marmalade (not too lumpy)
4 pears (cooking)

Cooking time: 45 minutes

Simmer the cider, sugar and marmalade into a syrup, having cut small any large piece of peel in the marmalade.

Peel, core and quarter the pears. Pack them in a close-fitting ovenproof ceramic pot. Cover the pears with the syrup and bake in a medium oven until the pears are cooked – about 30 minutes. The pot should be covered with loose-fitting foil or greaseproof rather than a lid.

Serve the pears hot – or very cold.

273

Rhubarb

First fruit of the year, rhubarb is often miscooked and tends, therefore, to have low status in the kitchen. It can be very good, however, if protected from water.

Cut it into thin slices, having peeled it, if stringy, and toss it in one-quarter to one-third its weight of sugar. Put rhubarb and all the sugar into saucepan with close-fitting lid, and cook gently for 10 minutes.

Remove the lid, increase the heat, and cook for a further 5 minutes, stirring with a wooden spoon to produce a dryish purée. A hint of lemon is pleasantly fresh, but orange is better; introduce citrus at the beginning of the process or when you have removed the lid, and include a little peel as well as a little juice.

A second method is to sweat rhubarb (chopped small or diced) in a little butter. Shake the pan from time to time, and remove it from the heat while the fruit is still firm and crisp. Sweeten with warm honey acidulated with lemon or orange juice.

Alternatively, boil 4½oz (120g) sugar in ¼pt (14cl) cider (or water) to produce a syrup. Pour the syrup, boiling hot, over 5oz (140g) rhubarb cut into short sticks, and the rind of an orange cut into matchsticks. Leave the rhubarb to cool in the syrup.

Each method does full justice to a usually wronged stalk. The rhubarb can then be eaten with cream, real custard or junket; put in tartlets, flans, pies or crumbles, fresh as spring.

CIDER WITH ROSES

6 (or more) well-scented roses
1pt (56cl) cider – sweet, still, rough if possible
4oz (112g) caster sugar
½oz (14g) or 1 sachet gelatine
strawberries, raspberries or blackberries

Preparation time: allow 2 days

Remove petals from 3 roses and put them into a 1-pt jar with a ground glass stopper. Pour cider over the petals and insert stopper. Leave in a warmish place for 8–12 hours.

Strain petals out of cider – and repeat the process with second 3 roses (but the same cider). After another 8 hours or more, remove second batch of petals and use the scented cider to make jelly with the sugar and gelatine as follows.

Add sugar to cider and raise the temperature to about blood heat. Soak the gelatine in water, if using the leaf variety. When the sugar is dissolved and the cider warm, add the gelatine. (Or follow instructions for jelly-making according to the type and brand of gelatine/jello you are using.)

Pour jelly into mould, adding strawberries and/or raspberries. (Bisect strawberries if large.) Alternatively, later in the year simmer a handful of blackberries in slightly sweetened water for a few minutes. Don't sweeten or cook them very much.

Pour the jelly into a mould.

Drain and slightly dry the blackberries. Toss them in sugar. Add them to the jelly before it has set, stirring very gently to ensure a fairly even distribution without letting the colour run too much.

A few extra rose petals put into the jelly mould before the jelly itself is a justifiable cosmetic.

BAKED BLACKBERRY AND APPLE

1 lb (448 g) blackberries
14 oz (400 g) (or more) sugar
½ pt (28 cl) water
lemon juice
4 large cooking apples
caster sugar
cream

Preparation and cooking time: 1¼ hours

Family fare rather than a party pudding, this is a good way of enjoying one of autumn's most numinous unions.

Prepare a blackberry cullis by simmering the berries in sugar and water with a squeeze of lemon for 20 minutes, stirring occasionally. Reduce to a purée in blender. Re-heat for 5 minutes, then strain through a fine sieve. Check that it is very sweet.

Wash, don't dry, but core the apples. Dust the skins with caster sugar. Fill the cavities with blackberry cullis. Bake in a medium-hot oven for 45 minutes or until the apples are cooked.

Mix the remaining blackberry cullis with cream and serve with the apples.

Cherries

Cherries show us how sweet life can be, how ephemeral it *must* be. They are the fulfilment of spring, the unforbidden fruit of innocence – for man and bird alike. Sweet ones are best eaten out of doors, near open windows, or on lazy summer train journeys – shared with the opposite sex. It is impossible to eat too many. Make the most of your next cherry season and take it not for granted.

The sour, black (usually) Morello-type cherry is almost as welcome as the sweet, though not quite so innocent. Use it for flans and jams, even in sauces for duck when entertaining adventurous but inexperienced eaters such as teenagers. Or try . . .

CHERRY BOUNCE

This was originally a slow-maturing, rum- or brandy-based cordial along the lines of sloe gin. We made it one year when the birds allowed us some of our Morellos – and found it dangerously attractive the following year. Here it's turned into a summery pudding ready in a few hours.

14 oz (400 g) Morello cherries
1 pt (56 cl) sweet cider
3½ oz (100 g) brown sugar
4 tablespoons light brown rum

Preparation and cooking time: 40 minutes; cooling time: at least 40 minutes

Simmer the cherries for 5 minutes in cider and sugar, having first melted the sugar in the cider. Drain the cherries and stone them as soon as they are cool enough. Put the stones to one side. (Stoning may be done with a special gadget, with fingers, or with a piece of wire such as a paper clip attached to a cork at one end. It's a fiddly business but worth taking trouble.)

Reduce the cider to a syrup by fast boiling until you have about ½pt (28cl) left. Let it cool down to blood temperature then add the rum to it.

Crack about half the cherry stones and add the kernels to the cherries themselves. Put cherries and kernels into 4 large wine glasses. Add the rum-flavoured syrup, and chill till needed.

Just before serving top the cherries with unsweetened whipped cream or a rum-flavoured, not very sweet, syllabub. (Similar puddings could, of course, be made with cherries preserved in brandy or with tinned black cherries.)

BANANA CUSTARD PIE

4 eggs
6oz (168g) caster sugar
½pt (28cl) milk
½pt (28cl) single cream
1½ tablespoons light rum
4 bananas
3 or 4 tablespoons fruit cullis or red jam
juice of ½ lemon

Preparation and cooking time: 45 minutes

Separate egg yolks from whites. Whisk 2 of the whites as for meringues. Add 4oz (112g) sugar.

Beat the egg yolks and 2 of the whites into a little of the cold milk. Heat the remainder of the milk, the cream and the rum to near boiling point, stirring well. Add remaining sugar and make sure it has dissolved before removing milk from heat. Stir in the egg yolks and cold milk.

Slice the bananas and simmer them in cullis or jam and lemon juice for 5 minutes. Then put them into a custard dish or Pyrex dish. Pour the custard mixture over the bananas and jam. Cover with greaseproof paper and bake in low to medium oven for 15 minutes, using the bain-marie method (i.e. in larger dish and surrounded by warm water). As soon as the custard has indisputably begun to set, take it out of the oven for a moment and spread it thinly with the meringue mixture. Then let it continue to bake until the meringue has set.

Eat hot or cold.

PRUNE PEKOE

1 lb (450 g) prunes
3 teaspoons orange pekoe tea
¾ pt (42 cl) sweet cider

Preparation and cooking time: at least 24 hours

Make a pot of orange pekoe tea. Pour it over the prunes, to cover. Marinate the prunes in tea for 12–24 hours. Then drain them.

Simmer the prunes in sweet cider for 15 minutes. Remove from heat and leave to marinate for a further 12 hours.

Serve the prunes in their cider marinade with wedges of orange.

ICED PRUNE PEKOE

Preparation and cooking time: at least 27 hours

Proceed as above. After the second marination, stone the prunes and blend them to a purée with a little of the marinade and the juice of 1 orange. Mix the purée with ½ pt (28 cl) double cream, and freeze. If you have no ice-cream machine, follow the usual rule for freezer-made ices, and mash the mixture 2 or 3 times while it is descending in temperature, to prevent ice crystals forming.

II

BREAKFAST & TEA

Until recently, tea was an important and greatly liked, middle-class meal of unashamed farinaceousness. Its main elements – bread and butter, hot-buttered toast, bridge rolls, sandwiches, crumpets, scones, buns, cakes and biscuits – were all versions of each other, individually delicious, collectively repetitive, redundant, absurd, unbalanced, fattening and irresistibly frivolous. Eaten by people who had three other large meals every day, the charm of the meal was its uselessness. Art triumphed over utility in a conspiracy to tempt: crisp white cloth, silver tableware, weightless cups, wafer-thin sandwiches, and is there Rupert Brooke for tea . . . As a meal for grown-ups in this purposeful age, tea has all but disappeared. Is there a case for renewing or rethinking it now?

I think not. There is clearly no need for a fourth meal. A serious tea spoils the appetite for dinner or supper. Tea interrupts the afternoon whether one is at work or play, and is disproportionately time-consuming to prepare. And, frankly, I cannot think of any changes or reforms which wouldn't make tea into another form of breakfast, lunch, or supper. So let's leave the meal nostalgically alone and hope somebody asks us to an old-fashioned tea very soon (with chocolate Bath Olivers, please).

High Tea

This is a combination of afternoon tea and supper for those who usually have neither. It is taken later than tea but well before any other evening meal. High tea comprises at least one savoury dish – meat, fish, eggs, cheese – sometimes a salad such as beetroot, a good selection of bready and cakey things – and tea to drink.

The practical aspect of high tea is that it leaves the evening free for other things. People who see this as an advantage are usually more interested in television or pubs than in cooking and eating.

Breakfast

Does Britain really make the world's best breakfasts or is it just that our simple forms of cooking suit breakfast particularly well? Certainly one doesn't want elaborate dishes or sophisticated sauces as one opens the morning's bills – bacon and eggs or kedgeree seem just right at that difficult hour. However, the fact that these dishes – and British breakfasts generally – are in decline gives the lie to some of the more extravagant claims advanced on their behalf.

On the other hand, 'continental' breakfasts are precious little help against the grim reality of morning meals: squabbling children, too little sleep, bad-news papers, cats which must be fed before anyone else, final notices. Minor tribulations maybe, but they loom large at 8 o'clock – even if you have friends staying with you and everyone pretends to be bright, chatty and eager for the day ahead. What you need at that dread hour is the maximum choice of therapeutic goodies with the minimum amount of trouble and no undue expense. Choice is the key to accentuating the positive, eliminating the negative, surviving breakfast and emerging ready for the fray.

The mind goes back to that golden era before the war – the real war, not Hitler's sequel – when one came down to a groaning sideboard laid by loyal, early-rising, virtually unpaid minions; a sideboard replete with eggs in many guises and bacon in many cuts, with porridge and salmon and fish cakes and kidneys and game and kippers . . . choice for any and every mood. At least there always seems to be in period films, Edwardian self-service being a favourite vehicle for character-revealing chat. In practice only one per cent of the population lived in that sort of style and most of the food in those silver chafing dishes must have been past its best long before family and guests deigned to descend. Anyone insisting on such display now ends up in court (bankruptcy, divorce or both).

In Scandinavia, however, choice persists, though the individual items are mostly cold. This means they can be prepared in advance and kept for several days. Foreigners, even the English, fishing in Norway or travelling by Fred Olsen Line are invariably won over by the cold, multifarious, herring-rich breakfasts. Why not arrange a marriage of convenience between the Edwardian sideboard and the Scandinavian cold table?

The Great Ethnic English Breakfast

The strategy is to devote a couple of hours each week to preparing a few simple dishes which are excellent to eat cold, which keep well, and which are appropriate for breakfast. Then, when the dread hour arrives, three or four alternatives are produced from larder or refrigerator, and offered with toast. Everyone helps him or herself and afterwards everything goes back in larder or fridge. Next day out come a couple of already started pots and perhaps one or two new ones. People ring the changes on what they eat as they feel inclined.

Of course, marmalade, honey, fruit juice, tea, coffee can also be offered, but it's only the tea or coffee which involves cooking.

Things to be avoided at breakfast for all but the most Rabelaisian appetites are violent, spicy tastes, onion and – more debatably – English cheese. Nor would I recommend small beer. Here are eight suggestions:

potted trout (page 49)
buttered kedgeree
kipper (or bloater) paste
sardine butter
cold gammon or ham
potted tongue
hardboiled eggs
Arbroath smokies (when you can find them)

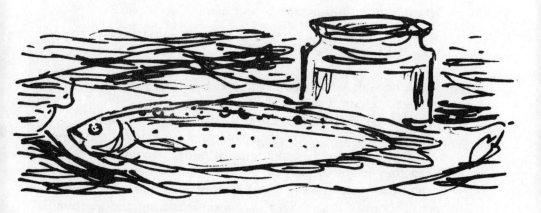

KIPPER PASTE

Blanch the kippers in 2 kettles of boiling water, leaving them in the first for 3 minutes, the second for longer – 8–10 minutes in all. When the kippers are cooked, remove skin and all bones. Blend the flesh with an equal weight of melted, unsalted butter and plenty of lemon juice.

Put the paste into several small pots rather than one large, and cover them with layers of clarified butter.

Other modestly priced smoked fish may be treated in the same way. The less salty varieties need only one kettle of boiling water.

BUTTERED KEDGEREE

Kedgeree was one of the favourite components of the Edwardian sideboard, and still turns up at present-day breakfasts from time to time, albeit as a leftover from supper. The Finnan haddock and eggs also combine to make excellent cold dishes of the potted fish family. Of the two versions given here, the first can be eaten with a fork, the second is best spread on toast.

1 large Finnan haddock (about 7oz/200g fish off the bone)
4 scant tablespoons rice
4 eggs
salt and pepper
2oz (56g) butter
clarified butter

Preparation time: 30–5 minutes; cooking time: at least 20 minutes

Simmer the haddock in a large pan of water until it is ready to come away easily from the bone. Take it out of the pan with a slotted spoon.

Use the same water to boil the rice, for about 10 minutes, until it is cooked. Drain it well.

Remove skin and bones from the fish; flake the flesh.

Break and beat the eggs, seasoning lightly with salt and pepper. Scramble them slowly using a lot of butter, stirring all the time. When they begin to thicken, add the cooked rice, distributing it evenly. Carry on scrambling and remove eggs from heat when they are stiff but not dry. Even then continue stirring and mashing so that it is free of lumps. Before the eggs have cooled, mash in some more softened butter.

Select a smallish, high-sided earthenware tureen with lid, or similar vessel. Put in eggs and fish in fairly thick alternate layers, beginning and ending with egg. Allow everything to cool before pouring melted, clarified butter over the top. Chill before use.

BUTTERED KEDGEREE WITHOUT RICE

1 large Finnan haddock (about 7 oz/200 g fish off the bone)
5 oz (140 g) unsalted butter
4 hardboiled eggs
pepper
½ oz (14 g) clarified butter

Preparation and cooking time: 15 minutes; cooling time: at least 20 minutes

Cook the haddock as above. Remove skin and bones.

Melt the unsalted butter. Remove yolks from hardboiled eggs.

Put flaked fish, mashed egg yolks and melted butter into a liquidiser. Season with pepper, and blend into a homogeneous mass. Put the mixture into 2 or 3 pots or ramekins. When cold, cover pots with melted, clarified butter.

While both these dishes are best made with whole Finnan haddock on the bone, smoked haddock fillets also give good results.

Arbroath (or Aberdeen) Smokies

Buy these delicious smoked, unsplit haddocks whenever you have the opportunity. Eat them cold with toast and butter. One smokie goes a surprisingly long way. (They can also be grilled and hot-buttered – a high-tea dish in Scotland.)

SARDINE BUTTER

Slit open tinned sardines through their tummies and remove the backbones. Mix them with at least half their weight in salted butter, a very little red pepper and lemon juice. This can be done with a fork, so long as the butter is soft; it's not worth dirtying the blender.

Refrigerate in small pots or ramekins; no need for clarified butter.

POTTED TONGUE

Mix cooked tongue with its own weight of butter, preferably clarified butter, seasoning it with salt, black pepper and nutmeg. Use a blender or liquidiser for the mixing process – which means that the butter must be fully melted. Put the mixture into small china pots and cover those not wanted for tomorrow's breakfast with melted butter, again clarified for preference. N.B. It is essential to clarify the top layer of butter if the potted material is going to be kept for more than 4–5 days. That way potted tongue and other potted dishes will keep (unstarted, of course) for several weeks and not even require refrigeration.

TO CLARIFY BUTTER

Melt ordinary salted or unsalted butter very slowly. Keep it in molten state for several minutes. Skim the surface a few times with the finest strainer you possess. Finally pour the butter through muslin or a strainer into a suitable storage vessel, taking care to leave solids and salty sediment in the bottom of the pan.

It is best to clarify butter in batches of not less than 8oz (250g), preferably more. It keeps for ages.

Beef dripping or pork lard may be clarified in the same way.

12
RULES & REGULATIONS

Disciplines for Preserving – but Developing and Enhancing – Englishness in the Kitchen

1) depend mainly on foodstuffs from (or readily producible in) the British Isles;

2) of exotic materials, only use those which have been continuously imported and widely used for around 100 years or more;

3) reject most outlandish, trendy, or 'new' foodstuffs;

4) avoid culinary processes and combinations which give particular ethnic effects (e.g. oriental or Mediterranean tastes);

5) use fresh, unprocessed, natural materials as much as possible;

6) eliminate, reduce, or question the flour-, fat-, sugar- and salt-content in traditional recipes, and in cooking generally;

7) respect the intrinsic tastes and textures of the materials used;

8) use animal fats for meat and game cookery;

9) allow fish, meat, or game a central role in most meals, but

10) improve the status of vegetables by faster cooking and finer cutting.

Many foods which grow or are made in or around the British Isles are also imported from overseas. No prohibition applies to such imports even if they are technically outlandish – to lamb from New Zealand, beef from South America, early vegetables from Spain (provided they are the right vegetables – see below), to prawns from Norway or Greenland, to butter-mountain butter. In many cases, no doubt, the home-produced version is to be preferred. The lists which follow are self-explanatory.

Index of Traditional Foods

Ingredients and materials which may be used without restriction in new English cookery:

bay leaf   horseradish
chives   lovage

marjoram
mustard (seed as well as powder)
parsley

rosemary
sage
thyme

barley
broad beans
broccoli
Brussels sprouts
cabbages
carrots
cauliflower
celeriac
celery
cress
cucumber
dried peas (and split)
dwarf beans (French)
garden peas
Jerusalem artichokes

leeks
lettuce
marrow
mushrooms and edible fungi
onion, spring onion
parsnips
potatoes
radishes
runner beans
shallots
sorrel
spinach
swedes
turnips
watercress

apples
blackberries
blackcurrants
cherries
damsons
gooseberries
loganberries
mulberries

pears
plums, gages
quince
raspberries
redcurrants
rhubarb
strawberries
(other orchard fruit)

bacon
beef
black pudding
ham
kidneys (lamb, veal)
lamb

liver (lamb, veal, pig's)
oxtail
pork
sausages
tripe

fish caught in territorial waters
freshwater fish (wild or farmed)
shellfish from territorial waters
bloaters
kippers

smoked cod's roe
smoked haddock
smoked mackerel
smoked salmon
smoked trout

chicken, capons
duck
goose
grouse
hare
mallard, wild duck

partridge
pheasant
pigeon
rabbit
turkey
venison

butter
cream
eggs

English cheeses
honey
milk

dripping (beef)
lard (pork)

lamb and mutton fat
suet

jams and jellies
marmalade
mushroom ketchup

mustard pickle (piccalilli)
sweet pickle, chutneys
Worcestershire sauce (also Harvey's, etc.)

beer
cider
cider vinegar
gin

ginger wine
home-made wines
sloe gin
whisky

arrowroot

Index of Naturalised Exotics
Not English-grown but no restrictions on use.

black pepper
cayenne pepper (chilli powder)
cloves
dried ginger

mace
nutmeg
white pepper

almonds
bananas
candied peel
capers
chocolate
coffee
currants

dates
lemons
oranges
prunes
raisins
sultanas
tea

tinned (and pickled) anchovies	tinned sardines
black treacle golden syrup	rum
Anglicised curry powders	mango chutney
lime juice port	Madeira sherry
Parmesan cheese	

Index of Borderlines

Use with caution, restraint and some reluctance.

apricots	lentils
butter beans	melon
coconuts	pineapple
courgettes	rice
figs	sweetcorn
globe artichokes	tomatoes
kidney beans	
basil	garlic
caraway	oregano
chervil	paprika
coriander	poppy seed
dill	tarragon
fennel	
carp	king prawns
crayfish	red mullet
duck or goose liver	veal
kid	
brandy	wine
olive oil	

Stores and Proprietary Foods

Part of the food industry is more concerned in the destruction than the renaissance of English cooking. In many ways the enemy of real food, it tempts its 'consumers' to abandon their stoves and leave cooking to the factory.

That said, there are a number of branded and factory-made items which are helpful and which can be kept in the store cupboard, refrigerator or freezer without damage to gastronomic integrity. It would be silly, for example, never to use Worcestershire Sauce (if liked) or to attempt a home-made version. Necessarily subjective, the list which follows includes several items already listed above. It is not meant to be a comprehensive analysis of what larder and freezer also need to be able to cope with reasonable contingencies or conceivable emergencies.

jams and jellies
marmalade (sweet and bitter)

pure lemon juice
vinegar (cider, wine, malt if liked)

anchovy essence
curry paste, curry powder (English-made)
gravy browning (harmless additive and effective cosmetic)
mango chutney
pickled onions

pickled walnuts
tomato purée (albeit for very sparing use in English cooking)
tabasco
Worcestershire sauce (or similar alternative)

candied peel
currants
dried fungi
dried herbs

dried peas
dried prunes
raisins

game soup
tinned anchovies
tinned consommé

tinned garden peas
tinned sardines

black treacle
rennet

stock cubes

frozen chicken livers
frozen fish, shellfish

frozen meat
frozen stock or cullis

The fruit and vegetables which freeze well include broad beans, gooseberries, blackberries, and the currant family – red, black, white.

293

Index Ciborum Prohibitorum

Not to be used in new English cookery.

aubergines
avocado pears
bamboo shoots
beanshoots/sprouts
borghul (cracked wheat)
chick peas
couscous
dried pulses other than peas
fresh limes
ful medames
hummus
kiwi fruit
kumquats
lychees

okra
olives
passion fruit
pasta
pimentos (peppers)
pine nuts
polenta
sauerkraut
soya beans and soy products
tamarind
truffles
wild rice
yams, sweet potato

cumin seed
fresh chillies
fresh ginger
garam masala (and genuine Indian
    spice mixtures/pickles)
green peppercorns

Japanese and Chinese condiments
red peppercorns
sambals and south-east Asian
    condiments
sesame
tahini

abalone
brisling
caviar
fresh sardines
John Dory
octopus

salt cod
sea urchins
squid
sturgeon
taramasalata
tuna

andouille
chorizo
foie gras
Frankfurter-type sausages
frogs' legs
garlic sausage

liver sausage
mortadella
raw ham (Parma, Bayonne, etc.)
salami
snails

Calvados
eau de vie

pastis

aïoli

béchamel-type sauces

cornflour

crème fraîche

fromage blanc

hollandaise-type sauces

non-English cheeses (except
   Parmesan)

raspberry vinegar

rouille

sour cream

yogurt

INDEX